OXFORD ENGLISH MONOGRAPHS

General Editors
CHRISTOPHER BUTLER   STEPHEN GILL
DOUGLAS GRAY   EMRYS JONES
ROGER LONSDALE

Mary Leapor:
A Study in Eighteenth-Century Women's Poetry

RICHARD GREENE

CLARENDON PRESS · OXFORD
1993

Oxford University Press, Walton Street, Oxford OX2 6DP
Oxford New York Toronto
Delhi Bombay Calcutta Madras Karachi
Kuala Lumpur Singapore Hong Kong Tokyo
Nairobi Dar es Salaam Cape Town
Melbourne Auckland Madrid
and associated companies in
Berlin Ibadan

Oxford is a trade mark of Oxford University Press

Published in the United States
by Oxford University Press Inc., New York

© Richard Greene 1993

All rights reserved. No part of this publication may be reproduced,
stored in a retrieval system, or transmitted, in any form or by any means,
without the prior permission in writing of Oxford University Press.
Within the UK, exceptions are allowed in respect of any fair dealing for the
purpose of research or private study, or criticism or review, as permitted
under the Copyright, Designs and Patents Act, 1988, or in the case of
reprographic reproduction in accordance with the terms of the licences
issued by the Copyright Licensing Agency. Enquiries concerning
reproduction outside these terms and in other countries should be
sent to the Rights Department, Oxford University Press,
at the address above

This book is sold subject to the condition that it shall not, by way
of trade or otherwise, be lent, re-sold, hired out or otherwise circulated
without the publisher's prior consent in any form of binding or cover
other than that in which it is published and without a similar condition
including this condition being imposed on the subsequent purchaser

British Library Cataloguing in Publication Data
Data available

Library of Congress Cataloging in Publication Data
Greene, Richard.
Mary Leapor : a study in eighteenth century women's poetry /
Richard Greene.
— (Oxford English monographs)
Includes bibliographical references and index.
(acid-free paper)
1. Leapor, Mrs. (Mary), 1722–1746. 2. Women and literature—
England—History—18th century. 3. Women poets, English—18th
century—Biography. I. Title. II. Series.
PR3539.L49Z66 1993
821'.5—dc20 [B]   92-29386
ISBN 0-19-811988-7

Typeset by Graphicraft Typesetters Ltd., Hong Kong
Printed in Great Britain
on acid-free paper by
Bookcraft Ltd.,
Midsomer Norton, Bath

For Deirdre

Preface

Eighteenth-century poets, apart from the insane and the eccentric, have been understood in terms of a succession of literary fashions: neo-classicism gives way at mid-century to sensibility, which becomes full-blown Romanticism toward the end of the century. There have been profound arguments about the details of this broad scheme, but until about 1980 there was general agreement about the outlines of the period. The discovery that there were a large number of poets, among them many women and labourers, whose works have been largely unknown to literary historians has made it necessary to reconsider some basic ideas about the period.

Mary Leapor (1722–46) was a poet of the mid-century. The daughter of a gardener and herself a domestic servant, she lived most of her twenty-four years in Brackley, Northamptonshire. Her works were not published until after her death; they were, however, fairly well received, and her reputation as a woman poet remained high for some years.

Leapor's poetry does not conform to the mid-century fashion. She seldom addresses abstractions and writes few odes. She writes poetry about her experiences as a labouring woman in a society which discriminates deeply on the basis of gender and class. In her taste for social satire and concrete description, as well as her preference for heroic couplets and octosyllabics, she is a follower of Pope and Swift. Although her admiration for these writers is intense, a number of her poems criticize their attitudes on social issues. Hence, as she works within a 'scriblerian' tradition she challenges aspects of the ideology of that mode. Her poetry represents a development of the tradition of Pope and Swift in the mid-century, that is, in the 'Age of Sensibility'. There were, of course, a number of well-known poets, such as Johnson, Churchill, and Crabbe, who realized new possibilities in the same tradition long after the deaths of Pope and Swift, though their works have been seen as somehow behind the times in which they were written. It is at least strange, however, to regard as moribund a literary tradition which continued to produce poets of such power. Although she would not share all of their attitudes,

Leapor, like many other 'submerged poets', is closer in poetic temperament to these writers than to the poets of sensibility.

Leapor, as a woman of the labouring class, remained firmly outside the social élite of her time. She has very strong affinities with some other poets whose works are now being brought into the canon of eighteenth-century verse. Many of these poets describe poverty or the injustices suffered by women in terms which are simply compelling. Indeed, Mary Leapor's own poetry is shaped by her experiences as an outsider.

This study approaches Leapor's poetry from a number of directions. The first chapter assembles the surviving fragments of her biography, and then examines her publication history and posthumous reputation. The second chapter discusses her attitudes towards issues of gender, especially marriage and the family, female friendship, and contemporary standards of feminine beauty. The third chapter considers her poetry against the background of her economic condition, with particular reference to domestic service, agriculture, and literary patronage. The fourth chapter examines Leapor's poetry in relation to the vogue of 'natural' poets, and goes on to argue that Leapor, despite being deprived of a complete formal education, had read more widely than was admitted at the time of her publication. The final chapter discusses how Leapor's poetry deals with her fear of imminent death, and how in the image of death the leveller she ultimately reconciles her desire for social change with the need for religious resignation.

Some of Leapor's concerns are shared by mainstream writers of the time and some are not. Indeed, the picture of the eighteenth century which is now emerging is complex and various. Recent studies of eighteenth-century writers, especially women, have recognized a great diversity—much was happening that cannot be accounted for by the standard paradigms of literary history. A number of eighteenth-century scholars have already devoted great efforts to broadening our sense of the period, and particularly to showing how these submerged poets should be understood. This book draws on their work and hopefully it will contribute to the same enterprise.

In researching and writing this book and the thesis which preceded it, I have benefited from the great generosity of a large

Preface

number of people. Above all, I am indebted to Karina Williamson, whose supervision of my work over three years was constructive, exact, and deeply supportive. I am also grateful to Peter Levi who supervised the initial stages of my work on Mary Leapor, and whose own daring emboldened me to take on this research. I am further indebted to a number of scholars who have shared their research with me or who have provided me with valuable advice, especially Betty Rizzo, Roger Lonsdale, John Clarke, Donna Landry, Mark Jenner, David Stewart, Valerie Rumbold, Christine Gerrard, Patrick O'Flaherty, and Donald Nichol. It is a pleasure to acknowledge the kindness of Francis Sitwell and Susanna Sitwell, who have explained to me the history of Weston Hall, and who have welcomed all my obscure queries. I am grateful to Jeremy Marshall and other lexicographers at the Oxford Dictionaries who have answered my questions with patience and interest. I acknowledge the courtesy of librarians and archivists at the Bodleian Library, the British Library, and the Northamptonshire Record Office. I also acknowledge my debt to the Rothermere Fellowships Trust, whose generous support over three years allowed me to undertake this project. For her proof-reading I thank Patricia Greene. My wife, Deirdre, has her own work, but has helped me with mine from the beginning. I am in the end left to thank my daughter Sarah for her patience; at the age of 9 she cannot remember when there was not a thesis or a book.

R.G.

Contents

Abbreviations	xii
1. Biography and Reputation	1
2. Problems of the Woman Poet	38
3. A Labouring Poet	98
4. Primitivism and Education	157
5. Poetry and the Last Things	186
Conclusion	205
Appendix: The Weston Hall Library	210
Bibliography	214
Index	235

Abbreviations

Baker — George Baker, *The History and Antiquities of the County of Northampton*, 2 vols. (London, 1822–41).

Clarke — John Clarke, *Yesterday's Brackley—The Last 300 Years* (Buckingham: Barracuda Books, 1990).

DNB — *Dictionary of National Biography*.

ECV — Roger Lonsdale, ed., *The New Oxford Book of Eighteenth-Century Verse* (Oxford and New York: Oxford University Press, 1984).

ECWP — Roger Lonsdale, ed., *Eighteenth-Century Women Poets: An Oxford Anthology* (Oxford and New York: Oxford University Press, 1989).

Eland — George Eland, ed., *Purefoy Letters 1735–1753*, 2 vols. (London: Sidgwick & Jackson, 1931).

GM — *The Gentleman's Magazine*, 1731– .

Hill — Bridget Hill, *Women, Work and Sexual Politics in Eighteenth-Century England* (Oxford: Basil Blackwell, 1989).

Johnson — Samuel Johnson, *The Yale Edition of the Works of Samuel Johnson*, 15 vols. to date (New Haven, Conn.: Yale University Press, 1958–).

Landry — Donna Landry, *The Muses of Resistance: Laboring-Class Women's Poetry in Britain, 1739–1796*, Cambridge Studies in Eighteenth-Century Literature and Thought (Cambridge: Cambridge University Press, 1990).

ML — Mary Leapor, *Poems Upon Several Occasions*, 2 vols. (London, 1748–51).

MR — *The Monthly Review*, 1749–1845.

Pope — Alexander Pope, *The Twickenham Edition of the Works of Alexander Pope*, gen. ed. John Butt, 11 vols. (London: Methuen, 1939–68).

Rizzo — Betty Rizzo, 'Molly Leapor: An Anxiety for Influence', *The Age of Johnson*, 4 (1991), 313–43.

Sitwell — George Sitwell, *A Brief History of Weston Hall, Northamptonshire, and of the Families that Possessed it* (London: p.p., 1927).

Swift — Jonathan Swift, *The Poems of Jonathan Swift*, ed. Harold Williams, 3 vols. (Oxford: Oxford University Press, 1958).

CHAPTER 1

BIOGRAPHY AND REPUTATION

Life

A mute inglorious Milton she was not, but at her death Mary Leapor was indeed 'A Youth to Fortune and to Fame unknown'. Whatever temporary vogue her poetry may have enjoyed following her death, the few historical traces of her life are contained within a very narrow compass. She can rarely have travelled, for example, more than fifteen miles from Brackley, Northamptonshire, where she lived for most of her twenty-four years. Since the records of her life are fragmentary and, in some cases, contradictory, it is necessary to consider first the character of Brackley and its neighbouring communities as the background to her life and poetry.

It is not possible to establish the exact population of Brackley in the middle of the eighteenth century; however, according to the census of 1801, there were by that year 1,495 people living there (Baker, i. 574). Since the town was expanding at the turn of the century, the population for the earlier time would have been slightly less. Brackley was surrounded by a number of smaller villages, such as Hinton with a population of approximately 175 (Baker, i. 635), the hamlet of Steane with only 15 (Baker, i. 686), or, somewhat further, the village where Leapor was born, Marston St Lawrence, where about 370 people lived (Baker, i. 642).

As a market town, Brackley was the centre of the local economy. Fairs were held there four times a year; supposedly, these were governed by a body known as the 'court of piepowder' (Clarke, 73). A large number of tradesmen and small merchants served the area's needs from the town. Brackley, however, was not notably prosperous. Its dominant family, the Bridgewaters, later known for huge commercial successes such as the Worsley coal-mines and the construction of canals in Lancashire, took various steps at the beginning of the century to invigorate its trade, including the construction of a new town hall. Nonetheless, Brackley remained 'obstinately stagnant'.[1]

The political life of the town was controlled by the Dukes of Bridgewater.[2] Although there were numerous landowners, including Magdalen College, Oxford, which maintained a school there,[3] the Bridgewaters' influence was predominant. In the first decade of the century the Bridgewaters aligned themselves with the Whigs. During the reign of Queen Anne parliamentary elections in Brackley were hotly contested by the Tories under John Welchman, senior, an attorney and sometime mayor of the town. After 1713, however, the corporation remained firmly in the hands of Bridgewater appointees. Only once in the century did they fail to return a Bridgewater candidate to Parliament. This occurred as a result of greater than usual bribery in the election of 1754.[4]

The religious character of Brackley was largely conformist. Although Northamptonshire had been a stronghold of Puritan sentiment during the Civil War, following the Restoration most of the county adhered to the episcopal Church.[5] Dissent in the county nonetheless survived powerfully throughout the eighteenth century in the persons of Phillip Doddridge and his followers. Prominent non-jurors included Nathaniel Crewe, who lived in Steane, and William Law.[6] While there was no dissenting church in Brackley, in a number of poems Mary Leapor discusses enthusiasm, usually without sympathy. The religious climate of the town doubtless owed much to the lingering High Church influence of Crewe. During the poet's lifetime the vicar of the town was Thomas Bowles (Baker, i. 576), a classicist whose preaching betrays some pedantry:

---

[1] John R. Lowerson, 'Enclosure and Farm Holdings in Brackley, 1829-51', *Northamptonshire Past and Present*, 6 (1978), 35.

[2] Ibid. 35-6; see also W. A. Speck, 'Brackley: A Study in the Growth of Oligarchy', *Midland History*, 3 (1975-6), 30-41.

[3] See Eric G. Forrester, *A History of Magdalen College School, Brackley, Northamptonshire, 1548-1949* (Buckingham: E. N. Hillier and Sons, 1950).

[4] Lewis Namier and John Brooke, *The House of Commons 1754-1790*, 2 vols. (London: HM Stationery Office, 1964), i. 343-4.

[5] R. M. Serjeantson and W. Ryland D. Atkins, 'Ecclesiastical History', in *The Victoria History of the County of Northampton*, ed. R. M. Serjeantson and W. Ryland D. Atkins, 4 vols. (London, 1902–), ii. (1906), 61-2.

[6] Ibid. 61-70.

The Star that appeared at [Christ's] Birth, and the Journey of the Chaldean wise Men, is mentioned by Chalcidius the Platonist. And Abul Pharajius tells us, that Zerdusht, or Zoroastres, (who was the great Patriarch of the Magians, who wrote the Book Zendavesta (which is the Bible of that Sect) and whose Name is still in the same Veneration among them, as that of Moses is among the Jews, and that of Muhammed among his Followers) foretold to his Magians the Coming of Christ . . .[7]

Bowles doubtless restrained his erudition when instructing the Brackley congregation, yet it remains a temptation to speculate on the manner in which Mary Leapor received her religion. To focus on this peculiar sermon is perhaps unfair to Bowles, as his Latin Grammar is certainly lucid and accessible.[8] In neighbouring Hinton, Dr Richard Grey was a divine of some significance. In 1744 he engaged William Warburton in a controversy over the Book of Job, conducting his argument with logic and civility.[9] He eventually became a prebend of St Paul's and Archdeacon of Leicester; had it not been for his friendship with Bishop Crewe, who sympathized with the Stuarts, he could have expected to become a bishop.[10] Grey's interests strayed into poetry. In 1754 he produced a verse translation of *De Animi Immortalitate* by Isaac Hawkins Browne,[11] the man who had edited Leapor's second volume. It is very probable that Grey took some part in Leapor's subscription. In the next generation Grey's daughter Bridget married Bowles's son Thomas, and among their children was the poet William Lisle Bowles.[12]

Brackley itself produced few people who impressed themselves on the historical record. Apart from Mary Leapor, the only native

[7] Thomas Bowles, *A Sermon on the Gradual Advances, and Distinct Periods of Divine Revelation* (Northampton, 1738), 22–4. This passage, in its printed form, is copiously annotated.
[8] See Thomas Bowles, *Grammaticæ Latin Syntaxis Commentariis Illustrata: Or, the Fundamental Rules of the Latin Grammar Made Plain and Easy* (Northampton, 1738). See also id., *A Compendious and Rational Institution of the Latin Tongue* (Oxford, 1740; rev. edn., 1748).
[9] See William Warburton, *Remarks on Several Occasional Reflections* (London, 1744), 37–70; Richard Grey, *An Answer To Mr. Warburton's Remarks on Several Occasions* (London, 1744).
[10] Philip Thicknesse, *Memoirs and Anecdotes* (Dublin, 1790), 8, 323. Thicknesse, also from Northamptonshire, was Grey's brother-in-law.
[11] Isaac Hawkins Browne, *De Animi Immortalitate* (London, 1754); id., *The Immortality of the Soul*, trans. Richard Grey (London, 1754).
[12] For reminiscences of the Bowles family, see William Lisle Bowles, *Scenes and Shadows of Days Departed* (London, 1835).

of Brackley to achieve prominence in the eighteenth century was Thomas Paine, whose book lists became a feature of the book trade for thirty-five years. He was baptized there in 1719 (Baker, i. 586), and his brother James maintained a bookshop in the town (Rizzo, 319).

To place Mary Leapor more specifically in this isolated world requires various types of evidence, including the poems, which must, of course, be used with caution. Most of what is known about Leapor derives from a letter by her friend and mentor, Bridget Freemantle, to a gentleman in London, probably John Duncombe though possibly John Blencowe. This letter was prefixed to the second volume of Leapor's verse published in 1751. A much shorter note had appeared in the first volume in 1748.

According to Freemantle, Leapor was born in Marston St Lawrence in Northamptonshire on 26 February 1722. Although the parish register was badly damaged by fire, there still exists the Bishop's transcript of that register in which Leapor's baptism is recorded on 16 March 1721[13] (the apparent discrepancy is accounted for by the change from old to new style calendars in 1752). The same transcript records the marriage of Philip Leapor and Anne Sharman on 29 September 1720.[14] Mary Leapor's mother is unfortunately an elusive figure. She was not born in Brackley or Marston St Lawrence. She may, however, have belonged to the Sharman family of Weston, Northamptonshire, where the poet subsequently worked as a kitchen-maid.[15] Another family of Sharmans is to be found in Sulgrave; however, the name is common throughout the county. No Sharmans subscribed to Leapor's poems, although a Margaret Sherman subscribed for two copies of the first volume. Freemantle reports that Anne Leapor predeceased her daughter by about four years. The Brackley Register records her burial on 26 December 1741.[16]

It is considerably easier to trace Philip Leapor. His parents, Philip Leapor and Elizabeth Whitehead, were married in Hinton

[13] 'Bishop's Transcripts of the Parish Register of Marston St. Lawrence 1706–1812', Northamptonshire Record Office, Delapré Abbey, Northampton.
[14] Ibid.
[15] 'Weston Poll-Book 1695', Northamptonshire Record Office, Delapré Abbey, Northampton.
[16] 'Brackley Parish Register 1727–1756', Northamptonshire Record Office, Delapré Abbey, Northampton.

in 1691.[17] Philip, their first surviving child, was born in Brackley on 18 March 1693. Alice, his sister, was born in 1695 and died apparently in 1708. The elder Philip Leapor died in 1696 and an Elizabeth Leapor died in 1701.[18] Philip Leapor may therefore have been orphaned at the age of 8. It should be noted, however, that there were several branches of the Leapor family in Brackley, and that the same Christian names were repeated over generations or within the same generation to such an extent that it is difficult to separate families, or even to identify individuals. Another Elizabeth Leapor, who died in November 1726, was probably the poet's grandmother.[19]

At some time before his marriage Philip Leapor moved to Marston St Lawrence, a village five miles from his home. There he worked as a gardener for Sir John Blencowe (1642–1726) who had been the Member of Parliament for Brackley from 1690 to 1695, and from 1696 to 1714 had served as a Baron of the Exchequer and Justice of Common Pleas (*DNB* ii. 672–3). Blencowe's wife Anne (d. 1718) was the daughter of Professor John Wallis (1616–1703) of Oxford, a polymath with expertise in classical and modern languages, astronomy, mathematics, cryptology, philosophy, and theology. Blencowe apparently owed his career as a judge to Wallis, who turned down a bishopric for himself but asked that his son-in-law be considered for a judicial appointment (*DNB* xx. 598–602). The attitude of Judge Blencowe towards his servants is suggested by his treatment of a man over 90 employed to break rocks. The man was decrepit and his efforts were spoiling the stones. Anne Blencowe suggested that the man be allowed to keep his wage of 8*d*. per day, but that he should remain at home. Blencowe responded, '... let him spoil on; he has a pleasure in thinking he earns his daily bread at four score years and ten; but if you turn him off, he will soon die with grief' (Baker, i. 639). The anecdote is recorded as an example of his humanity. By the standards of the time, therefore, he was probably a generous employer. By the end of his life Blencowe's faculties had decayed and he was convinced that he had invented longitude (*DNB* ii. 673).

---

[17] 'Hinton-in-the-Hedges Parish Register 1559–1812', Northamptonshire Record Office, Delapré Abbey, Northampton.
[18] 'Brackley Parish Register 1687–1702', Northamptonshire Record Office, Delapré Abbey, Northampton.   [19] Ibid.

Philip Leapor told Freemantle that he worked for the Blencowe family for five years following his daughter's birth. Since the judge died on 8 May 1726, it is possible that his son John, who inherited the house, decided against maintaining a full-time gardener. Leapor then returned with his wife and daughter to Brackley, in either 1726 or 1727, and opened his own nursery on a spot surrounded by the infant Ouse, about a quarter of a mile along the modern Hinton Road. The place is identified in the town as the site of a castle, of which no trace remained by the eighteenth century (Eland, i. 92). The Leapors' home was probably a short distance from the nursery. There is a very large map at the Northamptonshire Record Office, dated 1760, on which is marked the occupant of each premises in Brackley proper. In the area of the old castle there is a cluster of five properties marked 'Lepper' along Goose Green near a lane leading from Hinton. A sixth Leapor property is found nearby adjoining Cow Close. All the Leapors in Brackley are in this area.[20] If Philip Leapor's mother was indeed the woman who died in 1726, it is reasonable to believe that he took over a house which she had occupied, and leased a separate piece of ground for his nursery. It is not immediately apparent which house this might have been; however, the six properties are separated by little more than a hundred yards. Mary Leapor was an only child, but she grew up surrounded by a large extended family. It appears that none of the Leapors owned a freehold.[21]

There is a surprising body of circumstantial evidence concerning Philip Leapor in *The Purefoy Letters 1735–1753*, edited by George Eland. These are letters written by Henry Purefoy and his mother Elizabeth concerning all aspects of their substantial household in Shalstone, Buckinghamshire. They regularly employed Philip Leapor as a gardener, and the letters sent to him give some insight into his business. According to the Purefoy accounts, Leapor maintained an array of fruit trees. The following list dates from November 1734:

An Account of the Names of the Severall ffruit trees planted then by M^r. Lepper of Brackley

[20] 'Plan of Brackley 1760', Map 2985, Northamptonshire Record Office, Delapré Abbey, Northampton.
[21] *Northamptonshire Poll Books from 1702–1831* (Northampton, 1832); cited in Rizzo, 341–2.

> On the wall next the Stable yard
> Two old Newington Peach trees
> Two of the late Admirable Peach trees
> One red Roman Nectarine
> On the wall in ye Court
> A Newington Nectarine tree
> By the Pump
> One late fflanders Standard Cherry tree
> One May Duke Standard Cherry tree
> One Carnation Standard Cherry tree
> In the other Cherry walk
> ffour early Duke Standard Cherry trees
> One black heart Standard Cherry tree
> In the other Cherry walk
> One Crown Standard Cherry tree.   (Eland, i. 93)

Elsewhere, there are lists of plums, apples, pears, vines, and an assortment of vegetables, usually with reference to specific varieties. It is possible to see in a catalogue of this sort the origins of the very exact nomenclature found in many of Mary Leapor's landscape descriptions (see Chapter 3 below). This was the idiom of her father's trade.

The Purefoy Letters also give an idea of Philip Leapor's economic standing. In addition to his profit on the plants which he brought from his nursery, he charged the Purefoys 1s. 6d. for a day's labour in 1739 (Eland, i. 94), a rate that would have lifted his family to relative security, though certainly not prosperity. Such a wage would have been comparable to or even slightly better than that paid to other craftsmen in the area.[22] One letter indicates that he augmented his earnings as a gardener with clock repairs (Eland, i. 115). A rough estimate of his total annual income would be about £30, the sort of sum that curates received and complained of. Some letters, however, suggest that Leapor was rather dilatory, and may not have done much work in the winter. Henry Purefoy repeatedly urges him to perform tasks that have been delayed. He writes on 1 January 1745 (Eland, i. 94–5):

> Mr Leapor,
> I desire you will come over & thin ye cherry trees wch. you promised mee to have done long before this. I shall also want to talk with

---

[22] Nicholas Cooper, *Aynho: A Northamptonshire Village*, Banbury Historical Society, 20 (Banbury: Leopard's Head Press and Banbury Historical Society, 1984), 120.

you about the ffruit Trees I intend to plant against the wall next ye Pump Court. I desire you will send by ye bearer 2 quarts of Sugar Hotspur peas to set the first crop, & half a peck of Windsor Beans, & pray bring ye Hammer with you wch. I suppose you took by mistake. This will oblidge
Your freind to serve you
H. P.

It is, of course, possible that Leapor was not shiftless but very busy. Moreover, Purefoy may have made unreasonable demands on those who worked for him. L. G. Mitchell, commenting on Henry Purefoy's letters to craftsmen, suggests that the owner of an estate was obliged to suffer the seasonal idleness of a local craftsman since he was difficult to replace.[23] There were, however, at least three other gardeners in Brackley with whom Purefoy had dealings at different times.[24] Philip Leapor did not have a captive market.

On her deathbed Mary Leapor reportedly expressed concern for her father's advancing age. He survived his daughter, however, by thirty-four years and, according to the Brackley Register, was buried on 22 January 1771.[25] His enrolment as a burgess of Brackley in 1753 suggests that, contrary to the poet's fears, his fortunes did not collapse as he grew older, rather that his position was, if anything, improved.

The evidence relating to her father is almost the only approach to much of Mary Leapor's life, certainly to the first ten years. Beyond the information concerning her birth and the move to Brackley, the next thing known about the poet pertains to her education. Freemantle writes:

[Philip Leapor] informs me she was always fond of reading every thing that came in her way, as soon as she was capable of it; and that when she had learnt to write tolerably, which, as he remembers, was at about ten or eleven Years old, she would often be scribbling, and sometimes in Rhyme; which her Mother was at first pleas'd with: But finding this

---

[23] L. G. Mitchell, ed., *The Purefoy Letters 1735–53* (London: Sidgwick and Jackson, 1973), 70.

[24] George Eland, 'List of Brackley Tradesmen from Eland's *Purefoy Letters*, 1931', Northamptonshire Record Office, Delapré Abbey, Northampton. This list, in manuscript, was prepared for Dr. L. Parkhurst, whose history of Brackley was never completed.

[25] 'Brackley Parish Register: Burials 1771–1812', Northamptonshire Record Office, Delapré Abbey, Northampton.

Humour increase upon her as she grew up, when she thought her capable of more profitable Employment, she endeavour'd to break her of it; and that he likewise, having no Taste for Poetry, and not imagining it could ever be any Advantage to her, join'd in the same Design: But finding it impossible to alter her natural Inclination, he had of late desisted, and left her more at Liberty. (ML ii, pp. xxix–xxx)

Philip Leapor's surprisingly well-formed script is preserved in the records of the Brackley corporation.[26] From Freemantle's account, however, it seems that Anne Leapor was more involved in her daughter's reading; thus, it is possible that both of the poet's parents were at least minimally literate. In one of her letters the poet mentions having had a letter from an aunt whom she describes as 'sententious' (ML ii. 311). Since Philip Leapor's sister had died in childhood, this is probably a sister of the poet's mother, suggesting that the Sharman family was also literate. Perhaps this woman is the Margaret Sherman who subscribed. Of course, the aunt could be some other female relative on her father's side.

It is very likely that Mary Leapor attended the Free School in Brackley, operated by Magdalen College School and situated on the south side of the college chapel. At one point in the late seventeenth century three badly damaged volumes were purchased for the school, *Rider's Dictionary*, *Perottus upon Martial*, and *Erasmi Adagia*. While these books had probably disintegrated by Leapor's time, it is striking that poor scholars might be taught Latin. The schoolmaster's appointment was at times treated as a sinecure for the vicar of Evenley, a Magdalen living. Mary Leapor, however, would have studied under a man named Richard Cooper who made strenuous efforts to improve the school during the middle years of the century (Clarke, 146–7). What Leapor may have gained from Cooper is discussed in Chapter 4 below.

In an effort to market Leapor's poetry as that of a natural genius, the note to the first volume attempts to minimize her reading: 'Mrs. Leapor from a Child delighted in reading, and particularly Poetry, but had few Opportunities of procuring any Books of that kind' (ML i, p. i). To an extent, Freemantle

---

[26] 'Brackley Corporation 1729–1753: Register of Oaths and Declarations', Ellesmere Collection, Northamptonshire Record Office, Delapré Abbey, Northampton.

compounds this impression when she writes: 'Mrs. LEAPOR's whole Library consisted of about sixteen or seventeen single Volumes, among which were Part of Mr. *Pope*'s Works, *Dryden*'s Fables, some Volumes of Plays, &c.' (ML ii, p. xxxii). These were the books that she owned. It is hard to believe that she did not borrow others. Freemantle, drawing on Philip Leapor again, describes the poet's habits: 'she always chose to spend her leisure Hours in Writing and Reading, rather than in those Diversions which young People generally chuse; insomuch that some of the Neighbours that observ'd it, expressed their Concern, lest the Girl should over-study herself, and be mopish' (ML ii, p. xxx). Those neighbours were probably also members of the Leapor clan. The proposal for Leapor's subscription conveys a similar idea of her as an uneducated genius, given, nonetheless, to considerable reading:

[She] had no other Education than in common with those of her own Station; could borrow no Helps from the Converse of her Country Companions; yet, by the Strength of her own Parts, the Vivacity of her own Genius, and a perpetual Pursuit after Knowledge, not only acquired a Taste for the most exalted and refined Authors in our Language, but aspired to imitate 'em; and perhaps would have equall'd some of 'em, if the Length of her Life had borne any proportion to the Extent of her Abilities. What are now her Remains were the First fruits of her Studies...[27]

In Chapter 4, below, an examination of her poetry will demonstrate what sorts of books Leapor read, and, especially, which ones made a strong impact on her work.

Mary Leapor at some point in her adolescence became a domestic servant. Her first known employer was Susanna Jennens. The identity of this woman is known by a remarkable coincidence. Weston Hall in Northamptonshire passed in 1925 to Sacheverell Sitwell, a descendant of the Blencowe and Jennens families. The library of that house contains, among many other rare books, three sets of Leapor's poems. On the title-page to one of the first volumes is written, 'Once Kitchen maid at Weston'. That Leapor was employed in the house is entirely plausible, since Susanna Jennens was the daughter of Sir John Blencowe

---

[27] *Proposals For Printing by Subscription The Poetical Works, Serious and Humorous, Of Mrs. Leapor, lately Deceased* (London, 1747). A damaged copy of this is preserved at the Bodleian Library in Ballard MS 42.

who had employed the poet's father. She had been born in 1688 in Marston St Lawrence, and had married Richard Jennens of Mollington, Oxfordshire, in 1708 (Baker, i. 720). Following her husband's death, she is said to have been given Weston Hall as a Valentine present by her father [Sitwell, 5]. Mary Leapor would have been known, if not to Susanna Jennens, then to other members of the Blencowe family, who may have recommended her.

The village of Weston in which Leapor would have lived for some time was six miles north of Brackley. In the early eighteenth century about twenty families lived there, and, according to the census of 1801 it had a population of 137 (Baker, ii. 720). In many respects, Weston was more isolated than Brackley. Living in such a house would none the less have exposed Leapor to a more leisured way of life than she had known before, though as a servant her enjoyments would have been circumscribed. More importantly, she would have met relatively well educated people. It is very likely that she enjoyed access to books in the house (see Appendix).

Sir George Sitwell, the father of Edith, Osbert, and Sacheverell, was himself a poet and a formidable antiquary. In *A Brief History of Weston Hall* (1927) he brings together a great deal of information about this unusual house. He expresses considerable interest in the kitchen-maid poet: 'Mrs. Leapor shows in her verses an acquaintance which surprises one with the characters of classical mythology, and depicts with some success scenes of fashionable life. She can write lines so strong as to be almost terrifying...' (Sitwell, 31). Sitwell provides an extended description of the gardens as they would have been in Susanna Jennens's lifetime, a summary of the more interesting volumes in the library, and a general inventory of the house from Dutch paintings to kitchen pewter. According to Sitwell, Susanna Jennens lived alone in the house after 1732 (Sitwell, 21), that is, after the marriage of her daughter Mary to Arthur Barnardiston, a merchant with interests in Turkey. She did, however, often visit friends and members of her family, as well as receive visitors at Weston. In 1742 her son Richard purchased and occupied the nearby manor of Thorp Mandeville (Sitwell, 22). Susanna Jennens herself lived on a comfortable but not vast income of £300 (Sitwell, 21). Sitwell believes that most of her time was spent at needlework, reading, and gardening. Curiously, a cookbook compiled by Anne Blencowe, and to which Susanna Jennens made additions, was edited and published by George Saintsbury in 1925. Although it has not been seen for some time, the manuscript may contain a specimen of Mary Leapor's handwriting.[28] A large portrait of Susanna Jennens still hangs at Weston Hall, and has recently been restored.

If in some respects Jennens's life was quiet and domestic, she was also a woman of imagination. Inside a walnut cabinet at Weston the following account from 1747 or 1748 is pasted:

Mrs. Jennens, daughter of Judge Blencowe, dreamt that an express came with an account of the death of her sister, Lady Probyn; that the latter had appointed her sole Executrix and had left a cabinet to Mrs. Betty Blencowe in which were secret drawers containing several valuables. She told her dream to Mrs. Welch, then staying with her. A year afterwards, an express came, Mrs. Welch reminded her of her dream, and upon opening the Will it was found that the cabinet was left to Mrs. Blencowe and Mrs. Jennens was directed by her dream to the secret drawers, where she found diamonds and other valuables, which were afterwards given to her daughter Mrs. Peareth. (Sitwell, 33)

If nothing else, her imagination had a practical tendency.

In Susanna Jennens Leapor would have found a woman able to fend for herself in adversity. At her husband's death she had been left with four children under the age of 5. Despite having an income and for some years an indulgent father, the task of raising them cannot have been easy. This trial was repeated in the life of one of her daughters, Mary, who gave birth to a son a week after her husband, Arthur Barnardiston, died in 1737. It is possible that Leapor was employed at Weston at this time.

The Jennens family had a literary bent. There is a folder of very short poems at Weston Hall written by Jennens, her daughters, and other women of her acquaintance. Most of these are invitations or responses:

> Unhappy me
> That I can't be,

[28] George Saintsbury, ed., *The Receipt Book of Mrs. Ann Blencowe, A.D. 1694* (London: The Adelphi, Guy Chapman, 1925). See also Georgia Sitwell, Preface, in Francis Bamford (ed.), *Dear Miss Heber: An Eighteenth Century Correspondence* (London: Constable, 1936), pp. xiii-xxxi; this work is a selection of letters received by Susanna Jennens's great-granddaughter Mary Heber (1758-1809), who occupied Weston Hall during the latter part of the eighteenth century.

> With You at Tea,
> And must not see,
> Dear Miss Molly,
> Engag'd I be,
> As You may see,
> With our Johnny,
> But more to ye.[29]

It is not known who wrote these lines. The Molly is probably not Leapor but Mary Barnardiston. Charmingly, the verses are written along the edge of a circular piece of paper, which is folded three times to make the shape of a cone. The folding serves for an envelope. Obviously there is no literary merit in such rhymes, yet the folder of poems makes clear that there was a group of women poets associated with Weston Hall. There is also an older copybook of poems by Anne Blencowe, almost entirely on scriptural themes.[30] It is as if by working in Weston Hall Leapor came into contact with that family's modest literary tradition. If Susanna Jennens was alone much of the time, there is no reason to doubt that she gave attention to her kitchen-maid and that she encouraged her to read and to write poetry. By an acute reading of internal evidence, Betty Rizzo suggests that the 'Parthenissa' mentioned in 'The Proposal' and elsewhere in Leapor's poetry is the 'Mrs. J.' to whom Freemantle sent Leapor's manuscripts (see ML ii, p. xviii), and that the only probable candidate in the subscription lists is Susanna Jennens. Rizzo suggests that alternatively Parthenissa might be Elizabeth Lisle Bowles, wife of the Brackley vicar (Rizzo, 322). The new evidence from Weston Hall establishes a clear link between Jennens and Leapor; there is no reason now to doubt that Susanna Jennens is the woman mentioned in Leapor's poetry (see also Sitwell, 30).

That Jennens had some talent as a poet may be judged from 'Parthenissa's Answer to the Pocket-Book's Soliloquy', a poem in Leapor's second volume which can now be attributed to her. The poem is part of a humorous exchange with Leapor over the gift of a pocket-book, an exchange which took place after Leapor had left Weston Hall, possibly towards the end of the poet's life. Although she lacks Leapor's force, Jennens is competent and

---

[29] Manuscript poem, Weston Hall, Weston, Northamptonshire.
[30] Anne Blencowe, manuscript poems, Weston Hall, Weston, Northamptonshire.

amusing when she chides the book for complaining of its new owner. Her belief in Leapor's talent is suggested by one oddly poignant stanza:

> What better could thy Fate decree,
> What more Ambition hope?
> Know'st thou who 'twas accepted thee?
> The successor of Pope. (ML ii. 97)

Perhaps this is only a witty pleasantry; it may also be the delight this woman takes in her young friend's success. From 'The Muses Embassy' it is evident that Jennens corrected Leapor's verses. Iris, the messenger goddess, is sent by the muses to find a new poet; she discovers Mira's 'crippled Infants' and agrees to care for them:

> But to conform them into Rule,
> She set the wayward Brats to School.
> 'To whom?' The tuneful Virgins cry'd:
> To *Parthenissa*, she reply'd. (ML ii. 278)

If Jennens thought that Leapor had a future as a poet, Leapor also relied on this woman's criticism and encouragement.

At some point Leapor left Weston Hall and took work elsewhere. This was normal with jobs in domestic service and does not imply any disagreement with Jennens, though presumably there was a period when she saw little of her old employer. This part of Leapor's life is described in a letter to the *Gentleman's Magazine* in 1784. The writer, who is identified only as 'W.', is answering a request by the critic Thomas Holt White in the preceding issue for information on Leapor.[31] According to the correspondent the poet was 'some time cook-maid in a gentleman's family in the neighbourhood. Her fondness for writing verses there displayed itself by her sometimes taking up her pen while the jack was standing still, and the meat scorching' (*GM* 54 (1784), 807). He goes on to report the gentleman's recollections of his servant, perhaps revealing inadvertently something about Leapor's difficulties in the house:

---

[31] 'T.H.W.' responding to a quotation of Leapor along with Chaucer, Hesiod, and Shakespeare in the preceding issue, on the subject of gossamers, asks, 'Who is Molly Leapor, whom you mention in your note? I know no such person' (*GM* 54 (1784), 752). James M. Kuist identifies T.H.W. as Thomas Holt White, a regular contributor to the magazine: see *The Nichols File of The Gentleman's Magazine* (Madison and London: University of Wisconsin Press, 1982), 155.

He represented her as having been extremely swarthy, and quite emaciated, with a long crane-neck, and a short body, much resembling, in shape, a bass-viol. However, the talents of her mind amply compensated for the defects of her person; and if, with so few advantages, she was capable of writing with so much credit to herself, there can be no doubt but, if her career had been prolonged, she would have greatly distinguished herself in the annals of female literature. (*GM* 54 (1784), 807)

The correspondent intends not to be ungenerous. Trevor Hold, in his recent anthology *A Northamptonshire Garland*, identifies the house described in Leapor's poem 'Crumble Hall' as Edgcote House, on the grounds that the carved heads described at the beginning of the poem correspond to a drawing of Edgcote House by Peter Tillemans (*c.*1684-1733).[32] That Leapor actually worked at the house she describes as 'Crumble Hall' and that that is the place referred to in the *Gentleman's Magazine* is strongly suggested by internal evidence. In the poem she describes a woman named Sophronia making cheese-cakes (see ML ii. 118). The same woman appears in a number of poems, and in 'An Epistle to Artemisia. On Fame' she dismisses 'Mira', Leapor's persona, for writing while she should be working (see ML ii. 52). Leapor describes herself as the woman's 'Slave' in 'The Disappointment' (ML ii. 81). 'Advice to Sophronia' describes the woman as a decayed beauty of 55 who ought to prepare herself for a 'Virgin Grave'. Instead, she takes 'a beardless Clown' drawn by 'Gold's all-conqu'ring Charms' for her lover (ML ii. 56). Edgcote House was owned by Richard Chauncy (*c.*1690-1760), whose wife, Elizabeth (*c.*1693-1762), would have been about the age of Leapor's Sophronia (Baker, i. 493-5). The Sophronia in the poems, however, is unmarried, and it is therefore more likely that she was a housekeeper or a relative.

Unfortunately, it is more difficult to trace the Chauncys than the Blencowes, not least because they were less accomplished people. Toby Chauncy (1673-1733), a cousin of Richard Chauncy and a former owner of the house, had been elected Member

---

[32] Trevor Hold, ed., *A Northamptonshire Garland: An Anthology of Northamptonshire Poets with Biographical Notes* (Northampton: Northamptonshire Libraries, 1989), 103 n.; Hold refers to a forthcoming volume of Tillemans's drawings, edited by Bruce Bailey and to be published by the Northamptonshire Record Society.

of Parliament for Banbury in 1730 (Baker, i. 493-5). Richard Chauncy's eldest son, William Henry (1728-88), was matriculated at Oxford on 17 March 1743-4, but did not take a degree.[33] This man may be the 'W.' who wrote to the *Gentleman's Magazine*, though this is by no means certain.

Edgcote House, situated about 8 miles north-west of Brackley, was a somewhat larger house than Weston Hall. Its history, alluded to in 'Crumble Hall' (see ML ii. 112), was distinguished. It had been in the possession of Henry, Prince of Wales, prior to his accession as Henry V in 1413. Thomas Cromwell eventually purchased the manor, and installed a new kitchen with two huge chimneys, which were no longer used by the eighteenth century. In 1540 the house passed to Anne of Cleves as part of her settlement, after which it came into the hands of the Chauncy family.[34] Richard Chauncy tore down this house, and built the one that stands in its place at a cost of £20,000 between 1747 and 1752.[35] Leapor's objections to the plans are recorded in the last section of 'Crumble Hall' (see ML ii. 121-2). Richard Chauncy's improvements were taken a step further by William Henry Chauncy, who caused the village of Edgcote with its eighteen families to be removed from his prospect some time before 1788.[36] One of the few surviving descriptions of the old house is by Dr John Wallis, who took a scientific interest in the extraordinary chimneys.[37] From this it may be judged that the Chauncys had been friends of the Blencowe family, and that a reference from Susanna Jennens carried weight with them. Although Leapor was dismissed from Edgcote House, several members of the family subscribed to her poems. They may have been surprised by the contents of her second volume.

Most of Leapor's time at Weston Hall and Edgcote House would obviously have been spent working. A kitchen-maid was

[33] J. Foster, *Alumni Oxonienses 1715-1886*, 4 vols. (Oxford, 1888), i. 242.
[34] John Bridges, *The History and Antiquities of Northamptonshire*, ed. Peter Whalley, 2 vols. (Oxford, 1791), i, 117-21.
[35] Nikolaus Pevsner, *Northamptonshire*, rev. Bridget Cherry, *The Buildings of England*, ed. Nikolaus Pevsner and Judy Nairn (Harmondsworth: Penguin, 1961; rev. edn., 1973), 209.
[36] K. J. Allison *et al.*, *The Deserted Villages of Northamptonshire*, Department of English Local History Occasional Papers, no. 18 (Leicester: Leicester University Press, 1966), 38.
[37] John Wallis, 'An Extract of a Letter', *Philosophical Transactions*, 14 (20 Dec. 1684), 800-1.

usually the most menial servant in a house. The following job description is preserved with *The Purefoy Letters*:

The Cook Maid
To roast & boil butcher's meat & all manner of fowls.
To clean all the rooms below stairs.
To make the servants beds & to clean all the garrets.
To clean the great & little stairs.
To scour the pewter & brass.
To help wash, soap & buck.
Or to do anything she is ordered.
If she has never had the smallpox to sign a paper to leave the service if she has them.[38]

The tasks would have been fairly onerous and the rewards small. The Cartwright family, for example, who maintained a very large estate at Aynho, Northamptonshire, valued the work of a kitchen-maid at £3. 10s. per year.[39] While this was in addition to room and board, the amount itself was very small. In an excellent situation, a kitchen-maid might receive £10 per year (Hill, 133). It is well to remember that Susanna Jennens with her £300 per year was not extremely wealthy.

It is not known how long Leapor worked for Susanna Jennens and the Chauncys, or if she was also employed at other houses. That the job at Edgcote was her last is indicated by her poems, and it is possible to work out the approximate time that she left. Bridget Freemantle dates her own acquaintance with Leapor from fourteen months prior to the poet's death on 12 November 1746, that is, September 1745. In her 'Epistle to Artemisia. On Fame' Leapor follows the description of her dismissal directly with these lines:

> Thus wrapp'd in Sorrow, wretched *Mira* lay,
> Till *Artemisia* swept the Gloom away:
> The laughing Muse, by her Example led,
> Shakes her glad Wings, and quits the drowsy Bed.   (ML ii. 53)

Leapor was still downcast about the loss of her job, perhaps unable to write much poetry, when she met Freemantle. The interval between her leaving Edgcote and meeting Freemantle cannot have been great, a matter of months at most, unless Leapor's depression was vastly disproportionate to the space in

---

[38] Mitchell, ed., *Purefoy Letters*, 135.   [39] Cooper, *Aynho*, 117.

which she describes it. It is probable, then, that she returned to Brackley during the first six months of 1745. From this time until the end of her life she kept house for her father, and took some hand in his affairs. According to Freemantle, this work filled most of her time.

While Leapor may have felt embarrassed and withdrawn following her return from Edgcote, she was well known, even admired, for her writing in the area of her home. Of course, there also appear to have been a good number of people who regarded her as an eccentric or a 'mope'. It is none the less evident from her poetry that at different times she was visited by aspiring poets and dramatists. Again, it is possible to refer especially to her 'Epistle to Artemisia. On Fame'. Leapor's poetry and plays circulated in manuscript around Brackley, and Freemantle knew her writing long before they actually became friends. Judging from Freemantle's recollection, Leapor enjoyed some local celebrity:

> I remember I saw, two or three Years before my Acquaintance with her commenced, a Book about the Size of a common Copy-Book (but something thicker) fill'd with Poems of her writing, that much pleas'd me. I thought them extraordinary Performances for a Girl of her Age, and one that had so little Advantage (or rather none at all) either from Books or Conversation: But my bad State of Health prevented me from making any further Enquiry concerning this young Genius, till about fourteen Months before her Death, when I was first inform'd she had wrote a Tragedy.
>
> I could not help smiling at this; thinking it at least a very bold Attempt from a Person in her Situation. But however, it raised my Curiosity very much: And happening to meet with her a Day or two afterwards, I begg'd the Favour of seeing it; which was readily granted. You may easily guess how far it exceeded my Expectation. (ML ii, pp. xviii–xix)

Since Freemantle had to walk within a few yards of Leapor's door whenever she approached Brackley from Hinton, it is perhaps odd that they had not met at least in passing. At any rate, Mary Leapor's friendship with Bridget Freemantle marks a turning point in her life. She may have written some very promising poetry, but she had had little personal support for her writing while she was at Edgcote. Freemantle not only provided Leapor with a receptive audience for her mature work but actively promoted it.

Bridget Freemantle appears constantly in Leapor's later poems as 'Artemisia', a name that refers to a ruler of Rhodes known for having fostered the arts. The name was often given to women by eighteenth-century writers, and may have lost its original significance. Betty Rizzo has identified Freemantle from a letter of Samuel Richardson, who published Leapor's second volume, to Isaac Hawkins Browne.[40]

Bridget Freemantle was born in 1698 in Hinton. Her father, Thomas Freemantle, was a native of Moreton Pinkeney in Northamptonshire. He had been a fellow of Lincoln College, Oxford, and, from 1692 until his death in 1719 at the age of 56, was the rector of Hinton. His wife, Mary Newton, died on 19 May 1746, at the age of 77 (Baker, i. 636–8). Among the letters published with Leapor's second volume is one consoling her friend on the sickness of her mother (ML ii. 321–4). The death of Bridget Freemantle's mother was probably an important event in the course of her friendship with the poet, and it is possible that one of the epitaphs Leapor wrote was for Mary Freemantle, rather than for her own mother, as first seems likely (ML i. 263). Bridget Freemantle, like the poet, did not marry. She died in Hinton in 1779 at the age of 81 (Baker, i. 638).

Freemantle's friendship with Mary Leapor blossomed quickly. Shortly after reading the play she paid a visit to the poet, expressed a warm opinion of the piece, and asked for more of her work. She was pleased by what she was shown, and suggested a subscription might be organized. The idea prompted Leapor to write a rather long poem about the follies of ambition, entitled 'Mopsus; or, The Castle Builder'. Freemantle writes:

I indulg'd my Curiosity in calling upon her often, to see how she carried it on. . . . My expressing some Fear of being troublesome in coming so frequently, occasioned a great Variety of Invitations, both in Verse and Prose; which I could seldom resist: And indeed her whole Behaviour to me was so extremely good-natur'd and obliging, that I must have been the most ungrateful Person in the World, if I had not endeavour'd to make some Return.

From this Time to that of her Death, few Days pass'd in which I did not either see or hear from her; for she gave me the Pleasure of seeing all her Poems as soon as they were finish'd. (ML ii, pp. xx–xxi)

[40] See Betty Rizzo, 'Christopher Smart, The "C.S." Poems, and Molly Leapor's Epitaph', *The Library*, ser. 6/5 (1983), 25.

Freemantle goes on to assert that she was never extremely fond of poetry, and could claim no expertise in literature. It must be observed to the contrary that Leapor's 'Phoebus to Artemisia' describes her as a writer of verses:

> So may thy Verse through distant Ages run,
> Still the bright Image of its Parent Sun;
> Whilst I with Pleasure shall its Birth declare,
> And guard my Offspring with a Father's Care.   (ML ii. 6)

One is not obliged to believe that Freemantle was a good poet. Her modesty preserves the image of Leapor developing in isolation, or, to borrow the pastoral language of the subscription proposal, as one who 'could borrow no Helps from the Converse of her Country Companions'. It is interesting that Freemantle's grandfather also wrote some poems. In the first volume of Leapor's work there are three pastorals which Leapor rewrote from the manuscripts of a Mr Newton. This man would be unidentifiable except for the inscription on Mary Freemantle's tomb in the church at Hinton: 'Mary Freemantle, d. of John Newton Gent. & relict of Thomas F. late rector 19 May 1746 aet. 77' (Baker, ii. 638). There is, then, no reason to believe Freemantle when she claims to have had little interest in poetry.

Bridget Freemantle was probably a well-read woman and must have had an intellectual as well as a personal influence over Mary Leapor. Her father, having been an Oxford don, doubtless had a library of some kind, and presumably this was not dispersed after his death. The Freemantles' religious and political opinions also merit some attention. Along the path of academic and ecclesiastical preferment, Nathaniel Crewe had served as Rector of Lincoln College from 1668 to 1672, and afterwards maintained some influence there. Crewe eventually presented Thomas Freemantle to the living of Hinton in 1692. Freemantle and the newly ordained Richard Grey remained Crewe's closest confidants through the last years of his life. Although he reached an uneasy peace with the Hanoverians, Crewe held privately to his old loyalties, and on his death bed he is reported to have called out to Grey: 'Dick, don't you go over to them, don't you go over to them' (Clarke, 85). Thomas Freemantle, who died three years before Crewe, was probably a Jacobite, and was at least an active High Tory. Whether by the 1740s Bridget Freemantle and her mother still entertained enthusiasm for the Stuart cause is unknown. Leapor herself did not hold such opinions, since she praises the Duke of Cumberland in 'Cicely, Joan, and Deborah: An Eclogue' (see ML ii. 87). She argues in 'August 1746' that the rebels should be shown mercy (see ML ii. 61–3), but one did not need to be a Jacobite to object to the blood sports of public execution. To a labouring woman, the world of high politics may have seemed distant, for she touches on it rarely. Therefore, the question of Bridget Freemantle's influence on this point, though intriguing, is not crucial to an understanding of Leapor's poetry.

Freemantle's efforts towards a subscription were coupled with an attempt to have Leapor's play produced. The tragedy was sent to London, apparently to Colley Cibber, for a reading. The poet describes her anxiety in waiting for a reply:

I cast a languishing Eye upon the Waggon Yesterday. It is impossible to express the Hopes, the Fears, the various Conjectures, and Reveries, that your humble Servant must undergo this important Season, I am like the unhappy Gentleman mentioned in the *Guardian*; and can scarce endure the bare Pronunciation of the Letter S: The hissing of the Tea-kettle distracts me; and if I meet a Goose, I shun him as I would a Lion, or a Crocodile. I intend speedily to provide a Quantity of Hysteric Drops, being apprehensive of Fits at the Sound of the Post-horn. I can't hear the Playhouse spoke of without trembling; and shall not dare to look into a News-paper, for fear of meeting with the Name of *Cibber*. (ML ii. 311–12)

While Cibber later subscribed, he must have decided against producing the play. It was, in fact, never performed.[41] 'Upon her Play being returned to her, stained with Claret', one of Leapor's most attractive compositions, is a direct response to this rejection.

More successful was the attempt to get Leapor into print. Among her letters are two 'On her Writings being to be printed'. It can be judged from these that plans for the subscription were fairly advanced before her death. The first indicates, however, that Leapor was not well. She writes to relieve Freemantle's fears for the success of her publication:

Let the worst happen, I am but as I was before: I shall eat as long as I can, and sleep when I am easy. There is the same Air for me to breathe

---

[41] David Erskine Baker, *Biographia Dramatica: Or, A Companion to the Playhouse*, rev. Isaac Reed and Stephen Jones, 3 vols. (London, 1764; rev. edn., 1812), iii. 369.

in, and the same all chearing Sun. And as my few Acquaintance did not take to me upon the Account of Poetry, so they will scarcely fall off upon its ill Success. (ML ii. 313)

The second letter is difficult to place, since Leapor is responding to a gentleman whose comments on her work are relayed by someone else, or to whom she refers in the third person for reasons of politeness. The letter is concerned with the total number of lines she has written and with choosing one or two pieces which will represent her best work. The most likely interpretation is that it relates to the subscription proposals.

Leapor, however, did not live to see her work in print. Although her poetry often speaks of ill health and many times looks forward to the poet's early death, she died of measles, a sudden illness she was too weak to withstand. Freemantle describes her a day or two before her death asking that the subscription be continued:

> But I have still one Favour to beg of you. I find I am going. I always lov'd my Father; but I feel it now more than ever. He is growing into Years. My Heart bleeds to see the Concern he is in; and it would be the utmost Satisfaction to me, if I could hope any thing of mine could contribute to his comfortable Subsistence in his old Age: I therefore beg of you to take the Key of my Buroe; and if any thing is to be made of my poor Papers, that you will, for my sake, endeavour to promote a Subscription for his Benefit, which you so kindly have propos'd for mine. (ML ii, p. xxviii)

The Brackley register records Leapor's burial on 14 November 1746.[42]

Publication and Reputation

Leapor's death preceded by only two months the first appearances of her work in print. The *London Magazine* in its January 1747 issue printed the poem which in Leapor's second volume bears the title, 'To Lucinda'. In the magazine it is entitled 'The Rural Maid's Reflexions', and the author is identified only as 'a Gardener's Daughter'.[43] Since no comment is made on the

---

[42] 'Brackley Parish Register 1727–1756', Northamptonshire Record Office, Delapré Abbey, Northampton.
[43] 'The Rural Maid's Reflexions', *London Magazine*, 16 (1747), 45.

author being recently dead, it can be assumed that publication had been arranged while Leapor was still alive. It is addressed to some learned woman of a higher station who appears to be a new acquaintance; it is therefore possible that Leapor had had correspondence with a literary woman in London who arranged for the poem's publication. There is a small possibility that she had actually met such a person.

More importantly, the 'Proposals for Printing by Subscription The Poetical Works, Serious and Humorous, Of Mrs. Leapor, lately Deceased' finally appeared bearing the date 1 January 1746–7. Along with a note on the poet from which a passage has been quoted above, there also appeared 'An Ode on Mercy' as a sample of her skills. There was a promise of only one octavo volume at a price of 5*s*., to be delivered 'September next'. It can be assumed that the proposals were drawn up by David Garrick. When Thomas Holt White asked for information on Leapor in the *Gentleman's Magazine* in 1784 there were actually two replies. The second, signed 'Crito', makes this point:

> Molly Leapor... was a most extraordinary, uncultivated genius, who 'warbled her native wood-notes wild.' The first volume of her poems was published by subscription (the proposals for which were drawn up by Mr. Garrick) under the patronage of several persons of rank and taste, in 1748; as was also the second volume, of which the late Mr. Hawkins Browne was the editor in 175... both of them after her death, which happened prematurely by the meazles, at the age of 24. She has been celebrated by Mr. Duncombe in the *Feminead*. (*GM* 54 (1784), 806)

Reference to the *Nichols File* shows that 'Crito' was John Duncombe himself.[44] Duncombe's authority can be accepted for two reasons. First, he was a close friend of Samuel Richardson, who published the later volume. Second, his wife, Susanna Highmore, was also an intimate of Richardson's and had correspondence with him about Leapor (see below). While no confirmation has been found among records of Garrick's career, it can be taken on Duncombe's word that the actor prepared the proposals. It is strange, however, that Garrick did not subscribe for Leapor's volumes, since at almost the same time he subscribed for the Irish bricklayer poet, Henry Jones, though this may have

---

[44] Kuist, *Nichols File*, 57.

been done to please Chesterfield.[45] Duncombe raises other problems in this passage that must be returned to.

The first volume was clearly a success, attracting almost 600 subscribers, among them the Dukes of Bridgewater and Leeds, the Earls of Chesterfield, Arran, Gainsborough, Granville, and Pomfret, the Bishop of Gloucester, and many persons bearing lesser titles. Among the subscribers there is, of course, a large contingent of the Blencowe family, including the Jennens, Barnardiston, and Holbech branches connected by marriage. The Cartwrights of Aynho appear in the list, as well as the Purefoys, who, according to their letters, pressed the subscription among their acquaintances (Eland, ii. 278).

The 'Persons of Rank and of distinguished Taste and Judgement' who took an interest in Leapor's writing and promoted the subscription were most likely members of the Blencowe family. Certainly Susanna Jennens was involved in the subscription from an early stage. Indeed, she was the first to speak about the financial aspects of the project. Leapor writes in 'The Penitent':

> When *Parthenissa* talk'd today
> Of Profits and of *Mira*'s Lay,
> And list'ning *Mira* heard the Sound
> Of number Ten with added Pound,
> The saucy Minx betray'd her Pride,
> And turn'd her scornful Head aside... (ML i. 118-19)

Two or even three years' salary for a kitchen maid, £10 was, in fact, too low an estimate of the potential profit (see Rizzo, 323). Leapor had probably done some arithmetic of her own, and indulged the hope that the subscription might secure her future. What she would have done with the money can be surmised. In 'Mira's Will' she gives the peculiar instruction: 'Six comick Poets may the Corse surround, | And all Free-holders, if they can be found' (ML i. 9). Betty Rizzo observes that Philip Leapor voted for the first time in the 1749 election for Knight of the Shire, and judges from this that he had used the capital from the subscription to buy his freehold (Rizzo, 323). If Philip Leapor had earlier been hostile to his daughter's poetry, fearing it was unprofitable, but had then left her at liberty, it was probably because she had

---

[45] See Henry Jones, *Poems on Several Occasions* (London, 1749), 15.

convinced him that she could earn money with her pen. Specifically, they probably decided to buy the freehold.

The size of the subscription of the first volume, if not that of the second, can be compared to another effort undertaken by the Blencowes early in the next century. *The Casket* (1828) was a miscellany prepared by a Mrs Blencowe. That this was the same family can be judged from the inclusion of a poem by R. W. Blencowe, jun.,[46] who can be located in the genealogies.[47] The miscellany printed poems by Wordsworth, Crabbe, and Byron, as well as many others whose popularity has faded. On this occasion the subscription included six members of the royal family, as well as 'H.M. Librarian'. The success of Leapor's subscription, though on a much smaller scale, probably owed a great deal to the Blencowes' wide social connections.

James Roberts delivered the first volume to the subscribers in April 1748 (*GM* 18 (1748), 192). The book's reception seems to have been good. Ralph Griffiths's *Monthly Review* reprinted three poems in November 1749 (*MR* 2 (1749–50), 14–15), and Christopher Smart, having been introduced to Leapor's work while visiting Samuel Richardson,[48] reprinted Colinetta with a very warm comment in his journal *The Midwife*. He speaks here through Mrs Midnight:

The following Pastoral Piece, written by Mrs. Leapor, exceeds every Thing of that kind, which has yet been exhibited by the Male Authors, and I think does a supreme Honour to our Sex. Where will you find in any of them so much Nature, Sweetness, Simplicity and Ease, and such a judicious Choice of new and enlivening Epithets? Our Readers will have a farther Account of this excellent Lady in a future Number.[49]

Smart's interest in Leapor evidently faded, as he did not fulfil the promise of a 'farther Account'.

---

[46] R. W. Blencowe, Jr., 'The Jew's Appeal to the Christian', in Mrs Blencowe (ed.), *The Casket: A Miscellany* (London, 1829), 128–31.
[47] Thomas Phillips, 'Pedigree of Blencowe of Marston St. Lawrence, Co. Northamptonshire', in *Genealogia: A Collection of Pedigrees of Families* (n.p., c.1871).
[48] Rizzo, 'Christopher Smart, The "C.S." Poems, and Molly Leapor's Epitaph', 25.
[49] Christopher Smart, *The Midwife*, i (1750), 81; cited by Rizzo in 'Christopher Smart, The "C.S." Poems, and Molly Leapor's Epitaph', 26.

The reception of Leapor's work was sufficiently warm for a second volume to be considered. Samuel Richardson, though not a subscriber to the first volume, had taken an interest in Leapor, who was in his eyes perhaps a more tragic Pamela. As a printer Richardson was notably successful. As he became more independent of booksellers he began to choose works for publication which suited his own taste.[50] He took an active interest in women writers, and at different times published works by Sarah Fielding, Charlotte Lennox, Susanna Centlivre, Eliza Haywood, Elizabeth Carter, and Mary Barber, among others.[51] It appears that he published Mary Leapor not only because he thought she would be a commercial success, but because he admired her work. In one letter to Susanna Highmore, he turns down the offer of a sonnet to be prefixed to Leapor's second volume:

Do I condemn your sonnet, Madam? Indeed I don't. I think it has no little merit; but as a copy to be prefixed to the sweetly easy poems of Molly Leaper, had it not been written, I should not have advised the measure; and yet I love that genius should shew its powers.[52]

Richardson rejects Highmore's sonnet, however delicately, because it will appear incompetent beside Mary Leapor's poems. This letter implies that Richardson saw Leapor as a poet of genuine merit.

William Sale suggests that the idea for a second volume originated with Richardson's friend Thomas Edwards,[53] who is now remembered as the author of some excellent sonnets. There were several problems associated with the attempt to publish another volume, not least the lack of material. Richardson wrote to Highmore on 22 June 1750: 'I am afraid we shall want matter of Molly Leaper's works to make out the bulk of the new volume. We must try, if so, to get more of her letters.'[54] Bridget Freemantle's letter, however, indicates that by 21 February 1749 she had already supplied all the manuscripts in her possession:

[50] William M. Sale, Jr., *Samuel Richardson: Master Printer*, Cornell Studies in English, 37 (Ithaca, NY: Cornell University Press, 1950), 3.
[51] Ibid. 106-14.
[52] Anna Laetitia Barbauld, ed., *The Correspondence of Samuel Richardson*, 6 vols. (London, 1804), ii. 253. For information on Highmore, see Wilfred Bland, 'Susanna Highmore's Literary Reputation', *Proceedings of the American Philosophical Society*, 122 (1978), 377-84.
[53] Sale, *Samuel Richardson*, 116.
[54] Barbauld, *Correspondence of Samuel Richardson*, ii. 246.

I shall readily contribute any thing in my Power, tho' I fear that is very little: But, upon making a thorough Search among my Papers, I have found Two or Three of hers, that were mislaid when the other were sent to Mrs. J——; which I here send you, with two or three Copies wrote in her Childhood, that have since been alter'd as they now stand in the printed Book. (ML ii, p. xviii)

The volume that was finally delivered in March 1751 (*GM* 21 (1751), 143) filled 324 pages excluding the thirty-five pages of preliminaries. The first volume had only 282 pages altogether. The second volume, however, had a number of letters as well as an unfinished play to make up the required length.

The second volume, according to Duncombe, was edited by Isaac Hawkins Browne, a poet and sometime Member of Parliament. Betty Rizzo believes it is possible that he edited both volumes.[55] The lack of information on this point makes it difficult to judge the accuracy of the printed text. Comparison of 'To Lucinda' with the first publication of 'The Rural Maid's Reflexions' shows that Browne, for whatever reason, changed at least one title, though he may have been returning to the original. Comparison of 'An Ode on Mercy' in the first volume and the version printed with the subscription proposals also reveals differences, though again it is difficult to know whether the editor of that volume was following Leapor's manuscript in preference to a version corrected possibly by Garrick. Without the recovery of manuscripts, an unlikely prospect after two hundred years, such questions cannot be settled. Given Richardson's concern to fill out the second volume, it may be assumed that very few of Mary Leapor's works escaped publication. Since Leapor, according to Freemantle, destroyed much of her juvenilia, it is possible she would have wanted to exercise similar judgement over the publication of her two volumes. This, of course, is a common difficulty with posthumous editions, and not a serious one.

A minor problem which threatened to delay the second volume of Mary Leapor's work was the epitaph (see ML ii. 324). In her letter Bridget Freemantle made this request: 'Mr. *Leapor* has put down a Grave-Stone in Memory of his Daughter; and I should be glad if any of the ingenious Gentlemen you mention would be so

[55] Rizzo, 'Christopher Smart, The "C.S." Poems, and Molly Leapor's Epitaph', 25.

good as to write a few Lines to be put upon it' (ML ii, p. xxxii). At their meeting in either 1749 or 1750, Christopher Smart accepted this task from Richardson; however, he delayed writing the piece which was to be printed in the volume. Indeed, by 10 December 1750, with most of the book already printed, Richardson had still not received the epitaph. Whether the epitaph that was printed is Smart's work at all is unknown. Rizzo maintains no more than that it is possible that he wrote the poem.[56] To the evidence which she assembles, it is possible to add one fact. Susanna Highmore asked Elizabeth Carter to write a piece on Leapor, probably an epitaph. Carter wrote to Highmore:

I congratulate you that there is so soon to appear another volume of your favourite Mrs. Leapor's poetry. It is with much concern that I find myself unable to comply with a request from you and Mr. Browne, but indeed you pay me too great a compliment in supposing me capable of writing upon any subject that is proposed to me. Tho' I highly respect Mrs. Leapor's character from the account you give of it, yet as she was absolutely unknown to myself, and I am but little acquainted even with her writings, I am upon this account as well as many others, entirely unfit for such an undertaking as you propose.[57]

From this letter it is clear that Smart was not the only person asked to write on Leapor. It is possible that others besides Carter were asked to write the piece. Hence, the likelihood of an attribution to Smart is reduced. There is, incidentally, a suggestion in Carter's letter that she understood Highmore to have been acquainted with Leapor, though this cannot be proved. In the end, Philip Leapor had the poet's stone engraved without the published epitaph. Baker's history of Northamptonshire records this inscription (i. 579):

> In Memory of
> Mary Leapor
> Daughter of
> Philip and Ann
> Leapor: who

[56] Ibid. 26–31.
[57] Emily Morse Symonds [George Paston], *Mrs. Delany (Mary Granville): A Memoir* (London: Grant Richards, 1900), 297; cited by Edmund Blunden in a manuscript revision to a reprint in the Bodleian Library of 'A Northamptonshire Poetess: Glimpses of an Eighteenth-Century Prodigy', *Journal of the Northamptonshire Natural History Society*, 28 (1936), 60.

Departed this Life
Nov. ye 26. 1746
Aged 24.

Either Baker or the engraver confused the date of death. The stone has now vanished and is believed to have been used for paving the walks of St James's Church in Brackley.[58]

A serious problem related to the publication of the second volume was the shortage of subscribers. The list shows less than half the number for the first volume. There were, of course, some interesting additions such as William Pitt, but on the whole the second volume was a disappointment, certainly in commercial terms. Thomas Edwards suggested that the fault lay in the way the book was assembled. He wrote to Richardson: 'I thank you for sending me Molly Leapor. How does the town receive her? I am sorry to see the number of subscribers fall so vastly short of what appeared to the other volume. What ignorants we are! If we had but thought of *vamping* her with cuts, we had done the business.'[59] Woodcuts would have been an interesting addition to Leapor's second volume, and in themselves would serve as evidence on how she was understood by her contemporaries.

The simplest reason for the disappointing subscription is that the novelty of a kitchen-maid poet had dissipated in the four years since the first subscription, especially among the gentry around Brackley who might now observe Philip Leapor enjoying the fruits of the first volume. Yet in some quarters the second volume confirmed the poet's reputation. Whereas in 1749 the *Monthly Review* had published three poems, 'leaving their merit to the decision of the public' (*MR* 2 (1749–50), 15), in 1751 the judgement was more explicit:

This second volume contains, besides several ingenious smaller pieces, written on particular occasions, *The Unhappy Father*, a tragedy, with three acts of a second play, written at the request of a friend, in about a fortnight, and some letters of this extraordinary young woman, which have a solidity in them far beyond what could be expected from one of her years, and so destitute of the advantages of education... (*MR* 5 (1751), 23)

---

[58] George Eland, 'Molly Leapor—Poetess', *Northampton County Magazine*, 5 (1932), 116. Dr John Clarke informs me that there is a small memorial plaque to Mary Leapor in St James's Church, but I have not been able to locate this.

[59] Barbauld, *Correspondence of Samuel Richardson*, 24.

There is also a comment on Leapor's tragedy:

> As to Mrs. *Leapor*'s dramatic writings, it would not be over-rating their merit to say that much worse plays have succeeded on the stage: yet it is probable her *Unhappy Father* would not have pleased in the acting. She seems to have been too ignorant of, or to have too little regard to, those rules of the drama, and that happy management of plot and catastrophe, which often ensure success to poetry and sentiments much inferior to her own. (*MR* 5 (1751), 30)

From a twentieth-century perspective it is often difficult to admire either the management of plot and catastrophe or the sentiments of plays written in the mid-eighteenth century. Yet the reviewer's regard for Leapor's work is worth noting. Along with these comments the magazine reprinted Freemantle's letter and two of Leapor's own letters, while for samples of her verse readers were referred to the three that had appeared in the earlier number. It should also be noted that the *Gentleman's Magazine* allowed an anonymous poet to indulge the sincerest form of flattery in 1752, by publishing a pastiche of Leapor's religious poetry (see *GM* 22 (1752), 529).

Leapor's work was generally not compared to that of men, though as a female writer she commanded a position of importance for some time. John Duncombe's poem, *The Feminiad*, appeared in 1754 celebrating women poets. This unusual composition has no striking literary merit, yet has real importance as an attempt to assert the value of women writers. Leapor is among those mythologized almost beyond recognition:

> Now in ecstatic visions let me rove,
> By Cynthia's beams, thro' Brackley's glimm'ring grove;
> Where still each night, by startled shepherds seen,
> Young LEAPOR's form flies shadowy o'er the green.
> Those envy'd honours Nature lov'd to pay
> The bryar-bound turf, where erst her Shakespeare lay,
> Now on her darling Mira she bestows;
> There o'er the hallow'd ground she fondly strows
> The choicest fragrance of the breathing spring,
> And bids each year her fav'rite linnet sing.[60]

---

[60] John Duncombe, *The Feminiad* (London, 1754; facsimile, Augustan Reprint Society Publication 207, Los Angeles: William Andrews Clark Memorial Library, 1981), 20–1.

If Duncombe was himself an unaccomplished poet, he certainly laboured to promote the work of women whom he believed had been undervalued. As his contribution to the *Gentleman's Magazine* quoted above shows, he was also capable of promoting his own work. Duncombe's poem was reprinted a number of times and thus kept Leapor's name before the reading public for several decades.

At least as significant with regard to Leapor's reputation was her position in *Poems by Eminent Ladies* (1755).[61] This anthology, edited by George Colman and Bonnell Thornton, devoted 118 pages to Leapor, more than to any other writer. Aphra Behn, for example, received 112 pages, Mary Barber 44, and the Countess of Winchilsea only 30. When a revised edition appeared c.1775, Leapor was still the most heavily represented poet. While the space devoted to most of the individual poets in the earlier edition was sharply reduced, twenty-five of the thirty-three poems by Leapor were retained. As a crude barometer of reputation, such a comparison suggests that Leapor's stature as a woman writer remained high almost thirty years after her death.[62]

There were other expressions of interest. Leapor's 'A Request to the Divine Being' was included in Dell's *A Select Collection of the Psalms of David* (1756), a religious anthology dominated, surprisingly, by the work of Elizabeth Tollet.[63] Leapor's long poem 'The Rival Brothers' appeared in *The Lady's Poetical Magazine* (1782).[64] In 1791 William Cowper set Mary Leapor apart from other 'natural' poets whose celebrity and achievement had been strictly ephemeral. He writes to John Johnson concerning Elizabeth Bentley, whose work was then being subscribed:

Many such phenomena have arisen within my remembrance, at which all the world has wonder'd for a season, and has then forgot them. The fact is, that though strong natural genius is always accompanied with strong natural tendency to its object, yet it often happens that the tendency is found where the Genius is wanting. In the present instance however, (the

[61] George Colman and Bonnell Thornton, ed., *Poems by Eminent Ladies* (London, 1755); rev. edn., *Poems by the Most Eminent Ladies of Great Britain and Ireland* (London, c.1775).
[62] Blunden, 'A Northamptonshire Poetess', MS revision, 62.
[63] See Henry Dell, *A Select Collection of the Psalms of David* (London, 1756), 244.
[64] *The Lady's Poetical Magazine: Or, Beauties of British Poetry*, 4 vols. (London, 1781–82), iv (1782), 411–25; cited in Landry, 78.

poems of a certain Mrs. Leapor excepted, who published some 40 years ago) I discern, I think, more marks of a true poetical talent than I remember to have observed in the verses of any, whether male or female, so disadvantageously circumstanced.[65]

In Cowper's view, then, Leapor was the single natural poet whose work had proved durable. It is interesting that Cowper, along with Colman and Thornton, belonged to the Nonsense Club in the 1750s. Mary Leapor was therefore an enthusiasm of this group as well as of Richardson's circle. Christopher Smart, it should be noted, had connections with both groups.

Leapor's reputation subsided in the nineteenth century, but she was noticed occasionally. In 1807 Robert Southey reprinted 'The Crucifixion and Resurrection' and 'The Beauties of the Spring' in his *Specimens of the Later English Poets*, with a warm comment on 'this extraordinary woman'.[66] Alexander Dyce in his *Specimens of British Poetesses* (1825) described her, perhaps unemphatically, as 'no ordinary talent' and reprinted two of her poems, 'The Temple of Love' and 'The Month of August'.[67] It is a measure of the variability of taste that the first of these now seems one of Leapor's least interesting poems. *Blackwood's Edinburgh Magazine* in 1837 quoted a passage from 'The Month of August' describing a harvest feast, with the simple observation: 'The lines are savoury.'[68] Frederick Rowton in *The Female Poets of Great Britain* (1848) wrote of Leapor, 'Her writings, of which two volumes have appeared, display very considerable genius.' Following Dyce, he reprinted 'The Temple of Love'.[69] J. Churton Collins included 'Silvia and the Bee' and part of 'An Hymn to the Morning' in *A Treasury of Minor British Poetry* (1896), with the comment: 'Mary Leapor (1722–1746) appears now to be entirely forgotten, but she is a poetess of some merit.'[70] At the end of the

---

[65] James King and Charles Ryskamp, ed., *The Letters and Prose Writings of William Cowper*, 5 vols. (Oxford: Oxford University Press, 1979–86), iii (1982), 485.
[66] Robert Southey, ed., *Specimens of the Later English Poets*, 3 vols. (London, 1807), ii. 91–5.
[67] Alexander Dyce, ed., *Specimens of British Poetesses* (London, 1825), 171–8.
[68] *Blackwood's Edinburgh Magazine*, 41 (Dec. 1836–June 1837), 408; cited by Landry, 78–9.
[69] Frederic Rowton, ed., *The Female Poets of Great Britain* (London, 1848), 121–4.
[70] J. Churton Collins, ed., *A Treasury of Minor British Poetry* (London and New York, 1896), 389.

nineteenth century, the editors thought Leapor worth an article in the *Dictionary of National Biography* (*DNB* xi. 766).

In the twentieth century there have been numerous if somewhat isolated expressions of interest in Leapor's work. What follows is not an exhaustive survey, though it includes those references which indicate Leapor's literary standing. In 1914 George Saintsbury, in his contribution to the *Cambridge History of English Literature*, lamented that Leapor, among others, had sunken into 'absolute forgetfulness'.[71] This comment may have drawn attention to Leapor for a few years. Myra Reynolds in 1920 described Leapor as minor but individual: 'She manages the heroic couplet with considerable correctness and ease...'.[72] John Squire's *A Book of Women's Verse* (1921) reprinted 'Upon her Play being returned to her, stained with Claret', as well as excerpts from her poems 'An Essay on Hope' and 'An Essay on Friendship'.[73] In 1923 Iolo Williams included 'The Month of August' in *The Shorter Poems of the Eighteenth Century*.[74] Oliver Elton wrote in 1928: '...actuality, with an added touch of grace, is found in the imperfect rhymes of Mrs. Mary Leapor.'[75] Evidently Reynolds and Elton thought differently of Leapor's ability to deal with poetic forms.

When David Nichol Smith assembled his influential *Oxford Book of Eighteenth-Century Verse* (1926), Mary Leapor was not included. Partly to correct this omission, Edmund Blunden wrote an article in 1936, 'A Northamptonshire Poetess: Glimpses of an Eighteenth Century Prodigy'. This is the first sustained work published on Leapor and some of its bibliographical observations are of great value. Presumably Blunden took an interest in her as a result of his research into John Clare. There is no question about Blunden's sympathy with Leapor, but he is not enamoured of the Augustan conventions:

[71] George Saintsbury, 'Southey: Lesser Poets of the Later Eighteenth Century', in A. W. Ward and A. R. Waller (ed.), *The Cambridge History of English Literature*, 15 vols. (Cambridge: Cambridge University Press, 1907–27), ix (1914), 172.
[72] Myra Reynolds, *The Learned Lady in England 1650–1760* (Boston, Mass. and New York: Houghton Mifflin, 1920), 246–7.
[73] John Squire, ed., *A Book of Women's Verse* (Oxford: Clarendon Press, 1921), 59–60.
[74] Iolo Williams, ed., *The Shorter Poems of the Eighteenth Century* (London: William Heinemann, 1923), 342–5.
[75] Oliver Elton, *A Survey of English Literature 1730–1780*, 2 vols. (London: Edward Arnold, 1928), ii. 25.

Mary Leapor, on the evidence of the verse we have of hers, was without that inner fountain of cadences. Her measures are simpler [than Clare's] and she appears not to think of anything more audacious than writing a few forms skilfully and with point. The iambic was Pope's mainstay and it was good enough for her. But Pope, now and then at least, deserted his couplets for stanzas with another movement, and so does she; and when she does her instinct for a completeness of design is notable.[76]

Blunden does not take the view that the couplet is capable of very great variety; nonetheless, Leapor uses it 'skilfully and with point'. From another able poet, that is reasonable praise.

Blunden's article was published in an obscure magazine, and certainly did not establish a position for Leapor in eighteenth-century studies. Hoxie Neale Fairchild felt no hesitation in describing her as a 'nonentity' in 1942.[77] Four years later, Geoffrey Grigson included a passage from 'Colinetta' in his anthology *Before the Romantics* (1946).[78] In 1964 Edmund Blunden and Bernard Mellor republished four of Leapor's poems in their anthology *Wayside Poems of the Early Eighteenth Century*: 'Proserpine's Ragout', 'An Hymn to the Morning', 'Silvia and the Bee', and 'A New Ballad'.[79] While these are all among Leapor's better poems, it is interesting that not one of them is marked by that sharp protest against social injustice or the suffering of women which, to a reader in the 1990s, seems one of the chief characteristics of her verse. 'A New Ballad', for example, is chosen for its prosodic similarity to 'La Belle Dame Sans Merci'.[80] It would, however, be absurd to complain that Blunden and Mellor chiefly admire skill in a poet. Their anthology, like Grigson's, is valuable in that it steps outside the ordinary canon of eighteenth-century verse to recover poets whose works bear consideration.

Mary Leapor has never been forgotten among local historians and scholars in Northamptonshire. The antiquary Baker

---

[76] Blunden, 'A Northamptonshire Poetess', 73.

[77] Hoxie Neale Fairchild, *Religious Trends in English Poetry*, 6 vols. (New York: Columbia University Press, 1939–68), vol. ii: *1740–1780: Religious Sentimentalism in the Age of Johnson* (1942), p. 52.

[78] Geoffrey Grigson, ed., *Before the Romantics: An Anthology of the Enlightenment* (London: George Routledge & Sons, 1946), 318–19.

[79] Edmund Blunden and Bernard Mellor, ed., *Wayside Poems of the Early Eighteenth Century* (Hong Kong: Hong Kong University Press, 1964), 45–50.

[80] Ibid. 129.

unfortunately gave her a brief and dismissive notice in his topographical history of the county in 1822 (i. 647). John Cole, who also wrote a memoir of Hester Mulso Chapone, included Leapor in his *Popular Biography of Northamptonshire* (1839), along with Chapone, Mark Akenside, and William Lisle Bowles. When one attempts to judge the solidity of a poet's reputation on the basis of occasional references in published sources, it is well to note that not all references are of equal value. In Coles's book, the poets are described in much the same terms as 'The Warkton Strong Man', 'The Stentorian Voiced Crier, Of Northampton', and 'The Astonishing Reaper, of Great Doddington'.[81] Leapor has, of course, received more valuable attention from local scholars, certainly from George Eland, who published a brief but informative article on her in 1931.[82] Most recently, Trevor Hold's anthology, *A Northamptonshire Garland* (1989), includes three of Leapor's poems, and makes the crucial identification of Edgcote House as the model for Crumble Hall.

In the 1980s Leapor's work received more attention that at any time since the 1750s. Betty Rizzo's research has, of course, opened the door to a new understanding of Leapor. Roger Lonsdale included three of Leapor's poems in *The New Oxford Book of Eighteenth-Century Verse* (1984), 'An Essay on Woman', 'Mira's Will', and 'An Epistle to a Lady' (*ECV* 408–12). This substantial representation drew the attention of at least two eminent reviewers. Peter Porter, though he ultimately disagreed with Lonsdale's decision to include so many unknown poets in the anthology, was emphatic:

A real discovery is Mary Leapor, dead at twenty-four, the daughter of a Northamptonshire gardener. More than Stephen Duck, if not as strongly as Clare, Leapor shows that poets from the lower orders can handle formal verse with the sophistication of their Augustan exemplars.[83]

A bold statement, but not nearly so bold as that of Kingsley Amis, who admires Lonsdale's whole project, and Leapor in

---

[81] John Cole, *Popular Biography of Northamptonshire* (London, 1839), 99 and *passim*.

[82] Eland, 'Molly Leapor—Poetess', 116–19. See also David Powell, 'Five Best Poets of Northamptonshire', *Northamptonshire and Bedfordshire Life*, 2 (Apr.–May 1972), 22–4.

[83] Peter Porter, 'Disturbing the Augustan Peace', review of *ECV*, *TLS*, (22 Feb. 1985), 188.

particular. Amis observes that many of the newly discovered poets in the anthology are not masters of form but must be read for their 'realism', that is, for content:

[To] Mary Leapor, I award the palm... she writes here with rare skill, reason and imagination on woman in society, knocking askew any easy line-up of 'new' with 'realist' by doing so in the general manner of Pope, with whom she has no need to fear comparison.[84]

Roger Lonsdale's subsequent anthology, *Eighteenth-Century Women Poets* (1989), has raised Leapor's stature even further. She is given 22 full pages, slightly more than the Countess of Winchilsea (pp. 194–217; 4–26). No other poet in the century comes close to this representation. Reviewers have again fixed on Leapor as a figure of considerable interest. Margaret Anne Doody has called for a new edition of Leapor's poetry.[85] Malcolm Rutherford was especially struck by Leapor's satires: 'I was impressed again by Mary Leapor... It is rare to come across such a combative, talkative, witty form of verse, which seems to me quite as satirical as anything in Jane Austen's novels.'[86] Rutherford, like Porter, Amis, Doody, and others, believes that Leapor is a new light in the literary firmament.

It is a sign that Leapor's reputation has reached something of a plateau that it is possible for scholars to disagree about the correct reading of her work. In *The Muses of Resistance: Laboring-Class Women's Poetry in Britain 1739–1796* (1990) Donna Landry gives extensive consideration to Leapor. Although Landry approaches her subject from a very different perspective than does this study, her work is certainly bold, thoughtful, and provocative.

[84] Kingsley Amis, review of *ECV*, *The Listener*, (6 Dec. 1984), 27.
[85] Margaret Anne Doody, 'Tit for Tat', review of *ECWP*, *London Review of Books*, (21 Dec. 1989), 4. For positive comments on Leapor in other reviews of this anthology, see Terry Castle, 'Unruly and Unresigned', *TLS*, (10–16 Nov. 1989), 1228; Janet Barron, 'They Kept Scribbling', *Literary Review*, no. 136 (Jan. 1990), 57–8; Harriet Devine Jump, '107 Grandmothers', *Oxford Magazine*, no. 55 (Hilary Term 1990), 15; R. E. Pritchard, 'A Lettered Bride', *PN Review* 16/4 (1990), 60–1; Karina Williamson, *Essays in Criticism* (forthcoming). Leapor was also singled out by Margaret Forster as the best poet in the anthology in a discussion on BBC Radio 3, 'Critics' Forum', 7 Oct. 1989. For a round dismissal of Leapor, Lonsdale, and much else, see Germaine Greer, 'No Laments for Dead Birds', *Daily Telegraph* (21 Oct. 1989), Weekend sect., p. XIII.
[86] Malcolm Rutherford, 'Light on Female Bards', review of *ECWP*, *Financial Times* (16 Dec. 1989), Weekend sect., p. x.

Obviously, contemporary interest in Leapor owes a great deal to a general shift in eighteenth-century studies. There is a new interest among scholars in seeking out forgotten writers whose works represent the experiences of women or of the poor. It cannot be claimed that Leapor is the most obscure of these writers; indeed, her work has been noticed in the past by some highly regarded poets and critics. Until the 1980s, however, the vast majority of specialists in the period had not known of her existence. At best, she had what could be described as deuterocanonical status; she was unquestionably outside the usual canon of poets, but occasionally she was rediscovered, even admired. In all, it seems that Leapor has, at last, been recognized as a poet worthy of serious consideration. She has come a long way from 1766, when John Whiston described her poetry as 'extremely fit for young ladies'.[87]

[87] John Whiston, *Directions for a Proper Choice of Authors to Form a Library* (London, 1766), 41.

CHAPTER 2

PROBLEMS OF THE WOMAN POET

The poet was a member of polite society addressing himself to his equals, and though poetry was a special mode of communication it did not exempt him from all the normal usages of polite society. If you invited him to make one at a dinner-party, you expected him to talk intelligibly; if he published a volume of poems you expected him to write the sort of thing that the average well-educated man could understand because it came within the orbit of his own experience. If he had (as we all have) some purely private thoughts and feelings and relationships and experiences, you expected him to keep those to himself, and not embarrass your dinner-party with them, or even bring them into his poems.[1]

James Sutherland's description of eighteenth-century poetry as a dinner-party to which only men are invited may be justified in relation to the traditional canon of polite verse. This gathering, above all, does not wish to be disturbed or embarrassed or confused. Yet one may imagine that the dinner-party takes place in a large house, and that in another room the ladies are engaged in their own conversations. One woman, the wife of the host, is giving instructions to the upper servants. She may feel, like the Countess of Winchilsea, that her gifts are not valued: '... the dull mannage, of a servile house | Is held by some, our outmost art, and use.'[2] She may think herself wasted in a world where good help is hard to find. On the night of the dinner-party, it seems, the kitchen-maid has allowed the meat to scorch.

That women writers all suffered the same disadvantages, entertained approximately the same ambitions, and approached their writing out of basically the same experiences, is manifestly untrue. While many concerns are shared, their lives are often as different as those of the Countess of Winchilsea and the kitchen maid from Brackley. Although most scholars are aware of this problem

---

[1] James Sutherland, *A Preface to Eighteenth-Century Poetry* (Oxford: Clarendon Press, 1948), 105.

[2] Anne Finch, *The Poems of Anne Countess of Winchilsea*, ed. Myra Reynolds (Chicago: University of Chicago Press, 1903), 5.

with respect to women's writing, some prefer simpler terms. The editors of *Kissing the Rod: An Anthology of Seventeenth-Century Women's Verse* choose a military metaphor to describe the activity of women poets in their period: 'We have aimed to show who the women were who tried to storm the highest bastion of the cultural establishment, the citadel of "sacred poetry". They were all *guerilleras*, untrained, ill-equipped, isolated and vulnerable.'[3] Given the number of titled ladies in the volume, it is hard to believe that their struggles were absolutely equivalent to that of, say, Aphra Behn, who at the end of her life was brought to desperate circumstances. Ann Messenger describes the condition of women writers in the seventeenth and eighteenth centuries in very different terms:

no single critical or historical label fits. There were isolated, confessional, misunderstood, suffering women writers, and there were successful amateurs and professionals, welcomed and supported as part of the community. There were fighters and rebels who were writers, and there were contented wives, mothers, and Sunday school teachers who were writers. There was a sense of sisterhood, of a women's literary tradition, and there was overt rejection of the idea. The only truly valid generalization that can be drawn is that no truly valid generalization is possible.[4]

Messenger is not, of course, suggesting that women's writing in the period is so fragmented that the concept is basically useless, but that the writing of women cannot be reduced to a single critical proposition.

Some critics of women's writing in the eighteenth century approach their material with a narrowly ideological set of criteria. In a paper awarded a prize by the women's caucus of the MLA, Beth Kowaleski-Wallace writes: 'Eighteenth-century literary biography reiterates the preoccupation with the benevolent patriarch by providing examples of men-centered women, "daddy's girls", among them Elizabeth Carter, Hannah More, Maria Edgeworth, and Fanny Burney.'[5] It is hard to imagine that a term like

---

[3] Germaine Greer *et al.*, ed., Introduction, in *Kissing the Rod: An Anthology of Seventeenth-Century Women's Verse* (London: Virago, 1988), 1.

[4] Ann Messenger, 'Introduction: Restoring the Picture', in *His and Hers: Essays in Restoration and Eighteenth-Century Literature* (Lexington: The University of Kentucky Press, 1986), 9.

[5] Beth Kowaleski-Wallace, 'Milton's Daughters: The Education of Eighteenth-Century Women Writers', *Feminist Studies*, 12 (1986), 275–93.

'daddy's girls' can be applied with fairness, let alone exactitude. While it is certainly necessary to chart shifts in women's position in literature and society through history, it is crudely ahistorical to judge writers of the past exclusively through terms arrived at in the late twentieth century. Jessica Munns asks an important question in a generally sympathetic review of Jacqueline Pearson's *The Prostituted Muse: Images of Women and Women Dramatists 1642–1737*: 'What are modern feminists, busily undoing gender systems, doing setting up systematics of feminism and then, as it were, awarding or withholding Brownie points for their fulfilment or omission?'[6] To treat women of the eighteenth century narrowly as pioneers or precursors of modern feminism has the unfortunate effect of visiting a new teleology on eighteenth-century studies. Whereas the view of mid-century literature as pre-Romantic was effectively demolished by Northrop Frye,[7] there is a danger now of regarding women writers as pilgrims on the way to modern feminism, or at least to some recognizable place in the history of women's writing. The essential point is not that a feminist reading of the eighteenth century is impossible, but that it must, as Munns suggests, recognize not only sexual difference but the difference between one century and another.[8]

The crucial historical issue in relation to women writers of the eighteenth century is marriage. Lawrence Stone has put forward a highly influential argument that the eighteenth century saw the rise of the companionate marriage, and that affection between husband and wife was for the first time widely judged as important as economic considerations.[9] This argument has been challenged in relation to all classes by historians examining various kinds of evidence from the seventeenth century and earlier.[10]

---

[6] Jessica Munns, review of *The Prostituted Muse: Images of Women and Women Dramatists 1642–1737*, by Jacqueline Pearson, *Restoration and 18th Century Theatre Research*, ser. 2/4 (1989), 64.

[7] See Northrop Frye, 'Towards Defining an Age of Sensibility', *ELH* 23 (1956), 144–52.

[8] Munns, review of *The Prostituted Muse*, 64.

[9] Lawrence Stone, *The Family, Sex and Marriage in England 1500–1800* (London: Weidenfeld & Nicolson, 1977), 270–404. See also Randolph Trumbach, *The Rise of the Egalitarian Family: Aristocratic Kinship and Domestic Relations in Eighteenth-Century England* (New York, San Francisco, and London: Academic Press, 1978).

[10] See Kathleen M. Davies, 'The Sacred Condition of Equality: how Original were Puritan Doctrines of Marriage?', *Social History*, no. 5 (May 1977), 563–80;

Problems of the Woman Poet 41

The belief that affection as an ideal of marriage was basically invented by the middle and upper classes in the eighteenth century has, however, led some critics into simplistic views. Eva Figes, for example, bases her interpretation of women's writing until 1850 on the belief that 'Until the eighteenth century marriage, like life, tended to be brutish and short'.[11] Katherine Rogers, though a well-informed critic, is likewise misled on this point. She believes that the sudden growth in women's writing and the interest in issues relating to women was largely owing to the rise of the companionate marriage. The first sentence of *Feminism in Eighteenth-Century England* makes her position clear: 'A significant new interest in woman's nature and position, caused in part by a radical change in attitudes toward marriage, appears in eighteenth-century literature.'[12] Women did find a new means of articulating their experiences by publishing, yet it is a mistake to believe that the huge growth in women's writing went hand in hand with equally momentous shifts in attitudes towards marriage.[13]

Given that the ideal of the companionate marriage had existed

---

E. P. Thompson, 'Happy Families', review of *The Family, Sex and Marriage in England 1500–1800*, by Lawrence Stone, *New Society* (8 Sept. 1977), 499; Keith Wrightson, *English Society 1580–1680* (London: Hutchinson, 1980), 70–86; Margaret Spufford, *Small Books and Pleasant Histories: Popular Fiction and its Readership in Seventeenth-Century England* (London: Methuen, 1981), 157–61; J. A. Sharpe, 'Plebeian Marriage in Stuart England: Some Evidence from Popular Literature', *Transactions of the Royal Historical Society*, ser. 5/36 (1986), 69–90; also of interest is Miriam Slater, who puts forward an argument similar to that of Stone in 'The Weightiest Business: Marriage in an Upper-Gentry Family in Seventeenth-Century England', *Past & Present*, no. 72 (Aug. 1976), 25–54; Sara Heller Mendelson responds to Slater in 'The Weightiest Business: Marriage in an Upper-Gentry Family in Seventeenth-Century England', *Past & Present*, no. 85 (Nov. 1979), 126–35; Miriam Slater, 'A Rejoinder', *Past & Present*, no. 85 (Nov. 1979), 136–40.

[11] Eva Figes, *Sex and Subterfuge: Women Novelists to 1850* (London and Basingstoke: Macmillan, 1982), 5–6.

[12] Katherine Lyle M. Rogers, *Feminism in Eighteenth-Century England* (Brighton: Harvester, 1982), 1.

[13] See Judith Phillips Stanton, 'Statistical Profile of Women Writing in English from 1660 to 1800', in Frederick M. Keener and Susan E. Lorsch (ed.), *Eighteenth-Century Women and the Arts* (Westport, Conn.: Greenwood Press, 1988), 247–54. Stanton argues that the publication of women authors achieved momentum by itself; the appearance of one woman in print would encourage a number of others to make the attempt. This argument implies that the growth of publishing rather than a new attitude towards marriage itself was crucial to the growth of women's writing.

before the eighteenth century, it must be recognized that women's position within marriage was inferior to that of men. At marriage a woman's legal identity was submerged in that of her husband. A married woman's position before the law was approximately that of a child or an incompetent. The husband had coercive powers to govern most aspects of a woman's life, particularly through his control of money. Although they had certain rights, especially under equity law, few women were willing to go to court against their husbands.[14] At lower levels of society the forms of marriage tended to be more relaxed. Common-law marriage or simple espousal allowed women to retain financial independence.[15] By definition, of course, women at the lower levels of society would have had fewer assets to control.

Within marriage a wife was generally expected to obey her husband. The biblical teaching on this was unambiguous: Genesis 3: 16 and Galatians 5: 22-3 as well as other passages firmly established the husband as the dominant partner. Biblical authority was very difficult to resist, and presented particular problems to orthodox moralists who were also aware of the dangers of domestic tyranny. Samuel Johnson treads carefully in one of his sermons, affirming the woman's duty of obedience while arguing strongly that a husband's authority also has its limits: 'But though obedience may be justly required, servility is not to be exacted; and though it may be lawful to exert authority, it must be remembered, that to govern and to tyrannize are very different, and that oppression will naturally provoke rebellion' (Johnson, xiv. 14). Basic affection and normal standards of decency often allowed balanced relationships to evolve. Some husbands, however, would feel no hesitation in exacting the obedience decreed by scripture, even by the domestic chastisement permitted under law. The potential for oppression was enormous. Bridget Hill maintains that wife-beating was common

---

[14] Janelle Greenberg, 'The Legal Status of the English Woman in Early Eighteenth-Century Common Law and Equity', *Studies in Eighteenth-Century Culture*, 4, Proceedings of the American Society for Eighteenth Century Studies (Madison and London: University of Wisconsin Press, 1975), 175.
[15] See John R. Gillis, 'Married but not Churched: Plebeian Sexual Relations and Marital Nonconformity in Eighteenth-Century Britain', in Robert MacCubbin (ed.), *'Tis Nature's Fault: Unauthorized Sexuality during the Enlightenment* (Cambridge and New York: Cambridge University Press, 1987), 31-42.

Problems of the Woman Poet

through all levels of society, though it was rather better concealed among the affluent (Hill, 199–200).

Moral standards imposed a further and more subtle restriction on women. Whereas standards of ethical behaviour for men were essentially active, a woman was obliged above all to remain chaste. According to Katherine Rogers, a zealous defence of sexual reputation entailed a negative moral standard: virtue consisted in what was not done. In order to preserve her reputation, a woman was obliged to refrain from most types of work that might bring financial independence. As one rose in society this problem, paradoxically, became more acute as the possibilities of domestic service or involvement in a family enterprise were reduced.[16] Although writing remained an outlet for women's talents, many women who published were attacked as whores. Early in the century especially, there was the real danger of being compared with Aphra Behn or Delarivière Manley or other writers whose sexual conduct had caused scandal. There had been women writers of the Restoration whose reputations were unassailable, notably Katherine Phillips, but to publish was indeed a risk. By the second quarter of the century there were more examples of women writers whose morality was unimpeachable, including Elizabeth Rowe and Elizabeth Carter. Yet there were also instances of women writers falling into disgrace, most famously Laetitia Pilkington, a protégée of Jonathan Swift. The opprobrium that went with sexual scandal was usually difficult to bear. Catherine Jemmat in her 'Essay in Vindication of the Female Sex' (1766) described her own 'ruin':

> The villain who was the occasion of my ruin and disgrace, and has imparted the self-same treatment on many others of my sex, is considered by the world as a man of unspotted honour. The public may be assured that he has been very frequently engaged in what is gently termed *gallantry* and *intrigue*; but yet these (give me leave to call them capital crimes) are not in the least considered in him as deserving of censure.[17]

Jemmat's frank protest against a double standard is certainly unusual. It shows nonetheless that, in matters of scandal, women

---

[16] Rogers, *Feminism in Eighteenth-Century England*, 36–8.
[17] Catherine Jemmat, 'Essay in Vindication of the Female Sex', in *Miscellanies, in Prose and Verse* (London, 1766), 103–4.

had everything to lose, and men almost nothing. Women writers were expected to remain within strict bounds of modesty. It was normal for women to write about love, but they were expected always to be decorous. It was acceptable for Alexander Pope to describe female desire in 'Eloisa to Abelard', but no woman might approach the subject without considerable danger to her reputation.

An adult woman was normally expected to be a wife and mother. Yet in the first half of the century the number of unmarried women increased substantially, so that they formed a significant minority group.[18] Spinsters maintained an anomalous social position and were often seen as a threat to a society that assumed all women would marry and be subject to the control of their husbands (Hill, 229-30). Spinsters and widows enjoyed the legal status of *femme sole* in which they had control of their own affairs. Where a woman could expect a jointure, the death of a husband had distinct benefits, yet a woman who had lost a husband, or failed to get one at all, might find herself in genuine distress. Olwen Hufton observes that outside domestic service single working women had difficulty surviving on their wages. One common solution to this was 'spinster clustering', that is, single women sharing accommodation and expenses. An alternative was for a widowed mother and unmarried daughter to maintain a household, as, indeed, Bridget Freemantle did with her mother. Many women would assume control of the family business upon the death of a spouse. Widows were numerous, for example, in the publishing business. They were often to be found operating shops and farms. Hufton notes more surprising instances of widows continuing in their husbands' occupation as gaolers. Unmarried women, especially widows, had some prospect of an independent life. However, the numbers of women choosing not to marry receded in times of rising real wages, and the same conditions lowered the average age at marriage.[19] Hence, it is wise to remember that many women remained unmarried only because they did not have the means to start a new household with a husband. In the upper classes women often remained unmarried because their families could not provide sufficient

---

[18] Olwen Hufton, 'Women without Men: Widows and Spinsters in Britain and France in the Eighteenth Century', *Journal of Family History*, 9 (1984), 357-8.
[19] Ibid. 355-66.

dowries. Nonetheless, there were also women who chose not to marry in order to retain personal freedom. Defoe's Roxana explains why she has turned down an offer of marriage from a Dutch merchant: '... I had no need to give him twenty Thousand Pound to marry me, which had been buying my Lodging too dear a great deal.'[20] The case for women to eschew marriage was, of course, made most forcefully by Mary Astell, who, unlike Roxana, was not inclined to consider the merits of being a mistress. Rather, she proposed the establishment of an institution resembling a convent where women might study and develop themselves spiritually. Astell's college, though it was never established, became a landmark in feminist thinking of the period.[21]

The education of women at all levels of society was plainly inadequate. The universities excluded them altogether. This exclusion entailed that women writers would be less burdened by long-established literary models and possibly more disposed to develop their own forms and techniques. That a university education was not absolutely necessary for literary success can be seen in the career of Alexander Pope or Samuel Richardson. Yet systematic exclusion of women from higher education can only be seen as having forced the great majority of capable women out of the intellectual mainstream. Women's academies, in general, prepared the daughters of the wealthy to make their way in society, and sought to enhance their prospects of marriage. Whereas young men as a matter of course would study the classics, women would be instructed in painting, music, dancing, modern languages, or other accomplishments, but rarely would they be expected to achieve real competence.[22] Indeed, a learned woman was likely to experience difficulty finding a husband, and education might cease to be any advantage. There were, nonetheless, women who managed to become well educated. Mary Wortley Montagu taught herself Latin and other languages, and read extensively in her father's library. Mehetabel Wright was instructed by her father, Samuel Wesley, and is said to

---

[20] Daniel Defoe, *Roxana*, ed. Jane Jack (London, New York, and Toronto: Oxford University Press, 1964; paperback edn., 1981), 144.
[21] See Bridget Hill, 'A Refuge from Men: The Idea of a Protestant Nunnery', *Past & Present*, no. 117 (Nov. 1987), 107–30.
[22] Janet Todd, ed., *A Dictionary of British and American Women Writers 1660–1800* (London: Methuen, 1984), Introduction, 3–4.

have understood Greek by the age of 8. Elizabeth Carter and Constantia Grierson established themselves as classical scholars. Elizabeth Montagu became a leading Shakespearian critic. Most women who desired learning, however, acquired it by struggle, and in a manner which promoted a sense of inferiority even among the most gifted and widely read women. Indeed, the colourful story of Susanna Centlivre's sojourn at Cambridge supposedly disguised as a man presents an image of the woman entering the intellectual world by stealth. There is, however, no need to look for metaphors in the struggles of labouring women, including Mary Leapor, for whom education was a barely attainable luxury.

Women writers of the period, as well as sympathetic men, argued for better education as a means of improving the lot of women. It is significant that Charlotte Lennox's *The Female Quixote*, one of the most interesting novels of its time, is essentially a satire on women's education. Arabella, the heroine, is remarkably gifted, yet her reading is confined to French romances. She understands the world through trivial fictions, and is trapped within a child's view of history and society. Near the end of the novel the unnamed clergyman who is attempting to show Arabella how unreasonable her notions are, is left 'in strange Embarrassment, not knowing how to account for a Mind at once so enlighten'd, and so ridiculous'.[23] The parson's words can surely be read as an indictment of women's education which, though it improved throughout the period, generally failed to realize their intellectual potential.

It is now well known that women of the eighteenth century produced books in almost all genres. Women's writing in the period has recently become an area of scholarly interest. There had been earlier studies of women writers, notably Myra Reynolds's *The Learned Lady in England 1650–1760* (1920), and occasional studies of individual writers, but only since the 1970s have the conditions obtained for a comprehensive re-examination of these writers. Of particular importance is Janet Todd's *A Dictionary of British and American Women Writers 1660–1800* (1984), which brings forward an enormous amount of information

---

[23] Charlotte Lennox, *The Female Quixote*, ed. Margaret Dalziel (London, New York, and Toronto: Oxford University Press, 1970), 367.

about writers, some of whom have been entirely unregarded for more than two centuries. In general, studies of women prose writers have outstripped by some distance studies of poets, apart from Lady Mary Wortley Montagu and the Countess of Winchilsea. This imbalance is unfortunate, since, as Pat Rogers observes: 'there were more first-rate women poets than novelists in the period, and... poetry was still the place where ideas were growing most vigorously'.[24]

A study of women writers can easily lose sight of broader literary relations, and inadvertently consign its subjects to a ghetto. Since 1987 there have been two valuable essays which examine women poets of the eighteenth century in relation to contemporary male writers. Jocelyn Harris takes as her point of departure Duncombe's *The Feminiad*.[25] Her approach is fruitful in that it explores major issues in women's poetry of the time and its relation to the literary mainstream. Also of considerable interest is Margaret Doody's 'Swift among the Women', which traces the Dean's influence on women poets of the time.[26] Both Harris and Doody take a particular interest in Mary Leapor's poetry.

The publication of Roger Lonsdale's *Eighteenth-Century Women Poets: An Oxford Anthology* (1989) was an event of considerable importance. The most obvious achievement of this book is that it located and republished many poets whose neglect was far deeper than that of Mary Leapor. Indeed, the appearance of Lonsdale's book revealed and at once remedied a huge gap in the study of women writers. Claire Tomalin, Mary Wollstonecraft's biographer, asks candidly in her review of the anthology: 'How many women poets of the eighteenth century can most of us name? I was stuck after Anne, Countess of Winchilsea, Lady Mary Wortley Montagu, Joanna Baillie, Mrs.

---

[24] Pat Rogers, 'Puellilia', review of *Mothers of the Novel: One Hundred Good Women Writers Before Jane Austen*, by Dale Spender, *London Review of Books* (7 Aug. 1986), 11.
[25] Jocelyn Harris, 'Sappho, Souls, and the Salic Law of Wit', in Alan C. Kors and Paul J. Korshin (ed.), *Anticipations of the Enlightenment in England, France, and Germany* (Philadelphia: University of Pennsylvania Press, 1987), 232–58.
[26] Margaret Anne Doody, 'Swift among the Women', *Yearbook of English Studies*, 18 (1988), 68–92. For two less interesting treatments of women poets in the period see Anke Janssen, 'Frühe Lyrikerinnen des 18. Jahrhunderts in ihrem Verhältnis zur Poetik und zur *Poetic Diction*', *Anglia*, 99 (1981), 111–33; and Karl Heinz Göller, 'The Emancipation of Women in Eighteenth-Century English Literature', *Anglia*, 101 (1983), 78–98.

Barbauld and Helen Maria Williams.'[27] Apart from the simple work of recovery, Lonsdale provides a good deal of new biographical information about the poets, and, perhaps most importantly, his long introduction supplies a comprehensive history of women poets throughout the century. He accepts that the material defies easy summary and generalization (*ECWP*, p. xxii), but proceeds to survey the actual work of women poets, recognizing that there are always some who stand outside general trends. From the beginning to the end of the century, he observes that there was a huge increase in the amount of poetry published by women. This, in itself, indicates a change in the literary status of women. In the first decades, Lonsdale notes that there were a number of poets, such as Lady Mary Chudleigh, Octavia Walsh, Elizabeth Tollet, and Mehetabel Wright, who worked very much in isolation; these are not, however, entirely representative, since the Restoration 'brought a new confidence and competence to women's verse' (*ECWP*, p. xxii). Sarah Fyge Egerton, Elizabeth Rowe, the Countess of Winchilsea, and others asserted themselves in the literary mainstream. In the 1730s women found new outlets for their work through periodicals, especially the *Gentleman's Magazine*, and through subscription publishing. By the 1740s the numbers were increasing, although the best women poets, including Mary Leapor and Mary Jones, tended to be somewhat behind the times, modelling their work on Pope and Swift rather than responding to the new trend towards sensibility at mid-century. The 1750s marked an important transition, as works by such men as Duncombe and Ballard celebrated the achievements of women writers, and Colman and Thornton published the first edition of *Poems by Eminent Ladies*. In the 1750s the place of women in contemporary literature was much more widely recognized. The literary circles of Richardson and Johnson proved especially welcoming to women poets such as Elizabeth Carter, Anna Williams, Charlotte Lennox, and Hester Mulso Chapone. As the century went on, women poets exercised much greater influence on the literary scene. The appearance of Anna Seward, Anna Aikin Barbauld, Hannah More, Charlotte Smith, Helen Maria Williams, and others entailed that women

[27] Claire Tomalin, 'A Buried Treasury of Wicked Wits', review of *ECWP*, *The Independent* (7 Oct. 1989), 34.

were largely setting the poetic fashion from the late 1770s to the early 1790s. Indeed, the influence of women writers at the time was rising in many areas, as Fanny Burney's *Evelina* (1778) and Hannah Cowley's dramatic works placed them in the forefront of contemporary literature. The appearance of new literary circles around Elizabeth Montagu and Hester Thrale Piozzi was a further sign of women's improved status in the literary world.

In Lonsdale's view, the 1790s saw a reaction against women writers. New theories about education challenged women's intellectual credentials, since most of them lacked a knowledge of the classics. Wordsworth's polemics at the turn of the century implied strong criticism of fashionable women poets:

> Superficially more democratic than Richard Steele's definition of the poet as a 'very well-bred Man', Wordsworth's notion of the poet may seem even more relentlessly masculine and, in the loftiness of his conception of poetic genius, even more exclusive ... In attacking the 'gaudy and inane phraseology' of fashionable poetry, Wordsworth (ostensibly attacking Thomas Gray) was in fact echoing the charge repeatedly levelled at women poets by reviewers and others in the 1780s and 1790s ... (*ECWP*, p. xl)

Before long, a good deal of the poetry that women had written would seem decidedly out of date. Its exclusion from major anthologies made doubly sure that, after a generation or so, it would be read by almost no one.

Lonsdale's history of women poets through the century allows them to be understood against developments in the poetry written by men, whose dominance of fashion was challenged for only a short time towards the end of the period. Yet he also makes clear that a number of the best poets in his anthology were unbothered by developments in London: 'Some homely writers had clearly never heard about the requirements of polite taste' (*ECWP*, p. xxvi). Among these, towards the end of the period, are Susanna Blamire and Joanna Baillie, who are among the most heavily represented poets in the anthology. Indeed, if one considers the whole century, a surprising number of the heavily represented poets remained largely unaffected by changes in fashion, among them Mary Leapor, Mary Jones, Esther Lewis, Susanna Blamire, Elizabeth Hands, and Joanna Baillie. These poets generally prefer concrete description, and a versification reminiscent of Swift and Pope, to odes, abstraction, and sublime rhetoric. As a question of aesthetic value, it is hard to dispute Lonsdale's decision to give prominence to this material. Yet if one accepts that a number of very accomplished poets remained firmly off the routes of mainstream development, it must also be accepted that the history of women's poetry, and of poetry in general throughout the eighteenth century, has been written in a simplistic manner. Indeed, if so much is happening on the edges, one is obliged to ask again what is really characteristic of the period.

The rest of this chapter will discuss Mary Leapor's work in so far as it responds specifically to her experience of being a woman. The first section will discuss Leapor's attitudes towards marriage and the family. The second will discuss her views of female friendship. The final section will consider her representation of the female body, especially in relation to contemporary ideals of beauty.

Marriage, Family, and Sexuality

Mary Leapor's writings are given an extended feminist materialist reading by Donna Landry in *The Muses of Resistance: Laboring-Class Women's Poetry in Britain, 1739–1796* (1990). In a sense, one can only be delighted that Leapor and other poets like her are receiving such serious attention. Yet, in view of the problems discussed in the first section of this chapter, it will be necessary to disagree with a number of Landry's principal arguments. First, her approach is decidedly teleological, and she makes no secret of her attempt to understand Leapor against the backdrop of recent feminist discourse: 'Of the plebeian female poets of the period, Mary Leapor possesses the most writerly *œuvre*. Hers is also the body of work most easily assimilable to what we commonly describe today as "radical feminism," with its polemics against patriarchy, male violence, and heterosexist containments of economies of desire' (p. 119). Although Landry makes clear that the shoe does not always fit, this sort of approach, as suggested above, is dangerous in that it shapes what a scholar is willing to see. This danger is most obvious in Landry's consistent use of the terms 'heterosexual union', 'heterosexual attachment', and 'heterosexual couple', where Leapor's meaning is simply marriage or married couple. Landry's concern is to explore sexual difference:

'the extent to which Leapor's writing represents female eroticism as transgressive, situates it in relation to sapphic textuality, and exposes the necessary construction of such alternative desires within as well as against the very terms of heterosexual propriety from which they are generated' (p. 84). The binary opposite of heterosexual is homosexual or lesbian; the binary opposite of married is single. It appears that Landry is intent on manipulating such terms, in order to perform an ideological deconstruction. Again, she makes no secret of this:

> We are reminded by the silences in Leapor's texts that the pursuit of happiness as an enabling myth, in terms of official precept accessible to women through romantic love and marriage, remains in this period largely a privilege of bourgeois male subjects. For women and the lower classes, unhappiness is to be endured, not abandoned, even for the pursuit of imaginary alternatives. (p. 88)

This reading of silences depends on the argument that the companionate ideal of marriage developed first among the privileged classes, and that in the eighteenth century lower-class women could expect little affection in marriage. Even if the historical argument were sound, an objection could be raised to the critical method: silences are sometimes extremely difficult to interpret. Indeed, Landry is mistaken even when she claims that the poems are silent on the question of lower-class marriage: in 'The Month of August', for example, Phillis, a country girl, believes that she will be happy in marriage to a man of her own class, and Leapor does not undermine that suggestion. Although in other poems Leapor shows that labouring-class women can be desperately unhappy in marriage, she is not unequivocal. Depending upon one's theoretical persuasion, Landry's approach is either deconstructive, and rather exciting, or merely tendentious.

Landry represents Leapor as the thoroughgoing enemy of patriarchy who 'laughs at the fathers'. Yet, to promote this idea, she puts forward some very strange arguments. She provides a lopsided interpretation of Freemantle's report that on her death-bed the poet expressed concern for her father and asked that the subscription be carried on for his sake:

> In the light of Leapor's harrowing narratives of heterosexual attachment gone awry, as in 'The Temple of Love,' and family feeling deformed by familial conflict, as in *The Unhappy Father* and *The Cruel Parent*, it is

possible to read into this last wish a peculiar kind of vindication. If we are to take this speech as accurate reportage within the conventions of deathbed narratives, is there not something a little remarkable in Leapor's assuring her friend and patron that she has always loved her father, though never so much as now, when she is dying? And the work that he had tried to prevent will now, ironically, endow his old age, even afford him a comfortable subsistence: this work which was viewed as such unprofitable employment. (pp. 104-5)

In its way, this view of Leapor's last wishes is almost breathtaking. With a gesture to the conventions of death-bed narratives, Landry reads Freemantle's account as if it were a twentieth-century novel. Freemantle's letter shows that although Philip and Anne Leapor *both* attempted to break their daughter of the habit of writing verses, towards the end of the poet's life some accommodation was reached: 'But finding it impossible to alter her natural Inclination, [her father] had of late desisted and left her more at Liberty' (ii, p. xxx). Leapor's poetry makes clear that she suffered many distressing lectures from her father, yet if the two had reached an understanding—indeed, if they intended to use the money from the subscription to buy their freehold and have security for their life together—Landry's interpretation of this episode is simply captious. The same attempt to represent fathers in Leapor's writing purely as tyrants can likewise be seen in her interpretation of *The Unhappy Father*, which will be discussed below.

If Landry consistently overstates Leapor's radicalism, it remains true that by the standards of her time Leapor's views on marriage and the family were critical and hard-edged. That she could deal with the philosophical and ideological issues related to women's position in the family is evident from the poem 'Man the Monarch', in which she debunks the view that men's sovereignty over women derives from Adam:

> When our Grandsire nam'd the feather'd Kind,
> Pond'ring their Natures in his careful Mind,
> 'Twas then, if on our Author we rely,
> He view'd his Consort with an envious Eye;
> Greedy of Pow'r, he hugg'd the tott'ring Throne;
> Pleased with Homage, and would reign alone;
> And, better to secure his doubtful Rule,
> Roll'd his wise Eye-balls, and pronounc'd her *Fool*.

The regal Blood to distant Ages runs:
Sires, Brothers, Husbands, and commanding Sons,
The Sceptre claim; and ev'ry Cottage brings
A long Succession of domestic Kings. (ML ii. 10)

The poem is a response to some book Leapor has been reading. Jocelyn Harris is almost certainly right when she suggests that she is, in fact, responding to John Locke,[28] who writes 'Of Adam's Title to Sovereignty by the Subjection of Eve':

> if this be the *Original Grant of Government* and the *Foundation of Monarchical Power*, there will be as many Monarchs as there are Husbands. If therefore these words [Genesis 3: 16] give any Power to *Adam*, it can only be a Conjugal Power, not Political, the Power that every Husband hath to order the things of private Concernment in his Family, as the Proprietor of the Goods and Land there, and to have his Will take place before that of his wife in all things of their common Concernment; but not a Political Power of Life and Death over her, much less over any body else.[29]

As is widely observed, rationalist philosophy paved the way for a re-examination of women's place in society and in the family.[30] If Locke could subject the divine right of kings to a critical examination, the rights of husbands were likewise vulnerable to a reasoned critique. The language of kingship, sovereignty, and liberty is taken from political philosophy and applied to marriage. Mary Astell writes: 'how much soever Arbitrary Power may be dislik'd on a Throne, Not *Milton* himself wou'd cry up Liberty to poor *Female Slaves*, or plead for the Lawfulness of Resisting a Private Tyranny.'[31] Leapor's contempt for the idea of 'A long Succession of domestic Kings' is close in spirit to a passage by 'Sophia', the pamphleteer:

> I myself was accidentally witness to the diverting scene of a journeyman taylor's beating his wife about the ears with a neck of mutton, to make her know, as he said, her *sovereign lord* and *master*. And yet this,

---

[28] Jocelyn Harris, *Samuel Richardson* (Cambridge: Cambridge University Press, 1987), 18.
[29] John Locke, 'The First Treatise', in *Two Treatises of Government*, ed. Peter Laslett (Cambridge: Cambridge University Press, 1960; 2nd edn., 1967), 192.
[30] See Rogers, *Feminism in Eighteenth-Century England*, 53–84; Alice Browne, *The Eighteenth Century Feminist Mind* (Brighton: Harvester, 1987), pp. 20–1.
[31] Mary Astell, *Some Reflections Upon Marriage* (London, 1700; 2nd edn., 1703), 29.

perhaps, is as strong an argument as the best of their sex is able to produce, tho' convey'd in a greasy light.[32]

Both Leapor and 'Sophia' find something contemptible in the claims of men to automatic mastery over their wives. Indeed, for both it is ridiculous that a man who has no claim on the world's attention, should none the less be able to exact full obedience from his wife. This attitude, especially in 'Sophia's' case, may owe something to class-distinction, that is, a duke beating a duchess with a neck of mutton might prove less illustrative than a journeyman tailor doing such a thing to his wife. Yet the central point is that it is absurd to assume that any woman is less competent to direct her life than any man she marries.

In her rejection of a purely romantic view of the relations of men and women, Leapor's opinions on marriage are at a very great distance from those of more conventional women poets in her time. Mary Jones complains in a letter dated 1735 of the tediousness of most women's verse:

Whenever I meet with a Sister in print, I always expect to hear that *Corydon* has prov'd false; or that *Sylvia*'s cruel Parents have had prudence enough to keep two mad People from playing the Fool together, for Life. I've often wish'd, for the honour of our Sex, that these Subjects had been exhausted seventeen hundred years ago; but am afraid that seventeen hundred years hence, we shall have the same false *Corydon*'s, and the same complaining *Sylvia*'s. 'Tis pity, that this passion alone should set us to Rhyming.[33]

There were, of course, a good number of poets who moved beyond such limitations. Jones's comments are actually part of a favourable reaction to Mary Barber's poems. None the less, a woman poet who attacks the naïvety of a purely romantic view of marriage is, in some sense, going against the grain.

Jonathan Swift often presents a decidedly unpleasant view of women's sexuality, yet his poetry provided a model for women poets of the time who wished to expose the deceptions of romantic love, and the concealed dangers of marriage. For Swift, of course, the disillusionment will come when the man discovers that the woman he worshipped as a goddess is only too physical, as in 'The Lady's Dressing Room':

[32] 'Sophia', *Woman Not Inferior to Man* (London, 1739), 15.
[33] Mary Jones, 'To Hon. Miss Lovelace', in *Miscellanies in Prose and Verse* (Oxford, 1750), 321.

> Thus finishing his grand Survey,
> Disgusted *Strephon* stole away
> Repeating in his amourous Fits,
> Oh! *Celia, Celia, Celia* shits!   (Swift, ii. 529)

'The Lady's Dressing Room' drew the fire of Mary Wortley Montagu and the unidentified Miss W——, both of whom wrote parodies of the poem.[34] Mary Leapor, in an octosyllabic satire, 'The Mistaken Lover', responds, according to Margaret Doody, to Swift's 'Strephon and Chloe', a poem which describes fashionable courtship and marriage.[35] Swift's Chloe manages to conceal perfectly all of her less attractive bodily functions:

> Her graceful Mein, her Shape, and Face,
> Confest her of no mortal Race:
> And then, so nice, and so genteel;
> Such Cleanliness from Head to Heel:
> No Humours gross, or frowzy Steams,
> No noisom Whiffs, or sweaty Streams,
> Before, behind, above, below,
> Could from her taintless Body flow.   (Swift, ii. 584)

Chloe's beauty is a matter of hiding the dirty facts of the body. Strephon allows himself to be duped by the charms of this woman who, in Swift's view, seems immortal because she appears clean. In Leapor's poem, the deceptive exterior is not the woman's beauty but the beau's appearance. Having been wounded by her killing eyes, Strephon chooses his course:

> What shou'd he do?—'Commence the Beau,
> 'For Women oft are caught by Show.'
> The wounded *Strephon* now behold,
> Array'd in Coat of Green and Gold,
> (Of which we something might advance)
> The Sleeve was *a-la-mode de France*.
> We leave it here—and haste to tell,
> How smartly round his Temples fell
> The modish Wig.—Yet we presume,

---

[34] See Mary Wortley Montagu, 'The Reasons that Induced Dr. S[wift] to write a Poem call'd the Lady's Dressing room', in *Essays and Poems and Simplicity, A Comedy*, ed. Robert Halsband and Isobel Grundy (Oxford: Clarendon Press, 1977), 273–6; Miss W——, 'The Gentleman's Study, In Answer to [Swift's] The Lady's Dressing Room', *ECWP* 130–4.

[35] Doody, 'Swift among the Women', 79–80.

> More graceful was the scarlet Plume:
> Tho' some rude Soldier (doom'd to bear
> The Southern and the Northern Air,
> And walk through ev'ry kind of Weather)
> Might jeer at *Strephon*'s scarlet Feather;
> And tell us such shou'd ne'er be wore,
> Unless you fought at *Marston-moor*. (ML i. 81–2)

Although she describes a stereotypical beau, Leapor emphasizes that Strephon's artificial appearance is part of his strategy to deceive Celia. That he wears a soldier's plume without meriting it is meant to show that he is a bluff. In a passage which departs from Swift's model and follows John Gay's 'The Fan' (see Chapter 5 below), Strephon pays court to Celia with serenades and sonnets, and all 'the Lover's Cant'. In short order, Celia agrees, the documents are drawn up, and the wedding proceeds:

> But I shall pass the Wedding-day,
> Nor stay to paint the Ladies gay,
> Nor Splendor of the lighted Hall,
> The Feast, the Fiddles, nor the Ball.
> A lovely Theme!—'Tis true, but then
> We'll leave it to a softer Pen:
> Those transient Joys will fade too soon,
> We'll therefore skip the Hony-Moon. (ML i. 83)

Leapor is here parting company with conventional love poetry, leaving that to others who have 'a softer Pen'; Swift himself gives some space to describing wedding festivities, though the bitter revelation is expected shortly.

At this point in the poem Leapor, like Swift, attempts to account for the eventual unhappiness of the marriage. For Swift, the reason is that the marriage is based on an idealization of the woman. Marriage brings with it a disconcerting reality:

> How great a Change! how quickly made!
> They learn to call a Spade, a Spade.
> They soon from all Constraint are freed;
> Can see each other *do their Need*. (Swift, ii. 590)

The magic wears off, and Swift advises women that they have only themselves to blame for a husband's loss of enthusiasm if they do not keep themselves clean:

> UNJUSTLY all our Nymphs complain,
> Their Empire holds so short a Reign;
> Is after Marriage lost so soon,
> It hardly holds the Honey-moon:
> For, if they keep not what they caught,
> It is entirely their own Fault. (Swift, ii. 591)

Leapor, however, will have none of this. The truths that are recognized after marriage have very little to do with chamber pots. Rather, the husband's motives are exposed. Strephon has married Celia because she could bring 'Five thousand Pounds of Sterling clear, | To bless the Mansion of her Dear'. For Leapor, this is the hidden danger where a woman surrenders financial control in marriage:

> Some tell us Wives their Beauties lose,
> When they have spoil'd their bridal Shoes:
> Some learned Casuists make it clear,
> A Wife might please for half a Year:
> And others say, her Charms will hold
> As long as the suspended Gold;
> But that her Bloom is soon decay'd,
> And wither'd when her Fortune's paid. (ML i. 84)

Leapor rejects Swift's view: Strephon, having secured his wife's money, offers the feeble excuse for his dissipated behaviour that he was mistaken about her physical charms before they were married:

> 'But Ma'm, the Reason was, I find,
> That while a Lover I was blind:
> And now the Fault is not in me,
> 'Tis only this—that I can see.
> I thought you once a Goddess trim,
> The Graces dwelt on ev'ry Limb:
> But, Madam, if you e'er was such,
> Methinks you're alter'd very much...' (ML i. 87–8)

Strephon goes on to recount the various features which once inspired his love but now leave him cold:

> 'As first (I beg your Pardon tho')
> You hold your Head extremely low:
> And tho' your Shape is not awry,
> Your Shoulders stand prodigious high:

> Your curling Hair I durst have swore,
> Was blacker than the sable Moor:
> But now I find 'tis only brown,
> A Colour common through the Town:
> 'Tis true you're mighty fair—But now
> I spy a Freckle on your Brow;
> Your Lips I own are red and thin,
> But there's a Pimple on your Chin:
> Besides your Eyes are gray—Alack!
> 'Till now I always thought 'em black. (ML i. 88)

Nowhere in this catalogue of imperfections is there anything particularly unpleasant, certainly nothing to convince the reader that Strephon has discovered something repulsive about Celia's body. Strephon is simply attempting to excuse his loss of interest in Celia. In the end, Leapor proposes an explanation for marital disaffection far simpler than Swift's:

> 'Thus, Madam, I the Truth have told;
> 'Tis true, I thank you for your Gold;
> But find in searching of my Breast,
> That I could part with all the Rest.' (ML i. 88)

Doody notes that Leapor picks up Swift's characters or anti-characters and turns them to her own purposes.[36] As a subversion of what is already a mock form, Leapor's poem has its own sophistication. She agrees with Swift that coquettes and beaux tend not to live happily ever after, but she takes an altogether different view of the reasons. She believes that women with property or money are especially attractive to men, and that once that advantage has been surrendered, the husband may simply lose interest.

Leapor also produced several shorter satires on fashionable courtship and marriage. The tone is evident from some of the titles: 'Proper Ingredients for the Head of a Beau, found among the Rules of Prometheus'; 'The Sow and the Peacock'; 'Strephon to Celia: A modern Love Letter'. In each of these she takes aim at that object of Scriblerian mockery, the beau. Her satire, however, is always underpinned by an awareness of women's vulnerability.

Leapor's belief that a man's attractive appearance or manner

---

[36] Ibid., 79.

may conceal something treacherous is reiterated throughout her writing. Her treatment of courtship and betrayal in 'Complaining Daphne' bears careful examination. In this pastoral Daphne is longing for the return of her 'cruel, marble-hearted Swain' [ii. 74]. She comes to believe, however, that she is probably better off without him:

> Yet he may wear a Heart replete with Guile,
> And cover Mischief with a fraudful Smile:
> And foolish *Daphne* to her cost shall find
> Her heav'nly *Cynthio* like his earthly Kind. (ML ii. 76)

Cynthio has something in common with Strephon in 'The Mistaken Lover'. His pleasant appearance and delightful manner conceal bad motives. Daphne has no money for him to take, but there is the perennial fear of seduction. In a striking passage Daphne recalls working in the fields with her mother, falling ill from the heat, and being consoled by stories about love. Interestingly, John Clare also describes old women singing and telling stories during the weeding and haymaking.[37] Evidently 'Complaining Daphne', though a pastoral, has an actual connection with the life of agricultural labour in Northamptonshire. Clare does not specify what the songs and stories were; Leapor's account emphasizes tales of betrayal in love:

> Long Tales she told, to kill the tedious Hour;
> Of lovely Maids to early Ruin led,
> Who once were harmless as the Flocks they fed;
> Of some induc'd with gaudy Knights to roam
> From their dear Parents, and their blissful Home;
> Till, each deserted by her changing Friend,
> The pageant Wretches met a woful End.
> And still howe'er the mournful Tale began,
> She always ended—*Child, beware of Man.* (ML ii. 77-8)

The poem, at this point, is by no means radical. Leapor has described a pining country girl and 'her cruel, marble-hearted

---

[37] See John Clare, 'The Autobiography 1793-1824', in *The Prose of John Clare*, ed. J. W. Tibble and Anne Tibble (London: Routledge & Kegan Paul, 1951), 19. It should be noted that stories told (or read) at harvest time may also have been conventional in some kinds of poetry: see Christopher Smart, 'A Noon-Piece', in *The Poetical Works of Christopher Smart*, ed. Karina Williamson and Marcus Walsh, 5 vols. (Oxford: Oxford University Press, 1980–), vol. iv: *Miscellaneous Poems English and Latin*, ed. Karina Williamson (1987), 143.

Swain', both of the sort Mary Jones found so tedious: 'the same false *Corydon*'s, and the same complaining *Sylvia*'s'. The essential affirmation in the poem is that a young woman should preserve her virginity, again nothing remarkable. A mother advising her daughter to beware of men is likewise in the normal course of things. Donna Landry sees the poem rather differently:

> Daphne's response to this remembrance is to pledge obedience to her mother's memory by forgetting Cynthio and embracing her sister shepherdesses. In a triumph of renunciation of heterosexual closure in marriage, the poem ends with a celebration of the tranquillity and harmony to be found when women choose to live only for each other, in a feminine pastoral paradise, a sapphic idyll . . . (Landry, 90)

It must be observed that the point of the mother's stories was not that Daphne should embrace her sister shepherdesses in a sapphic idyll, but, very simply, that she should not allow herself to be seduced. The conclusion of the poem does, however, point to a repudiation of sexual passion:

> Ye Sylvan Sisters! come; ye gentle Dames,
> Whose tender Souls are spotless as your Names!
> Henceforth shall *Daphne* only live for you;
> Content—and bid the lordly Race Adieu;
> See the clear Streams in gentler Murmurs flow,
> And fresher Gales from od'rous Mountains blow.
> Now the charm'd Tempest from my Bosom flies:
> Sweet Slumber seizes on my willing Eyes. (ML ii. 78–9)

The sylvan sisters are 'spotless' and an alternative to guilty passion with Cynthio; Daphne will be safe from sexual feeling and sexual betrayal in their company. Her options are not precisely heterosexuality and lesbianism, but rather seduction and chastity. Leapor characteristically affirms the value of female friendship, while rejecting idealized romantic love. Although the poem is conventional in several respects, it ends critically, not with the shepherdess cheered up by a song or by the sight of another attractive shepherd, but with Daphne recognizing that she has been gullible about her young man. That Daphne repudiates 'the lordly Race' indicates that she sees sexual betrayal as a form of domination.

Leapor's views on marriage are ambiguous. That she could not find a simple solution to the problems of women in marriage can

Problems of the Woman Poet

be seen from two poems entitled 'Mira to Octavia' which advise a young woman who has fallen in love with an unsuitable man. The poem which appears in the first volume is relatively simple in its advice. The one in the second volume is longer and far more detailed, suggesting that Octavia had rejected the reasoning of the earlier piece. In the first poem Leapor writes:

> your Servant has been told,
> That you, (despising Settlements and Gold)
> Determine *Florio* witty, young and gay,
> To have and hold for ever and for ay ...   (ML i. 258)

Octavia is willing to marry a dashing young man for love. In Leapor's view, her friend has failed to recognize that beneath the charming exterior there may be something very unpleasant:

> I know, to shun, you hold it as a Rule,
> The arrant Coxcomb and the stupid Fool:
> No such is *Florio*, he has Wit—'tis true,
> Enough, Octavia, to impose on you:
> Yet such a Wit you'll, by Experience, find
> Worse than a Fool that's complaisant and kind:
> It only serves to gild his Vices o'er,
> And teach his malice how to wound the more.   (ML i. 258)

A marriage begun without financial security looks hazardous to the poet, let alone one where the man seems cunning and manipulative. She foresees a future when those qualities Octavia admires in Florio will be only an irrelevance:

> Now cou'd your *Florio* by his Wit inspire
> The chilly Hearth, to blaze with lasting Fire:
> Or when his Children round the Table throng,
> By an Allusion or a sprightly Song,
> Adorn the Board, i'th' twinkling of an Eye,
> With a hot Pasty or a Warden Pye,
> There might be Reason on *Octavia*'s Side,
> And not a Sage cou'd blame the prudent Bride.   (ML i. 259)

Leapor goes on to observe that although knights in romances may '... sup on Grass and breakfast on the Breeze', that is nothing which Octavia could bear. Instead, she should consider the merits of another suitor, Dusterandus, who, though less charming than Florio, is more likely to prove a good husband:

> He whose stedfast Mind
> Is yet untainted, tho' not much refin'd;
> Whose Soul ne'er roves beyond his native Fields;
> Nor asks for Joys but what his Pasture yields;
> On Life's dull Cares with Patience can attend,
> A gentle Master and a constant Friend... (ML i. 260)

Leapor is adamant that her friend will be happier with a man who is dependable and who lives within his means. She also sees a contrast between the wounding tongue of Florio and the more gentle, if less polished, manner of Dusterandus. The prospect of lasting affection is greater with Dusterandus. At all costs, she would dispel her friend's idealized view of marriage: 'In spite of all romantick Poets sing; | This Gold, my Dearest, is an useful thing' (ML i. 261). In this poem, therefore, Leapor argues that happiness in marriage is available to Octavia if she chooses wisely.

The second poem to Octavia opens with little change from the first. Mira may not, however, continue to criticize the man Octavia wants to marry:

> Frown not, sweet Virgin; we'll Decorums keep;
> *Philander's* Faults shall in Oblivion sleep.
> Peace to his Name!—These only are design'd
> A simple Lecture to our easy Kind. (ML ii. 102)

Leapor's first poem was evidently not well received. In the second, the attack on Florio's character is dropped, and the man is now called Philander, a possible borrowing from Aphra Behn. Dusterandus is not mentioned, perhaps because Octavia simply did not care even to consider his merits as a husband. Leapor adopts the less offensive course of a generalized commentary: 'Of Wives I sing, and Husbands, not a Few: | Examples rare! some fictious, and some true' (ML ii. 102). Through the rest of the poem she offers examples of marriages in which a promising husband proves neglectful or vicious. The first of these seems to take account of Octavia's objections to Dusterandus. Leapor describes the condition of a woman named Pamela who marries a stupid man:

> But could our Eyes behold the deep Recess,
> Where soft *Pamela's* thoughts in private rest,
> You'd find, in spite of *Hymen's* sacred Vows,
> Ten Hours in Twelve that she abhors her Spouse. (ML ii. 103)

Problems of the Woman Poet

Leapor goes on to describe a woman married to a clergyman who is universally virtuous and 'Pleasant to all except his doating Bride' (ML ii. 104). Another woman, Virgo, marries Tycho, an astronomer, who has time for nothing lower than the stars and the planets. A prude, Chloe, marries a zealot, Enthusiano, who eventually locks her up with directions to say her prayers, as he goes to his mistress. Leapor insists that she has not exaggerated the perils of marriage:

> Poets and Painters then, perhaps you'll cry,
> Oft in their Satire, and their Canvas, lye.
> But, dear *Octavia*, in the Case of Wife,
> I fear the Shade but faintly Apes the Life. (ML ii. 108)

Leapor is attempting to dissuade her friend from a particular marriage through generalized arguments. She uses the vignettes to explode a naïve view of romantic fulfilment in marriage. Since she is not to discuss the faults of the particular man involved, and since nothing is to be gained by arguing for the uninspiring Dusterandus, she attempts to convince her friend that marriage *per se* is risky, even if there is some chance of a happy outcome:

> Yet, not a Rebel to your *Hymen*'s Law,
> His sacred Altars I behold with Awe:
> Nor Foe to Man; for I acknowledge yet
> Some Men have Honour, as some Maids have Wit.
> But then remember, these, my learned Fair,
> Old Authors tell us, are extremely rare. (ML ii. 109)

Leapor does not make the case that women are always unhappy in marriage. Since she is not going to advise Octavia to marry the suspect Philander, she suggests celibacy:

> And shall *Octavia* prostitute her Store,
> To buy a Tyrant with the tempting Ore?
> Besides, I fear your Shackles will be found
> Too dearly purchas'd with a thousand Pound.
>   Then be the charming Mistress of thy Gold;
> While young, admir'd; and rev'renc'd, when you're Old.
> The Grave and Sprightly shall thy Board attend,
> The gay Companion, and the serious Friend. (ML ii. 109)

Leapor makes general assertions about marriage in this poem partly because she cannot make further particular observations without offending Octavia. How, then, are these assertions to be understood—as a radical statement of separatist principles, or as a rhetorical posture? In both poems, Leapor attempts to debunk unreal expectations of marriage. She considers it to be a gamble for any woman, a gamble which can only be justified where the woman examines the character and prospects of the man she is to marry. In some cases, it is best to remain celibate. Since Octavia will save a substantial dowry, she will have a prosperous independence. The one indisputable position which connects the two poems is that Octavia should not marry Florio or Philander on the slender hope that love will prevail.

In Leapor's view, the problems of women in relation to marriage are not immediately curable. There is no obvious choice which will set women free. 'An Essay on Woman', though very much a poem of protest against the injustices women suffer, offers no simple solutions. The poem opens with a grim summary of the lot of a woman:

> WOMAN—a pleasing, but a short-liv'd Flow'r,
> Too soft for Business, and too weak for Pow'r:
> A Wife in Bondage, or neglected Maid;
> Despis'd, if ugly; if she's fair—betray'd.   (ML ii. 64)

Marriage exposes the woman to tyranny, while celibacy leaves her scarcely better off. Olwen Hufton maintains that in the eighteenth century the stereotypical spinster was 'one to be despised, pitied, and avoided as a sempiternal spoilsport in the orgy of life'.[38] It is hard to imagine that Leapor would sentimentalize the condition of celibacy, especially if she found herself mocked as an old maid. Indeed, she, like Johnson, is aware how few the pleasures would be. Celibacy is, at best, the lesser evil; by no means is it regarded as a panacea. Women who are courted by men are, however, in greater danger of being deceived and exploited:

> 'Tis Wealth alone inspires ev'ry Grace,
> And calls the Raptures to her plenteous Face.
> What Numbers for those charming Features pine,
> If blooming Acres round her Temples twine?   (ML ii. 64)

A woman without wealth will have few suitors, but a woman who can produce a large dowry will have more than her share of

---

[38] Hufton, 'Women without Men', 356.

acquisitive Strephons writing sonnets. Compliments, however, last only

> Till mighty Hymen lifts his sceptred Rod,
> And sinks her Glories with a fatal Nod;
> Dissolves her Triumphs; sweeps her Charms away,
> And turns the Goddess to her native Clay. (ML ii. 65)

Flattery conceals greed, and marriage will bring a hard realization to women who readily believe the compliments of their suitors or, indeed, their promises of fidelity. Moreover, Leapor can see no means of improving the situation. Wealth, beauty, and wit are all shown to be insufficient means for securing affection and happiness. Sylvia, for example, is beautiful: 'And yet That Face her partial Husband tires, | And those bright Eyes, that all the World admires' (ML ii. 65). Pamphilia, a self-portrait of the poet, seems to annoy both men and women by her learning:

> *Pamphilia*'s Wit who does not strive to shun,
> Like Death's Infection, or a Dog-Day's Sun?
> The Damsels view her with malignant Eyes:
> The Men are vex'd to find a Nymph so wise:
> And Wisdom only serves to make her know
> The keen Sensation of superior Woe. (ML ii. 65–6)

Leapor was without question committed to educating herself, and yet here she asks whether her struggle is worth the insults and the discouragement. A woman who wishes to achieve an enjoyable life by accumulating wealth is likewise deceived. Leapor sees such a woman degrading herself as a miser:

> Then let her quit Extravagance and Play;
> The brisk Companion; and expensive Tea;
> To feast with *Cordia* in her filthy Sty
> On stew'd Potatoes, or on mouldy Pye;
> Whose eager Eyes stare ghastly at the Poor,
> And fright the Beggars from her hated Door:
> In greasy Clouts she wraps her smoky Chin,
> And holds, that Pride's a never-pardon'd Sin. (ML ii. 66)

This image of the financially independent woman is repugnant to Leapor, who would rather remain poor but take some enjoyment from her life:

> If this be Wealth, no matter where it falls;
> But save, ye Muses, save your *Mira's* Walls:

> Still give me pleasing Indolence, and Ease;
> A Fire to warm me, and a Friend to please. (ML ii. 67)

The means of escaping poverty are not worth pursuing by a woman who genuinely wishes to be happy. In the end, there is nothing better to be expected than dignified poverty with the consolation of friendship. This is the best that can be hoped for, even if it is a long way from a fully satisfying life. At the end of the poem every difficulty remains:

> Since, whether sunk in Avarice, or Pride;
> A wanton Virgin, or a starving Bride;
> Or, wond'ring Crouds attend her charming Tongue;
> Or deem'd an Idiot, ever speaks the Wrong:
> Tho' Nature arm'd us for the growing Ill,
> With fraudful Cunning, and a headstrong Will;
> Yet, with ten thousand Follies to her Charge,
> Unhappy Woman's but a Slave at large. (ML ii. 67)

Leapor's rage is unmistakable: women are essentially trapped. Yet she is prepared to fight for her dignity, and, indeed, believes it is in women's characters to resist a tyranny, even if they are deprived of the hope of success. These lines make the poem's opening reference to women's softness and weakness sound like an ironic echo of Pope's 'Epistle to a Lady':

> Nothing so true as what you once let fall,
> Most Women have no Characters at all.
> Matter too soft a lasting mark to bear,
> And best distinguish'd by black, brown, or fair. (Pope, iii. ii. 46)

If Leapor can find no clear path to freedom she is willing at least to raise a forceful argument against the way women are understood. The title of the poem, 'An Essay on Woman', is certainly a reference to Pope. Leapor's 'An Essay on Friendship' is a more comprehensive rebuttal of Pope's 'Epistle to a Lady' (see below), yet it is evident that she also has the poem in mind when she is writing 'An Essay on Woman'. This may be judged simply on the basis of two small echoes: Pope has characters named Simplicius and Papillia, Leapor has Simplicus and Pamphilia. More importantly, Pope writes:

> See how the World its Veterans rewards!
> A Youth of frolicks, an old Age of Cards,

> Fair to no purpose, artful to no end,
> Young without Lovers, old without a Friend,
> A Fop their Passion, but their Prize a Sot,
> Alive, ridiculous, and dead, forgot.   (Pope, iii. ii. 69-70)

Leapor and Pope see the general condition of women as a series of contradictions. For Pope, these contradictions are follies to be satirized; for Leapor, they are injustices to be protested against. As Pope can imagine a Martha Blount who is an exception to the follies of her sex, so, in Leapor's poetry, the happy woman is an exception because she has escaped the general trap. It would, of course, be wrong to view Pope or even Swift as a simple woman-hater. Leapor, whose own techniques and interests have been deeply influenced by both poets, none the less disputes their general understanding of women's unhappiness. For her, women are not merely the authors of their own misfortunes or, at best, 'softer men', but the victims of an unjust order.

Leapor's treatment of the family is not limited to the relations of husbands and wives. In her poem 'The Cruel Parent', she describes the suffering of a young woman who is starved by her father. To what extent this relates to Leapor's own circumstances is not certain. The poem is not addressed to Artemisia and is, on that account, probably from some time before that friendship commenced. The poem is set in the night and opens: 'lonely *Mira* with her Head reclin'd, | And mourn'd the Sorrows of her helpless Kind' (i. 273). What Mira's own immediate sorrows are is not stated: rather, she describes the pains of Celia:

> Then to her Fancy *Celia*'s Woes appear,
> The Nymph, whose Tale deserves a pitying Tear;
> Whose early Beauties met a swift Decay;
> A Rose that faded at the rising Day,
> While Grief and Shame oppress'd her tender Age,
> Pursu'd by Famine and a Father's Rage ...   (ML i. 274)

Evidently Celia suffers more terribly than Mira, though the poet identifies with her. Mira falls asleep and dreams luridly about Celia, whose father, Lysegus, keeps her locked in a room in a castle, and refuses to feed her. Instead, he berates her and describes the misery she might expect as a beggar. Eventually she drops dead, and Lysegus is speared by a supernatural visitor.

Since there is no indication what Mira is unhappy about, or

whether Leapor was thinking of any real person in Celia, it is very difficult to judge the significance of this poem. It could be speculated that it was written after Leapor's dismissal from Edgcote House, and that her father was extremely angry at her returning as his dependant. By this reasoning, Leapor's only way of striking back at the father to whom she was looking for support was to write a poem as a cathartic fantasy. Donna Landry believes that the poem 'presents an iconography of paternal despotism and daughterly humiliation scarcely to be met with elsewhere in eighteenth-century verse' (Landry, 103). Unarguably, the father in the poem is a despot, and the daughter is humiliated. Landry's views on Leapor are most nearly justified in relation to this piece. Yet the poem stands apart from the attitudes most commonly expressed in her work, and, given its obscurity, it is necessary to be cautious with respect to its specific meaning. Contrary to Landry's claim, moreover, Leapor's treatment of conflict between a father and daughter is by no means unique in eighteenth-century poetry. Lady Dorothea Dubois, for example, describes an attempt to be reconciled with her bigamous father, the Earl of Anglesey, as he is dying. The old man repudiates her, and she is driven out of the house by her half-brother and a gang of servants:

> His base-born Son, a Pistol e'en presents,
> Behind her Head; but watchful Heav'n prevents
> The Fiend from executing his Intents.
> They pull and drag her, tear her Hands and Cloak,
> Nay dare uplift their own to give a Stroke:
> Force her from Room to Room, then down the Stairs,
> Nor heed her piteous Cries, nor flowing Tears.
> Some, more humane, now shook indeed their Head
> As they pass'd by, but nothing still they said.
> (Scarce two Months past a dang'rous Lying-in,
> Such cruel Usage surely was a Sin.)
> . . . .
> Her Servants now are ty'd, her Horse's Ear
> Inhumanly cut off: 'tis much they spare
> *Dorinda*'s Life . . .[39]

---

[39] Lady Dorothea Dubois, 'A True Tale', in *Poems on Several Occasions* (Dublin, 1764), 13–14.

Dubois actually wrote a number of poems arguing her claims against her father. Somewhat earlier, Sarah Fyge Egerton had complained in poems, admittedly less violent, that her father had banished her from London for publishing 'The Female Advocate'. Accordingly, it is difficult to maintain that 'The Cruel Parent' is in any way unique. It is certainly Leapor's most angry description of a father figure, and must owe something to her disagreements with her own father. While it could be said that an extreme poem reveals hidden struggles most clearly, it may also be remote from the poet's characteristic beliefs and attitudes. At the very least, the poem can be said to show Leapor's awareness of the vulnerability of an unmarried woman who is dependent on her father for financial support. Whether it confirms her as the enemy of patriarchy, as one who 'laughs at the fathers', is doubtful.

Leapor's play *The Unhappy Father* provides a complex treatment of issues relating to marriage and the family. As Betty Rizzo observes, it is a domestic tragedy in the manner of Nicholas Rowe, a she-tragedy.[40] The woman at the centre of the work is Terentia, an orphan under the care of a widower, Dycarbas. His two sons, Polonius and Lycander, compete for Terentia's affections. In order to defuse this rivalry, Dycarbas resolves that both sons should leave home for a time. Terentia, who has chosen Polonius over Lycander, initially resents Dycarbas's action:

> Last Night I heard—I heard with wounded Ears,
> Your *cruel* Father (never so till then)
> Give the strict Orders for your hasty Voyage.
> My swelling Heart was stung with bitter Grief;
> But you receiv'd the Sentence with a Smile.   (ML ii. 131)

By the end of this scene, however, Terentia is expressing fulsome gratitude to Dycarbas for saving her from an uncle who had wanted to steal her inheritance. There is no doubt of her regard for Dycarbas:

> If Deeds like this demand a Blessing, then
> Sure Heav'n has Millions still in Store for you:
> For You, ascend the Pray'rs of hoary Age,
> Who share the Comfort of your bounteous Hand:

---

[40] Betty Rizzo, 'Leapor, Mary', in Todd (ed.), *A Dictionary of British and American Women Writers 1660–1800*, 192–3.

> Deserted Babes are taught to lisp your Name,
> And, smiling, stretch their little Hands to you.   (ML ii. 133)

Terentia goes offstage and, in a soliloquy, Dycarbas explains his actions. First, however, he asks for divine guidance: 'Assist me, Heav'n! and teach me how to act | In this so nice, so delicate affair' (ML ii. 134). He accepts Terentia's choice of Polonius: 'Her Inclination my Consent has joined | To give this beauteous Blessing to *Polonius*' (ML ii. 135). There is no question that Dycarbas has any intention of opposing Terentia's decision, though he is conscious of having authority in the matter. His purpose in sending his sons away is solely to prevent conflict between them until Lycander also accepts Terentia's decision. There are, then, no grounds to believe, as Landry does (p. 103), that he is wilful in his disposition of his children's affective lives; indeed, his most important act is essentially to defend Terentia's freedom.

To focus on Dycarbas is unfortunately something of a distraction; his supposedly 'fumbling interventions' (Landry, 103) have little to do with the outcome of the play, and the final disasters are exclusively the result of sexual jealousy among the young male characters. Lycander describes his passion for Terentia to his sister Emilia:

> O my *Emilia*, I've surviv'd myself,
> And know not how to act in this new Being.
> How comes it? I, whose Soul was only read
> In stern Philosophy, and sacred Morals;
> Who look'd on Beauty with a careless Eye,
> Nor paid the least Attention to its Charms;
> What Magic bids me now so fondly dote
> On what so lately I disdain'd to look on?
> Woman, a Feather in the Cap of Nature!
> I hate the Sex: And yet I love *Terentia*.   (ML ii. 156)

Lycander is cold and intellectual. Ordinarily he has no respect whatever for women: indeed, his attraction to Terentia goes against his reason, philosophy, and morality. Although he accepts his father's command, he delays his departure for one last meeting which Emilia, his accomplice, arranges with the reluctant Terentia. This act of disobedience leads to the subsequent massacre.

Perhaps the most interesting character in the play is Emilia, whose marriage to Eustathius is characterized by serious arguments and frequent reconciliations. Despite Dycarbas's efforts to persuade Eustathius and command Emilia, they cannot moderate their behaviour. When Leonardo, a cousin who had once wished to marry Emilia, appears, intent on revenge, it is very easy for him to provoke Eustathius' Othello-like jealousy. Leonardo forges a love letter from Emilia, and bribes a servant to deliver it to Eustathius along with Emilia's stolen glove. The letter invites Leonardo to a tryst in the grove where Terentia is to meet Lycander. Eustathius' anger reaches a new height and, after an exchange with him, Emilia complains:

> Is this the Treatment of unhappy Wives?
> Ah! who would then be counted in the Number?
> And why did Heav'n's creating Power form
> Amongst his Works, one Creature only doom'd
> To lasting Anguish, and perpetual Chains?
> And yet inspir'd us with a thinking Soul,
> To taste our Sorrows with a keener Relish?
> Our servile Tongues are taught to cry for Pardon
> Ere the weak Senses know the Use of Words:
> Our little Souls are tortur'd by Advice;
> And moral Lectures stun our Infant Years:
> Thro' check'd Desires, Threatnings, and Restraint,
> The Virgin runs; but ne'er outgrows her Shackles;
> They still will fit her, even to hoary Age.
> With lordly Rulers Women still are curs'd;
> But the last Tyrant always proves the worst. (ML ii. 190)

This soliloquy, one of Leapor's strongest statements on the treatment of women, was, as Betty Rizzo observes, mentioned by none of her eighteenth-century admirers (Rizzo, 328). Doubtless such a protest would have upset the meek image of the poet promoted during the subscriptions. Yet these lines contain an anger encountered again and again in her work, that, from the constraints of a girl's upbringing to the tyrannies of marriage, there is small hope of a woman achieving the life she wants. It is probable that the soliloquy is based on a speech of Calisto in Rowe's *The Fair Penitent*:

> How hard is the Condition of our Sex,
> Thro' ev'ry State of Life the Slaves of Man?
> In all the dear delightful Days of Youth,

> A rigid Father dictates to our Wills,
> And deals out Pleasure with a scanty Hand;
> To his, the Tyrant Husband's Reign succeeds
> Proud with Opinion of superior Reason,
> He holds Domestick Bus'ness and Devotion
> All we are capable to know, and shuts us,
> Like Cloyster'd Ideots, from the World's Acquaintance,
> And all the Joys of Freedom; wherefore are we
> Born with high Souls, but to assert our selves,
> Shake off this vile Obedience they exact,
> And claim an equal Empire o'er the World?[41]

Protests of this sort are difficult to contain within the patriarchal conventions of the tragedy. Emilia, it turns out, has moral defects: she fights with her husband and disobeys her father. That Emilia makes the speech suggests that Leapor at this point in her career is uncertain of how far she can press the argument. When it comes from Emilia's mouth, Leapor can partly disown the content of the speech as a manifestation of Emilia's moral failings. If an entirely innocent character, Terentia perhaps, embarked on an angry critique of patriarchy, it would be very difficult to remain within the tragic form, and ultimately impossible to interest a producer in the script. When the bloodbath begins, Emilia is stabbed by her husband, who is killed by Lycander, who then kills Leonardo and takes a mortal wound himself. In all of this sanguinary excess, it is the guilty who die. The only innocent person to perish in the play is Dycarbas, an old man already resigned to the will of God:

> For soon this feeble Case, worn out with Age,
> Shall sleep and moulder in its dusty Cell.
> Then the freed Spirit shall exulting fly... (ML ii. 206)

The reported death of Polonius causes Dycarbas's final collapse, and brings Terentia to the verge of suicide. The reassertion of order in the play comes with Polonius's return. He assumes the authority of the patriarch and saves Terentia from her weakness. At the end they look forward to a married life together in a world diminished by the events of the play. There is no question that Leapor's play concludes with a reaffirmation of patriarchal values. Yet the portrayal of sexual violence, combined with Emilia's

---

[41] Nicholas Rowe, 'The Fair Penitent', in *The Dramatick Works of Nicholas Rowe, Esq.*, 2 vols. (London, 1720), i. 30.

protest, leaves the impression that the conclusion does not entirely resolve thematic contradictions.

In her second play, untitled and completed only to the third act, Leapor finds scope within the historical events surrounding the short reign of the Saxon King Edwy or Eadwig (955-9) to study once more the problems of marriage and sexual violence. In this play, the king and his army do battle, presumably at Gloucester, with a larger force representing ambitious elements in the Church. The two soldiers leading the rebel armies, Odoff and Dusterandus, are motivated partly by a desire to take Edwy's wife, Elgiva, and her sister, Emmel, as spoils:

> O how 'twou'd please my Pride to clasp her here
> To this glad Breast!—While Horror, Rage, and Grief,
> Shall reign alternate in her glowing Eyes!
> Whilst raving, weeping, struggling in my Arms,
> I gaze with Rapture on her vary'd Charms.   (ML ii. 250)

The treatment of the two sisters as objects for possession and domination is given a further and perhaps more insidious turn by their mother, Eleonora, who by 'serpentizing Fraud' uses her daughters to gain political advantage. In the first instance she arranges the marriage of Elgiva to the sensitive and naïve king. While this proves a very happy marriage, it also gives Eleonora the influence she desires. At the beginning of the play she persuades Edwy to reject offers of peace from the rebellious monks, who are, in fact, her enemies far more than the king's. When it appears that Edwy will lose the battle, she tries to purchase her survival by delivering her daughters to Odoff and Dusterandus. The chiefs renege on the deal and she is stabbed as she tries to entice Odoff herself. From this point, the play is unfinished.

The events upon which the play is based suggest an interesting examination of the forces opposing happiness in marriage. Edwy survived and retreated from the battle at Gloucester, and a meeting of the Witan divided his kingdom. In the following year, 958, a bishop forced the separation of Edwy and his wife on the grounds of consanguinity. Edwy died in 959 at the age of 19 (*DNB* vi. 558). If the play had been completed, it would have shown the marriage of Edwy and Elgiva destroyed by parental manipulation and political intrigue.

Leapor portrays Edwy as a heroic figure and a good husband. Elgiva, like Terentia in the earlier play, is powerless: she is effectively sold by her mother and then held prisoner by men intent on raping her. Eleonora herself is the most concentrated depiction of evil in Leapor's writings. The play portrays a good marriage torn apart by external forces. It certainly embodies an affective ideal of marriage, yet it is also the work of a woman who was convinced that marriage is fraught with dangers.

Leapor does not utterly repudiate marriage: repeatedly in her work she offers examples of marriages which could bring a woman some kind of satisfaction. She is keenly aware, however, of the deceptions to which a woman is exposed in courtship, and of the possibility that a husband may simply prove a tyrant. Yet she cannot find an entirely satisfactory alternative, for the life of the spinster is often portrayed in stark terms. Although it appears that she reached a peace with her father, she found herself constrained within that relationship. Her ambivalence towards him is reflected in her work as she portrays several fathers who are sympathetic, and one especially who is repugnant. On balance, however, her poetry is pessimistic about marriage and women's place in the family. It is perhaps a measure of Leapor's character that, even where there is little hope that injustice will be overcome, she is willing to raise a protest.

Women's Friendship

Mary Leapor's poetry consistently affirms the value of women's friendship. Even though many writers before her had made a similar affirmation, not least Katherine Phillips and Mary Astell, it must be recognized that to make such claims was to dispute a widely held belief, based on Aristotelian physiology, that women were by nature soft and therefore inconstant.[42] The best-known statement of this view of women is Pope's 'Epistle to a Lady'. Some women actually accepted Pope's view, albeit with sorrow. Sarah Dixon, for example, wrote on the loss of a friend:

> Ingenious *Pope*! whose better Skill
> Can dive into a Woman's Will,

---

[42] See Carolyn Williams, 'The Changing Face of Change: Fe/male In/constancy', *British Journal for Eighteenth-Century Studies*, 12 (1989), 13–28.

How truly have the Numbers told
'Her Soul is of too soft a Mould,
A lasting Character to hold.'[43]

Other women were willing to argue that if there was truth in Pope's portraits of women, the cause of their failings was not, as he suggested, a weakness of nature. Lady Irwin in 'An Epistle to Mr. Pope' spoke of women 'Whose mind a savage waste unpeopled lies'. For her, any difference between men and women was accounted for by education:

What makes ye diff'rence then, you may enquire,
Between the hero, and the rural 'squire;
Between the maid bred up with courtly care,
Or she who earns by toil her daily fare:
Their power is stinted, but not so their will;
Ambitious thoughts the humblest cottage fill;
Far as they can they push their little fame,
And try to leave behind a deathless name.
In education all the diff'rence lies;
Women, if taught, would be as bold and wise
As haughty man, improv'd by art and rules;
Where God makes one, neglect makes twenty fools.   (*GM* 6 (1736), 745)

Irwin's poem, it should be noted, was written more than a decade before Gray's 'Elegy'. She sees similarities between the wasted potential of women and that of the poor. Although it would be wrong to see the injustices suffered by a Viscountess as equivalent to those of the poor, Irwin's willingness to examine questions of gender and class together make 'An Epistle to Mr. Pope' a striking and significant composition. Somewhat later, Mary Whateley, following Pope's style very closely, suggests that it is not necessary for women to respond in kind to misogynistic satire:

Satire on Men superfluous wou'd be,
What they approve, by our own Sex we see.
Since Woman's Happiness depends on Man;
'Tis easy to conclude where first began
This Group of Follies, that o'erspread the Earth:
From our wise Lords they first receiv'd their Birth;

---

[43] Sarah Dixon, 'On the Loss of Stella's Friendship', in *Poems on Several Occasions* (Canterbury, 1740), 54.

> These our fond Females, bent to please Mankind,
> Enlarg'd, exalted, soften'd, and refin'd.[44]

Trivial behaviour in women ultimately reveals the folly of men's minds: women have become what men desire. Pope's Epistle is probably the most important statement of the dominant view of women in the eighteenth century, and women writing explicitly about issues of gender often found it necessary to confront this poem.

Mary Leapor appears to have given a great deal of thought to Pope's 'Epistle to a Lady'. 'An Essay on Woman' rejects the belief that women are soft and incapable of an active life. In the second 'Mira to Octavia' poem, Leapor draws on Pope in a crucial passage:

> And shall *Octavia* prostitute her Store,
> To buy a Tyrant with the tempting Ore?
> Besides, I fear your Shackles will be found
> Too dearly purchas'd with a thousand Pound.   (ML ii. 109)

Although there are other possible sources, it is most likely that these lines are an echo of Pope's comments on Martha Blount's celibacy:

> Ascendant Phoebus watch'd that hour with care,
> Averted half your Parents simple Pray'r,
> And gave you Beauty, but deny'd the Pelf
> Which buys your sex a Tyrant o'er itself.   (Pope, iii. II. 73)

Leapor offers to her friend the choice Pope applauded in Martha Blount. Indeed, this debt must be recognized: while Leapor disagrees with much of 'Epistle to a Lady', she also accepts much. Throughout her work, she tends to regard the happy, mature, and stable woman as an ideal reached only occasionally, and to believe that most women are unhappy and inclined to unworthy behaviour. Whereas Pope sees this as an inevitable consequence of women's softness, Leapor believes that women can actually improve themselves.

'Essay on Friendship' is particularly significant among Leapor's works. Although its language is not as remarkable as that of some of her other poems, it reveals a great deal about her attitudes towards gender, and towards her own writing:

---

[44] Mary Whateley, 'The Vanity of external Accomplishments', in *Original Poems on Several Occasions* (London, 1764), 104.

> To *Artemisia*—'Tis to her we sing,
> For her once more we touch the sounding String.
> 'Tis not to *Cythera*'s Reign nor *Cupid*'s Fires,
> But sacred Friendship that our Muse inspires.
> A Theme that suits *Æmilia*'s pleasing Tongue:
> So to the Fair One's I devote my Song. (ML i. 74)

Leapor's development as a writer is closely connected to her friendships with other women. During her time at Weston Hall she was evidently influenced by Susanna Jennens and her circle of relatives and acquaintances who wrote verse in the normal course of friendship. It seems that Leapor's writings later circulated in manuscript around Brackley, although not exclusively among women. The poems of her last fourteen months are, with few exceptions, directed to Bridget Freemantle: ''Tis to her we sing...'. The implied reader of Leapor's poems is, generally speaking, a female friend.[45] Although some poems, especially her essays, suggest that she is also looking towards a wider audience, in the vast majority of poems she speaks specifically to some woman she knows. Not all of these addresses are meant to be read by the person involved: Sophronia would have dismissed Leapor all the sooner if she had read 'The Disappointment' and 'The Consolation'. Still, in an important way, Leapor's poetic voice is formed by her relations with other women. In the passage above, she makes clear that she is not interested in conventional love poetry, but in describing something closer to her actual way of life. She has taken some point made by a friend whom she names Æmilia and develops it into a full essay. Leapor's poem has its origin in conversation, so that literary creativity and friendship are in this case, as in many of her poems, inseparable. Leapor's plays have an obviously public character, yet it is interesting to observe that the second was written 'At the Request of a Friend' (ML ii. 225); presumably, that friend was Freemantle. It seems that the issue of friendship is significant in respect to almost every area of Leapor's writing. Moreover, she

---

[45] For discussions of the idea of an implied reader, see Wolfgang Iser, *The Implied Reader: Patterns of Communication in Prose Fiction from Bunyan to Beckett* (Baltimore and London: The Johns Hopkins University Press, 1974); Walter J. Ong, 'The Writer's Audience is Always a Fiction', in *Interfaces of the Word: Studies in the Evolution of Consciousness and Culture* (Ithaca, NY and London: Cornell University Press, 1977), 53–81.

understands friendship in literary terms. She knows about misogynistic satire:

> The Wise will seldom credit all they hear,
> Tho' saucy Wits shou'd tell them with a Sneer,
> That Womens Friendships, like a certain Fly,
> Are hatch'd i'th Morning and at Ev'ning die.
> 'Tis true, our Sex has been from early Time
> A constant Topick for Satirick Rhyme:
> Nor without Reason... (ML i. 74)

Betty Rizzo suggests that Leapor's metaphor is a sign of her limitations as a poet; she cannot bring herself to write the simple word 'mayfly' (Rizzo, 338). Yet this is not the actual struggle with convention going on in these lines. Leapor, surprisingly, includes Pope among saucy wits, for the mayfly as a metaphor for women's changeable nature is taken from his 'Epistle to a Lady':

> Rufa, whose eye quick-glancing o'er the Park,
> Attracts each light gay meteor of a Spark,
> Agrees as ill with Rufa studying Locke,
> As Sappho's diamonds with her dirty smock,
> Or Sappho at her toilet's greazy task,
> With Sappho fragrant at an ev'ning Mask:
> So morning Insects that in muck begun,
> Shine, buzz, and fly-blow in the setting-sun. (Pope, iii. II. 50–2)

Pope, in a Swiftian moment, connects women's changes with dirt and, in the image of fly-blow, putrefaction. This passage, among other things, mocks a woman who reads Locke. Leapor's reference to the fly is a signal that she is arguing against Pope's Epistle.

As a woman who had apparently chosen not to marry, Leapor looked for constancy primarily in relation to friendship. She describes friendship in terms which have rather less to do with sexuality than with religion. For Leapor, friendship is 'sacred'. Constancy is to be cultivated in the soul:

> we're often found,
> Or lost in Passion, or in Pleasures drown'd:
> And the fierce Winds that bid the Ocean roll,
> Are less inconstant than a Woman's Soul:
> Yet some there are who keep the mod'rate Way,
> Can think an Hour, and be calm a Day:

> Who ne'er were known to start into a Flame,
> Turn Pale or tremble at a losing Game.
> Run *Chloe*'s Shape or *Delia*'s Features down,
> Or change Complexion at *Celinda*'s Gown:
> But still serene, compassionate and kind,
> Walk through Life's Circuit with an equal Mind. (ML i. 75)

The concept of *aequa mens*, a balanced spirit, is originally Stoic, and is also very Horatian; in Leapor's work, however, the idea is usually associated with resignation to the will of God. It is interesting to connect this point with her 'An Epistle to a Lady'; as Leapor contemplates her own death, and the soul leaving the body, the last thing she wishes to see is her friend: 'Be you the last that leaves my closing Eyes' (ML i. 40). Friendship is seen as a spiritual comfort, steadying her spirit for its last journey.

In her 'Essay on Friendship' Leapor offers several characters of women to make an argument for behaviour that is temperate, honest, and cheerful. She claims that friendships should be in the same degree, and not 'Where heavy Pomp and sullen Form withholds | That chearful Ease and Sympathy of Souls' (ML i. 77). This may tell us something about Bridget Freemantle—that she did not stand on her dignity in her friendship with the poet, even though she came from a more genteel background, and was about the age of Leapor's parents. Like Pope, Leapor finds one woman who combines all that she could hope for:

> Celestial Friendship with its nicer Rules,
> Frequents not Dunghills nor the Clubs of Fools.
> It asks, to make this Union soft and long,
> A Mind susceptible, and Judgment strong;
> And then a Taste: but let that Taste be giv'n
> By mighty Nature and the Stamp of Heav'n:
> Possest of these, the justly temper'd Flame
> Will glow incessant, and be still the same:
> Not mov'd by Sorrow, Sickness, or by Age
> To sullen Coldness or distemper'd Rage.
> The Soul unstain'd with Envy or with Pride,
> Pleas'd with itself and all the World beside,
> Unmov'd can see gilt Chariots whirling by,
> Or view the wretched with a melting Eye,
> Discern a Failing and forgive it too:
> Such, *Artemisia*, we may find in you. (ML i. 77–8)

In this light, constancy in friendship is seen as a kind of grace or spiritual maturity, and inconstancy as sin. This is significant, since a weakness of nature cannot really be escaped, but sin, on the other hand, can be repented of. Although Leapor accepts that many women are guilty of inconstancy and immoderate behaviour, she none the less holds out the prospect of transformation. Whereas Pope's view of inconstancy begins in muck and ends in maggots, Leapor moves the discussion towards the higher and more generous ground of theology:

> But all have Failings, not the best are free,
> Or in a greater or a less Degree.
> What follows then?—Forgive, or unforgiven
> Expect no Passage at the Gate of Heav'n.   (ML i. 79)

Leapor accepts part of Pope's charge against women. She provides her own examples of sudden changes in behaviour, some of which are very close to Pope's characters. Leapor describes Armida: 'To-day more holy than a cloister'd Nun, | Almost an Atheist by to-morrow's Sun' (ML i. 78), while Pope writes of Narcissa: 'Now Conscience chills her, and now Passion burns; | And Atheism and Religion take their turns...' (Pope, iii. II. 55). Leapor, however, is not ultimately constrained by what Pope gives her. By seeing the failures of women as sins which may be repented of, rather than the unalterable course of nature, she advances a far more hopeful view of her sex than does Pope.

Leapor's 'Essay on Friendship' ends with a surprisingly modest claim: 'our chief Task is seldom to offend, | And Life's great Blessing a well-chosen Friend' (ML i. 80). It seems that one of the great pains of Leapor's life was the lack of such friendship. Her relationship with Freemantle seems to have provided her with shelter from an often upsetting social life in Brackley. 'The Visit' presents an unusual picture of Mira simply defeated by 'the scolding Dame' and the gossips and physiognomists of Brackley:

> O ARTEMISIA! dear to me,
> As to the Lawyer golden Fee;
> Whose Name dwells pleasant on my Tongue,
> And first, and last, shall grace my Song;
> Receive within your Friendly Door
> A Wretch that vows to rove no more:
> In some close Corner let me hide,

> Remote from Compliments and Pride;
> Where Morals grave, or Sonnets gay,
> Delude the guiltless chearful Day... (ML ii. 290)

Leapor and Freemantle spent a good deal of their time talking about poetry and religion. The word 'guiltless' is striking. Leapor in many places feels compelled to defend the pleasure she takes in writing poetry and reading books. In 'The Question. Occasion'd by a Serious Admonition', she writes:

> Let me enjoy the sweet Suspence of Woe,
> When Heav'n strikes me, I shall own the Blow:
> Till then let me indulge one simple Hour,
> Like the pleas'd Infant o'er a painted Flow'r:
> Idly 'tis true: But guiltlessly the Time
> Is spent in trifling with a harmless Rhyme. (ML i. 225)

It is easy in the quest for grave scholarly judgements to forget that Leapor wrote for pleasure. As the unemployed daughter of a gardener, her luxuries were few. A woman of her station was expected to work hard. Her father and mother objected to the way she used her spare time. Her neighbours observed her, and feared 'mopishness'; that this is even recorded implies that it was a matter of some discussion. Poems like 'The Visit', 'The Epistle of Deborah Dough', and 'Corydon. Phillario. Or, Mira's Picture', show that Leapor found herself talked about. In the narrow world of Brackley, this meant that she was an outsider. Her father, it should be noted, observed only one of his daughter's friends, who appears in the poetry as 'Fidelia' (see ML ii, p. xxx). The value Leapor places on authentic friendship arises from painful experience. When she criticizes the inconstancy of women, it is not because she is overwhelmed by Pope's influence, but because she has been, if not betrayed, at least disappointed in her friendships with other women. It is against this background of rejection that Leapor's celebrations of friendship must be understood.

Her poetry indicates that Leapor did have some friends before meeting Freemantle; Octavia, for example, respected her enough to listen to her advice, even if she probably did not accept it. Leapor often compliments other women in her poems, and two especially, 'Song to Cloe, playing on her Spinnet' and 'Silvia and the Bee', are given over to praising the beauty and the accomplishments of particular friends. In the first of these Leapor warns beaux to beware of Cloe's eyes that wound, and she goes on to describe her friend's musical skill:

> *Amphion* led the ravish'd Stones
> (They say)—and as he'd rise or fall,
> Bricks, Pebbles, Slats and Marrow-Bones
> Wou'd form a Steeple or a Wall:
>   But this, you know,
>   Is long ago:
> We fancy 'tis a Whim:
> O had they charming *Cloe* heard,
> They'd surely not have stir'd for him.
>   The *Thracian* Bard,
>   Whose Fate was hard,
> (And *Proserpine* severe)
> Had brought *Eurydice* back—alas!
> But *Cloe* was not there.   (ML i. 121–2)

In 'Silvia and the Bee', Silvia walking among flowers is stung by a bee seeking the sweetest honey. She kills it, and Mira reproaches her in a spirit of raillery for similar treatment of two admirers, Cynthio and Amintor:

> They tell you, those soft Lips may vie
>   With Pinks at op'ning Day;
> And yet you slew a simple Fly,
>   For proving what they say.
> Believe me, not a Bud like thee
>   In this fair Garden blows;
> Then blame no more the erring Bee,
>   Who took you for the Rose.   (ML i. 273)

Both poems are somewhat conventional in their idealized descriptions of a woman's beauty captivating young men. Yet, in their way, these poems are also rather accomplished. 'Song to Cloe, playing on her Spinnet' especially displays a delicate touch and a complete control of form. Both poems could be read for an underlying lesbian attraction, though such an argument would be difficult to sustain, since Cloe and Silvia are both praised for their ability to win young men's affections. In the end, the poems must be read as expressions of sheer delight in friendship.

Leapor's poems inviting friends to tea are written in a similar vein of pleasure or celebration. She writes 'To Artemisia':

> If *Artemisia*'s Soul can dwell
> Four Hours in a tiny Cell,
> (To give that Space of Bliss to me)
> I wait my Happiness at three.   (ML i. 106)

Such poems are a summons to conversation and Bohea. They are, in that respect, very ordinary; yet insofar as they represent the interior world of Leapor's friendships they are distinctive. John Stuart Mill's claim that eloquence is heard and poetry overheard can, in a sense, be applied to such poems. Although Mill may have been thinking of the Romantic poet speaking gloomily to himself, here Leapor holds out the prospect of good gossip, and the reader is set to overhear the conversation:

> What Nymph, that's eloquent and gay,
> But owes it chiefly to her Tea?
> With Satire that supplies our Tongues,
> And greatly helps the failing Lungs.
> By that assisted we can spy
> A Fault with microscopick Eye;
> Dissect a Prude with wond'rous Art,
> And read the Care of *Delia's* Heart.   (ML i. 108)

In 'The Proposal' Leapor actually characterizes her muse in comic terms as a gossip (see ML i. 173). Patricia Meyer Spacks sees a parallel between the 'exclusionary alliance' which exists in gossip, and the relation between a reader and narrator in fiction: 'what reader and narrator share is a set of responses to the private doings of richly imagined individuals'.[46] Although Spacks is mainly concerned with fiction, in Leapor's poetry a reader is often drawn into such a relationship with the poet, and into the privileged society of her closest friends.

Mary Leapor's muse is emphatically social. Although a handful of poems were written in times of solitude or loneliness, the great bulk of her poetry was written for Freemantle or for other friends. This is an important point. John Sitter writes:

By the mid-century, retirement has hardened into retreat. The poet characteristically longs to be not only far from the madding crowd, which Pope had wanted as much as Gray, but far from everybody. Accordingly, many of the poems that most reflect the 1740s and 1750s are not

---

[46] Patricia Meyer Spacks, *Gossip* (New York: Alfred P. Knopf, 1985), 22.

epistles—that is, not poems with an explicit audience and implicit social engagement—but soliloquies or lyrics, usually blank verse musings or odes addressed to personifications.[47]

Whereas Sutherland describes the Augustan poet as a man at dinner with his friends, Sitter leaves the impression of the mid-century poet alone in his rooms gnawing a joint. Leapor, of course, fits neither pattern. Having been dismissed as a kitchen-maid, she harnesses her poetry to her teapot. She is an outsider, but a sociable one. She does not fly from history, yet as a woman of the labouring class there is a great deal from which she is excluded. Her poetry is addressed immediately to her friends; the reading public, the anonymous book buyer, stand somewhere outside that circle, but within earshot.

A final question is whether Leapor's view of female friendship is in some sense lesbian. There is certainly no indication of a physical relationship between Leapor and Freemantle, or with any other woman mentioned in the poems. Lillian Faderman accepts that women's relations may have been less physical in the past, but asserts that it is possible that such relations were still lesbian: 'if by "lesbian" we mean an all-consuming emotional relationship in which two women are devoted to each other above anyone else, these ubiquitous sixteenth-, seventeenth-, eighteenth-, and nineteenth-century romantic friendships were "lesbian" '.[48] This broad definition may ultimately empty the term of meaning; one is left with a scholar pushing writers of the past through a psycho-sexual hoop. The majority of recent commentators have argued that evidence of lesbianism among eighteenth-century writers is very difficult to assess. Ruth Perry describes the problem in her biography of Mary Astell:

For one thing, intense, spiritualized friendships with other women were not unusual in that culture.... The fact is that men and women of that day inhabited separate worlds; their social rounds and domestic activities kept them in the society of their own sex much of the time. Social

---

[47] John Sitter, *Literary Loneliness in Mid-Eighteenth Century England* (Ithaca, NY and London: Cornell University Press, 1982), 85–6. I am indebted to Dr Roger Lonsdale for his comments on Sitter's argument in relation to problems of the poetic canon.

[48] Lillian Faderman, *Surpassing the Love of Men: Romantic Friendship and Love Between Women from the Renaissance to the Present* (New York: William Morrow and Company, 1981), 19.

intercourse with those of the opposite sex was strictly regulated before marriage. As a result, there were simply more same-sex intimacies and ones of greater intensity than we are used to in our modern world, steeped as it is in post-Freudian heterosexuality.[49]

Janet Todd likewise proceeds cautiously in discussing lesbianism. Female friendship is expressed in fiction and especially in letters through language in which by the mid-eighteenth century terms of ecstasy figured almost by convention: 'female friendship represented for most women simply a rapturous sentimental union, springing perhaps from fear of male aggression or neglect but fed primarily by yearning for a partner in sensibility, a confidante in literature'.[50] Donna Landry entertains very little doubt that Leapor's poetry is basically lesbian, though the case is not argued in depth. On the basis of a reference to Sappho in 'An Hymn to the Morning', Landry develops the concept of Sapphic textuality:

> Sappho's name also functions in this period as a sign of transgressive female desire. If we read 'An Hymn to the Morning' in the light of Mira's yearning to match Sappho in poetical sweetness, her technical rivalry with the Lesbian muse—and, more contentiously, her rivalry with Sappho as a wooer of women, her technical rivalry with the lesbian lover—the eroticism of Leapor's textuality becomes distinctly noticeable, though it remains safely mediated by conventional landscape cathexis. (Landry, 85)

Landry provides little evidence that the name Sappho actually had the connotation of 'transgressive female desire'. Use of the name was, in fact, standard for female poets: in a notable instance, John Dryden used it in his ode on the death of Anne Killigrew. Her claim on this point is doubtful, to say the least. The words 'more contentiously' are an admission that the whole case for lesbianism is not provable; indeed, with respect to the poem she is discussing, neither Sappho nor Mira woos in any discernible way. Landry reads concealed eroticism in various female personifications, and in a landscape which, she admits, contains at least one heterosexual image. Everything really depends on the final stanza:

[49] Ruth Perry, *The Celebrated Mary Astell: An Early English Feminist* (Chicago and London: University of Chicago Press, 1986), 140.
[50] Janet Todd, *Women's Friendship in Literature* (New York: Columbia University Press, 1980), 359-60.

> Thus sung *Mira* to her Lyre,
> Till the idle Numbers tire:
> Ah! *Sappho* sweeter sings, I cry,
> And the spiteful Rocks reply,
> (Responsive to the jarring Strings)
> Sweeter—*Sappho* sweeter sings.   (ML i. 25)

Sappho is invoked purely as a predecessor in women's poetry: sexual rivalry is not an issue. Landry writes of the whole poem: 'These verses are hardly sapphic in any technical sense. Indeed, the reference to Sappho in the last stanza may seem to come out of nowhere' (Landry, 84). If the reference comes out of nowhere, it is by no means a promising place to begin an interpretation of Leapor's poetry.

The evidence that Leapor was a lesbian in the strict sense, as opposed to Faderman's, is slight. She did not marry; she criticized aspects of the institution of marriage; and she formed close friendships with women, one of which was particularly important. In some poems she praises the beauty and accomplishments of other women, though in a manner which foregrounds heterosexual courtship. This evidence is simply not conclusive. To borrow a term from Nina Auerbach, lesbianism is a 'silent possibility'[51] in Leapor's writing. It is more probable, however, that Leapor's female friendships followed the pattern most usual in her time, and that in Bridget Freemantle she simply found 'a partner in sensibility, a confidante in literature'.

Images of the Female Body

She is the daughter of a gardener, but no such elegant creature as Tennyson's Rose. She has work to do indoors and out, and her life is eminently prosaic. She has a plain face, an awkward figure, and nondescript clothes. But she has no quarrel with fate or her mirror. She seems to have been a shrewd, sensible young woman, vivacious, quick-witted, with no illusions, no sentimentality, no dreams.[52]

Myra Reynolds's claim that Mary Leapor has no argument with her mirror just misses a useful insight about the poet. More

---

[51] Nina Auerbach, *Communities of Women: An Idea in Fiction* (Cambridge, Mass. and London: Harvard University Press, 1978), 7.
[52] Reynolds, *The Learned Lady in England 1650–1760*, 247.

Problems of the Woman Poet

recently, Jocelyn Harris has spoken of Leapor's 'self-loathing';[53] although this is a strong term to use, any close reading of Leapor's poetry will show that she was very sensitive about her appearance. This is a significant issue in a culture where women were taught to value themselves by their beauty. The Countess of Winchilsea describes the problem in 'An Epilogue to the Tragedy of Jane Shore':

> There is a season, which too fast approaches,
> And every list'ning beauty nearly touches;
> When handsome Ladies, falling to decay,
> Pass thro' new epithets to smooth the way:
> From *fair* and *young* transportedly confess'd,
> Dwindle to *fine*, *well fashion'd*, and *well dress'd*.
> Thence as their fortitude's extremest proof,
> To *well as yet*; from *well* to *well enough*;
> Till having on such weak foundation stood,
> Deplorably at last they sink to *good*.
> Abandon'd then, 'tis time to be retir'd,
> And seen no more, when not alas! admir'd.[54]

Amusing though this is, other women were embittered by the loss of their beauty. The most famous instance is Lady Mary Wortley Montagu, whose 'Saturday' eclogue describes a woman in despair over the damage smallpox has done to her face. Even late in her life, Montagu remained unable to accept her own loss of beauty. She wrote to her daughter in 1757: 'It is eleven Year since I have seen my Figure in a Glass. The last Refflection I saw there was so disagreeable, I resolv'd to spare my selfe such mortifications for the Future, and shall continue that resolution to my Live's end.'[55] Even women who are supposedly resigned to the ordinariness of their features register a quiet complaint. Elizabeth Teft asks:

> Was Nature angry when she form'd my Clay?
> Or, urg'd by Haste to finish, cou'd not stay?
> Or drest with all her Store some perfect she,
> So lavish there, she'd none to spare for me?

---

[53] Harris, 'Sappho, Souls, and the Salic Law of Wit', 242.
[54] Anne Finch, 'An Epilogue to the Tragedy of Jane Shore', in *Poems*, 101.
[55] Lady Mary Wortley Montagu, 'To Lady Bute', in *The Complete Letters of Lady Mary Wortley Montagu*, ed. Robert Halsband, 3 vols. (Oxford: Oxford University Press, 1965–7), iii (1967), 135.

> I oft converse with those she's deem'd to grace
> With Air and Shape, fine Mien, and charming Face:
> When self-survey'd, the Glass hears this Reply,
> Dear! what a strange, unpolish'd thing am I![56]

Mirrors often appear in the poetry of women in the eighteenth century. Terry Castle suggests that for these poets the mirror was at once an emblem of the psyche and the symbol of an alternative world: 'the mirror image both distilled a longing for purity and expressed a desire for escape'.[57] If women's lives were often painfully limited, it was possible to find or make a better self in the mirror. There, too, a woman could find plainness confirmed, or watch her beauty decay.

The tendency to judge a woman's worth, or for her to judge her own worth, by her appearance was by no means new. Roy Porter maintains, however, that in the eighteenth century the growth of fashion brought with it a new standard of beauty which emphasized the artificial, so that many Georgians feared a civilization of façades.[58] 'Georgian values glamorized fine ladies into sex objects. Mutating from household managers into mannequins, ladies slipped into a femininity worn for the gaze of men, which had traditionally been the prerogative of actresses and whores.'[59] Women wore cosmetics that were caked and heavily coloured, so that painted faces largely obscured the natural complexion. In addition, such equipment as wigs, visors, jewels, masks, patches, lace, and gauze tended to conceal defects in appearance and tantalize at the same time. Men often believed that a woman's modesty could be judged by her ability to blush under the right circumstances. Yet under thick cosmetics this physiognomic test was no longer possible. Artificial appearance thereby takes on a sexual overtone which Porter detects in the expression 'making faces', meaning to have sex.[60] Keith Thomas observes that by the eighteenth century bodily control became a symbol of social hierarchy.[61] An elegant person would not pass wind audibly, or

---

[56] Elizabeth Teft, 'On Viewing Herself in a Glass', in *Orinthia's Miscellanies* (London, 1747), 54.
[57] Castle, 'Unruly and Unresigned', review of *ECWP*, p. 1228.
[58] Roy Porter, 'Making Faces: Physiognomy and Fashion in Eighteenth-Century England', *Études Anglaises: Grande Bretagne, États-Unis*, 38 (1985), 387.
[59] Ibid. 389.   [60] Ibid.
[61] Keith Thomas, 'The Place of Laughter in Tudor and Stuart England', *TLS* (21 Jan. 1977), 80.

expose teeth while laughing. Women's clothing was, of course, constricting, doubtless an aspect of this fashion to control the body. Stays would be tightened mercilessly to achieve the desired figure, and the image of women fainting because of overtightened stays is a commonplace in the literature of the period. Nature was forced into the correct forms. There was hardware available to straighten women's backs, necks, and shoulders. Where this involved suspension by the chin, there was risk of strangulation. As well as maintaining a good posture, women were expected to move with grace, which was the principal reason for dancing lessons.[62] A woman attempting to achieve such perfection needed to spend a great deal of money, and so women of the labouring class were automatically excluded, even if they were possessed of 'natural' beauty. This highly artificial ideal can be seen, then, as an aspect both of the relations between men and women, and of the relations between classes.

Jonathan Swift's misogynistic satires often work simply by showing the difference between the physical woman and the dazzling effect created by make-up and dress. What Swift finds is, of course, the problem: 'Who sees, will spew; who smells, be poison'd' (Swift, ii. 583). For Swift, there is a connection between cosmetics and prostitution; the carefully assembled exterior often conceals both physical horror and moral contamination. Mary Leapor attempts to see beyond artificial appearance to what she believes is a more authentic femininity. Her poem 'Dorinda at her Glass' describes a faded beauty who can no longer marshal her charms. Whereas Pope's Belinda might worship her own image as an idol, Dorinda can now only grieve before the mirror:

> At length the Mourner rais'd her aking Head,
> And discontented left her hated Bed.
> But sighing shun'd the Relicks of her Pride,
> And left her Toilet for the Chimney Side:
> Her careless Locks upon her Shoulders lay
> Uncurl'd, alas! because they half were Gray;
> No magick Baths employ her skilful Hand,
> But useless Phials on her Table stand:
> She slights her Form, no more by Youth inspir'd,
> And loaths that Idol which she once admir'd. (ML i. 2–3)

---

[62] Browne, *The Eighteenth Century Feminist Mind*, 32–3; see also Fenela Ann Childs, 'Prescriptions for Manners in English Courtesy Literature, 1690–1760, and their Social Implications' (D.Phil. thesis, Oxford University, 1984), esp. 246–7.

Not even the most elaborate cosmetics can hide Dorinda's age. She has valued herself as a beauty, and now that her looks have departed she is left with nothing:

> To her lov'd Glass repair'd the weeping Maid,
> And with a Sigh address'd the alter'd Shade.
> Say, what art thou, that wear'st a gloomy Form,
> With low'ring Forehead, like a northern Storm;
> Cheeks pale and hollow, as the Face of Woe,
> And Lips that with no gay Vermilion glow?   (ML i. 3)

Dorinda only knows herself by the mirror: it has literally and figuratively provided her with a self-image. Of course, without her cosmetics there is nothing alarming about Dorinda. Unlike Swift, Leapor chooses to affirm Dorinda's worth. Indeed, Dorinda now advises other women to recognize that beauty cannot be made to last, and Leapor closes the poem urging women to improve themselves spiritually so that old age will be satisfying:

> Thus *Pope* has sung, thus let *Dorinda* sing;
> 'Virtue, brave Boys,—'tis Virtue makes a King:'
> Why not a Queen? fair Virtue is the same
> In the rough Hero, and the smiling Dame:
> *Dorinda*'s Soul her Beauties shall pursue,
> Tho' late I see her, and embrace her too . . .   (ML i. 7)

Leapor, a committed Anglican, believes that life's fundamental duties are spiritual. Worship at the shrine of beauty is a distraction from true worship. She often understands friendship as a spiritual comfort: accordingly, she advises women to pursue friendship, rather than beauty, since death is in sight: 'To smooth my Passage to the silent Gloom, | And give a Tear to grace the mournful Tomb' (ML i. 8). By emphasizing the spiritual potential of women, Leapor believes that she has found a more reasonable and more durable standard of value.

In 'Dorinda at her Glass', 'Advice to Sophronia', and other poems, Leapor asserts that women should preserve their dignity by accepting the loss of beauty. Yet she felt her own dignity threatened by standards of beauty. In 'The Visit', she is distressed by comments on her appearance, and it is for this reason that she needs shelter:

> Where careless Creatures, such as I,
> May 'scape the penetrating Eye

Of Students in Physiognomy;
Who read your want of Wit or Grace,
Not from your Manners, but your Face;
Whose Tongues are for a Week supply'd
From one poor Mouth that's stretch'd too wide;
Who greatly blame a freckled Hand,
A skinny Arm, full Shoulders; and,
Without a Microscope, can spy
A Nose that's plac'd an Inch awry. (ML ii. 291)

It seems that, in the view of some of her acquaintances, Leapor was simply an ugly woman. Yet the poet often sees her appearance in relation to her poverty, as one manifestation of a generally bleak and constrained way of life. In 'The Disappointment', she indulges a brief fantasy of being something more:

What Shadows swam before these dazled Eyes!
Fans, Laces, and Ribbands, in bright Order rise:
Methought these Limbs your silken Favours found,
And thro' streight Entries brush'd the rustling Gown,
While the gay Vestment of Delicious Hue
Sung thro' the Isle, and whistled in the Pew.
Then, who its Wearer, by her Form shall tell:
No longer *Mira*, but a shining Belle. (ML ii. 79)

Leapor dreams of escape from plainness; she dreams of being elegant, even beautiful. Of course, the promised gown is a cheat, and she is left with her old self. When she recounts her dismissal from Edgcote House in 'An Epistle to Artemisia. On Fame', she is criticized by Parthenia for her dirty shoes and by Sophronia for her posture: ' "Still o'er a Table leans your bending Neck: | Your Head will grow prepost'rous, like a Peck' (ML ii. 52). When the *Gentleman's Magazine* published the remarks of a former employer on Mary Leapor, much was made of the length of her neck and the shortness of her body. Leapor, a poor woman, could not dress to advantage; indeed, her employers' low regard for her as a servant is partly related to her appearance. Her shoes, posture, and proportions have a strange economic significance, since they all seem to have been factors in her dismissal. In 'The Mistaken Lover' Strephon attacks his wife's appearance to cover his actual greed. It may be that the spectacle of an intellectually ambitious kitchen-maid unnerved her employers, and that she posed a threat to their view of a proper social order. In a world where physiognomy was a respected practice, Leapor's appearance may have given the Chauncys grounds to believe that she really was a person of no significance and that she ought to learn her station.

Leapor's most telling examination of standards of beauty is 'Corydon. Phillario. Or, Mira's Picture'. In her letter Freemantle expresses concern that this poem will be misunderstood:

> I think it may give the Reader a worse Idea of her Person than it deserv'd, which was very far from being shocking; tho' there was nothing extraordinary in it. The Poem was occasioned by her happening to hear that a Gentleman who had seen some of her Poems, wanted to know what her Person was. (ML ii, p. xxxii)

This seems quaint, but at least one scholar has expressed confusion over whether this Mira is a real person.[63] To know the occasion of the poem is helpful in any case, since it allows the reader to see that not only is Leapor making a burlesque of her own appearance but satirizing the gentleman as well, and, in a broad sense, the male gaze. Corydon is a shepherd, and Phillario is a sophisticated man accustomed to polite society. The two are walking amid flowers and birds, and Phillario asks about the local beauties: 'What Nymph, O Shepherd! reigns | The rural Toast of these delightful Plains?' Phillario mentions several women who are admired variously for graceful ease, inspiring eyes, a charming voice, a fair face, or raven hair. Phillario, however, is startled by the sight of Mira:

> But who is she that walks from yonder Hill,
> With studious Brows, and Night-cap Dishabille?
> That looks a Stranger to the Beams of Day;
> And counts her Steps, and mutters all the Way?   (ML ii. 295-6)

Presumably Mira is composing a poem, counting the syllables as she walks. The gentleman who was impressed by Leapor's poems has given her an occasion to debunk any notion that intellectual or personal worth can be judged from physical appearance. In 'The Mistaken Lover' Leapor shows Strephon feebly criticizing his wife's appearance; in this poem she goes much further by asserting that she herself is an ugly woman, a slattern, and almost

---

[63] See Marion K. Bragg, *The Formal Eclogue in Eighteenth-Century England*, University of Maine Studies, ser. 26 (Orono, Me.: The University Press, 1926), 88.

dares the gentleman to stand by his favourable opinion of her intelligence. When Corydon asks Phillario if he likes Mira, the response is unmistakable:

> Like her!—I'd rather beg the friendly Rains
> To sweep that Nuisance from thy loaded Plains;
> That—
>   Corydon.
> —Hold, *Phillario*! She's a Neighbour's Child:
> 'Tis true, her Linen may be something soil'd.
>   Phillario.
> Her Linen, Corydon!—herself, you mean.
> Are such the Dryads of thy smiling Plain?   (ML ii. 296)

Twentieth-century readers may think of the eighteenth century as a time when dirt was everywhere and personal hygiene abysmal. Indeed, that would appear to be the origin of Swift's excremental vision. Johnson's famous comment about Kit Smart suggests that some people were actually content with their dirt: 'Another charge was, that he did not love clean linen; and I have no passion for it.'[64] Yet, by the eighteenth century, polite culture made much of personal cleanliness. In one conduct manual, we read: 'Cleanliness is a mark of politeness: and it is universally agreed upon, that no one, unadorned with this virtue, can go into company without being offensive. Besides, the easier or higher any one's fortune is, this duty rises in proportion.'[65] Hygiene becomes a matter of social distinction: polite people always wear clean linen. In her self-portrait Leapor is intent on flouting almost every aspect of contemporary standards of beauty. Moreover, she is willing to connect her poor appearance with her interest in literature. Corydon, speaking as well as he can in Mira's defence, observes:

> Her Eyes are dim, you'll say: Why, that is true:
> I've heard the Reason, and I'll tell it you.
> By a Rush-Candle (as her Father says)
> She sits whole Ev'nings, reading wicked Plays.   (ML ii. 297)

---

[64] James Boswell, *Boswell's Life of Johnson*, ed. G. B. Hill, rev. L. F. Powell, 6 vols. (Oxford: Clarendon Press 1934–50), i (1934), 397.

[65] *The Young Gentleman and Lady Instructed*, 2 vols. (London, 1747), ii. 162; cited by Childs, 'Prescriptions for Manners', 252.

It seems that a literary woman of Leapor's class can only read by night: there are simply too many things to be done during the day. The poems which impressed the gentleman could only have been produced by a poet with rings around her eyes. If women are to be judged by their appearance, Mira ought to give up books:

> Phillario.
> *She* read!—She'd better milk her brindled Cows:
> I wish the Candle does not singe her Brows,
> So like a dry Furze-faggot; and, beside,
> Not quite so even as a Mouse's Hide. (ML ii. 297)

Phillario goes on to denounce Mira's shape as so many mountains, and then looks into her mouth:

> Corydon.
> But she has teeth —
> Phillario.
> —Consid'ring how they grow,
> 'Tis no great matter if she has or no:
> They look decay'd with Posset, and with Plumbs,
> And seem prepar'd to quit her swelling Gums. (ML ii. 298)

Although eighteenth-century cooking tended to use a great deal of sugar, women were expected to keep their teeth in repair. John Breval writes in *The Art of Dress* (1717):

> Take, gentle Creatures, take a Friend's Advice,
> In polishing your Teeth be wond'rous nice;
> For no Defect in these (should such be known)
> Ten Thousand other Graces will attone;
> Oft let the Brush it's Morning Task repeat;
> And shun at Boards the too high-season'd Meat;
> *Ragouts*, and luscious Soups, make Teeth decay,
> And op'ning Lips the tainted Breath betray.[66]

Roy Porter suggests that the reasoning behind Chesterfield's advice to his son never to laugh was that laughter might reveal rotten teeth.[67] Bad teeth, like other unpleasant aspects of the body, ought to be concealed or controlled.

---

[66] John Breval, *The Art of Dress* (London, 1717), 19–20; for a discussion of Breval and the problems of tooth-brushing in the early eighteenth century see Childs, 'Prescriptions for Manners', 252.
[67] Porter, 'Making Faces', 391.

Such principles of fashion, of course, applied above all to women. Insofar as Leapor presents herself as genuinely ugly, she has a chance to confound the gentleman's expectation that a gifted writer will also have a charming appearance. As Margaret Anne Doody puts it: 'Leapor plays with the fascination of female ugliness in such a manner as to free herself from conventional claims of feminine proprieties.'[68] By emphasizing every defect in her body, she offers a challenge to polite culture. Whereas women are expected to conceal or control whatever defects their bodies may have, Leapor puts hers on display, and even amplifies them. This is a procedure like Swift's, except that Leapor is staking her claim to real dignity; she asserts that she does not wish to be valued for beauty, but for her wit and, as we glean from other poems, her morals. Maximilian Novak speaks of the eighteenth century as the 'Age of Disguise', and Terry Castle treats the masquerade as a central metaphor of eighteenth-century culture.[69] Leapor adamantly refuses to conceal herself. She insists on a dignity which has nothing to do with appearances. Bold though it is, Leapor's poem is remarkably pessimistic. Mira cannot enter Phillario's world on the strength of her intellect, because her features are too plain; although Corydon will not attack her appearance, he has no appreciation of her intellect since he believes that plays are wicked. The poem has an oddly sinister ending:

> Corydon.
> No more, my Friend! for see, the Sun grows high,
> And I must send the Weeders to my Rye:
> Those spurious Plants must from the Soil be torn,
> Lest the rude Brambles over-top the Corn.   (ML ii. 298)

Phillario has already wished that the rain would sweep Mira away, and now Corydon is intent on getting rid of weeds. Presumably Mira is such a 'spurious plant', unwelcome, and best plucked out. The poem is a counter-pastoral, and its underlying vision is of disharmony. As in 'An Essay on Woman', Leapor

---

[68] Doody, 'Swift among the Women', 79.
[69] See Maximilian Novak, ed., *English Literature in the Age of Disguise* (Berkeley and London: University of California Press, 1977); Terry Castle, *Masquerade and Civilization: The Carnivalesque in Eighteenth-Century English Culture and Fiction* (Stanford, Calif.: Stanford University Press, 1986).

raises her protest but can see no escape from her situation. In 'Mira's Picture' she is caught between classes and between standards of value: both Corydon and Phillario judge her to be worthless.

Margaret Anne Doody claims that eighteenth-century poetry is incarnational, not merely because it deals in particulars, 'but also because it celebrates, however ruefully, the experience of living a bodily and historical life'.[70] How much of eighteenth-century poetry can be accounted for by this term is arguable, yet the idea is certainly useful with respect to Mary Leapor. Doody believes that interest in incarnation can lead to an 'ironic self-awareness of the gap between that cultural icon, the beautiful female, and the strange physical self'.[71] Leapor's poetry can certainly be very physical, as in 'Mira's Picture'. She is aware of women's bodies. A classic instance of this is 'The Head-Ach', in which she humorously compares her own writing of poetry with a friend's gossip. Both are crimes for which they are punished in the natural course of things:

> Just so, *Aurelia*, you complain
> Of Vapours, Rheums, and gouty Pain;
> Yet I am patient, so shou'd you,
> For Cramps and Head-achs are our due:
> We suffer justly for our Crimes;
> For Scandal you, and I for Rhymes... (ML i. 102)

Leapor finds in her menstrual pains a bond with Aurelia, even if the poem is largely a gentle rebuke to her friend for malicious talk. In a very light-hearted manner, she connects her poetry with women's friendship, and with women's physical experience.

In Doody's view, women poets of the eighteenth century are often very conscious of dirt. In this, again, they resemble Swift, though they rarely share his horrified fascination. An awareness of dirt can often be detected in women's descriptions of their environment. Esther Lewis describes a stroll during the winter:

> Exalted now on iron stilts I move,
> Through dirt with cane supported fearless rove,
> Till rooted deep upon the yielding plain,
> A breathing monument awhile remain,

---

[70] Doody, 'Tit for Tat', review of *ECWP*, p. 3.   [71] Ibid., 4.

> To warn each wand'ring she my fate to shun,
> Nor such defiling dirty hazards run.[72]

Doody's notion of incarnation in poetry really does not account for the hundreds of poems written by women to the standard abstractions such as sleep, pity, and wisdom, yet there is certainly a strain in the poetry of eighteenth-century women which might take as its best emblem Esther Lewis perched on her stilts. Mary Leapor, too, knows that she lives in a dirty world. Her house, for example, would probably have had a clay floor, and if its lighting was primarily from rushes, it would have been dingy. As a gardener's daughter she would have been accustomed to muddy boots and black finger-nails. In 'The Pocket-Book's Petition to Parthenissa', the book begs Parthenissa to write something on one of its pages, after which it will be content: 'Nor once, repining at my Cell, | With Darkness, Dirt, and Mira, dwell' (ML ii. 94). In 'An Epistle to a Lady' Leapor indicates that in her house there is no hope of keeping things clean:

> Convinc'd too soon, her Eye unwilling falls
> On the blue Curtains and the dusty Walls:
> She wakes, alas! to Business and to Woes,
> To sweep her Kitchen, and to mend her Clothes. (ML i. 39)

'An Epistle to a Lady' is Leapor's most poignant meditation on death (see Chapter 5 below). She ponders her body's fragility, her intellectual struggles, the poverty and drabness of her environment, and her need for friendship; the poem ends with thoughts of the world to come. Apart from Doody's specific use of the word, 'incarnation' is a theological term describing the divinization of history and the material order. The paradox in Leapor's response to her experience is that she is firmly aware of its physical nature, yet she also insists on the intellectual and spiritual dignity of women. Leapor's poetry strives towards a vision of wholeness. Her protest is, in that sense, rooted in orthodoxy.

---

[72] Esther Lewis, 'A Letter to a Lady in London', in *Poems Moral and Entertaining* (Bath, 1789), 300.

CHAPTER 3

A LABOURING POET

> A servant write verses! say's Madam Du Bloom;
> Pray what is the subject?—a Mop, or a Broom?
> He, he, he,—say's Miss Flounce; I suppose we shall see
> An Ode on a Dishclout—what else can it be?[1]

These lines 'On the Supposition of an Advertisement appearing in a Morning Paper, of the Publication of a VOLUME of POEMS, by a SERVANT MAID' were written by Elizabeth Hands, sometime domestic servant, about forty years after the publication of Mary Leapor's first volume. Despite the significant number of labouring poets who published throughout the century, Hands assumed that her social position would constitute an obstacle to the acceptance of her work. Indeed, while she produced some poems of distinct merit, she, like most labouring poets of her time, had been forgotten until the 1980s.

Mary Leapor has, of course, fared somewhat better than Elizabeth Hands. Her presence in anthologies and her occasional mention in critical works have sustained a small reputation on the periphery of eighteenth-century literature. In this chapter, Leapor's work will be considered against the background of her economic circumstances as a kitchen-maid and the daughter of an agricultural craftsman. It will be argued that Leapor's work contributes to a fairly broad movement among labouring-class poets to provide an accurate account of work and social conditions in their time. While it would be erroneous to view this sort of poetry as a unified and self-conscious expression of cultural resistance, it remains possible to see in it assertions of identity and interest separate from those of more affluent writers.

There is always a problem of terminology and definitions. The term 'working-class literature', defined broadly, would be useful in this context. It carries such a weight of ideology, however, that

---

[1] Elizabeth Hands, 'A Poem, On the Supposition of an Advertisement appearing in a Morning Paper, of the Publication of a VOLUME of POEMS, by a SERVANT MAID', in *The Death of Amnon* (Coventry, 1789), 47.

there is great room for misunderstanding. The problem can be seen with a definition given by Phyllis Mary Ashraf: 'Working class literature is that writing which first appears within the modern working class in the process of its formation and carries the marks of its origin in its attitude to society, particularly to workers' problems, and in its manner of expression.'[2] The immediate difficulty with an ideological definition is that it can deflect attention from writers of the working class to those who write about the working class, a tendency which is prominent in Ashraf's own study. Furthermore, it introduces a circularity into the argument: working-class writers are defined as those who manifest a consciousness appropriate to the working class. Given that much of eighteenth-century society is pre-industrial, Ashraf's definition is not very useful.

For the purposes of this discussion it is best to avoid the term 'working-class literature', in favour of terms which are less polemically charged, such as labouring poets, or even labouring-class poets. A term which is used occasionally in scholarship, 'peasant poetry', will be avoided since it is simply too narrow. One scholar has found himself in the awkward position of having to describe William Falconer, author of *The Shipwreck*, as 'a peasant of the sea'.[3] It is, however, necessary to limit the term 'labouring poets' in certain respects. The figure of the impoverished poet is a commonplace in literature. If indigence were the sole criterion, then the category would include Oliver Goldsmith, the young Samuel Johnson, Christopher Smart, and numerous other poets who enjoyed the distinct privilege of a university education but were at times besieged by duns. Furthermore, many clerics in the eighteenth century held modest livings, although they too occupied a position of privilege in society. The most obvious definition for labouring poets is that it includes all those whose support normally depended on manual work, either their own or that of their families. This would include skilled workers as well as unskilled, small tenant farmers and other rural cottagers, servants in husbandry as well as lower domestic

---

[2] Phyllis Mary Ashraf, *Introduction to Working Class Literature in Great Britain*, 2 vols. (Berlin: Ministerium für Volksbildung, Hauptabteilung Lehrbildung, 1978–9), i (1978), 18.
[3] Rayner Unwin, *The Rural Muse: Studies in the Peasant Poetry of England* (London: George Allen and Unwin, 1954), 83.

servants, some small traders, and all the dependants of such people. Problems of classification remain, especially with poets whose circumstances and allegiances changed over time. An important example is George Crabbe, who grew up in poverty but eventually became a priest; although his poetry is deeply informed by the experience of poverty, he is alienated in many respects from the class into which he was born. In such a case, however, it is still possible to recognize much in his poetry that is a response to his origins. Since polite elements composed only a small segment of the population, the group of poets here being identified is those whose lives most represent the experiences of the great majority of people in eighteenth-century England.

Labouring poets in the eighteenth century have been the subject of lengthy considerations by a number of critics, commencing with Robert Southey's 'An Introductory Essay on the Lives and Works of Our Uneducated Poets' (1831). As an introduction to a nineteenth-century poet named John Jones, Southey discusses the careers of John Taylor, the seventeenth-century waterman poet, and then four eighteenth-century figures, Stephen Duck, James Woodhouse, John Frederick Bryant, and Ann Yearsley. This is a very small sample of labouring-class poetry in the eighteenth century, for, as A. J. Sambrook observes with just a little exaggeration, 'since the discovery in 1730 of Stephen Duck ... hardly a year had passed without some peasant poet being brought forward and hailed as a "natural genius"'.[4] Critics have unfortunately tended to restrict their attention to a group of poets only slightly larger than that identified by Southey. The title of Southey's essay suggests a second area of difficulty, since he defines his subject only in a privative sense. Rather than starting from the position that these poets write out of a different social and economic experience than their polite contemporaries, Southey focuses on their lack of formal education. Labouring poets are thus strictly defined by their handicaps.

A similar difficulty can be seen in the work of a twentieth-century critic, Rayner Unwin. Although his title, *The Rural Muse: Studies in the Peasant Poetry of England* (1954), implies that he has taken a positive view, he is hard pressed at times to defend the value of the peasant poet: 'His will be a limited but constant

[4] A. J. Sambrook, 'An Essay on Eighteenth-Century Pastoral, Pope to Wordsworth (II)', *Trivium*, 6 (1971), 107.

talent, valuable not so much in itself as in its resuscitative power. In their way Duck and Bloomfield... are the mouthpieces of external nature; touchstones of jasper that betray the gold in other men.'[5] Unwin's study, with its Romantic emphases on the imagination and the individual response to nature, often fails to account for the social and literary conflicts underlying the poetry written by labouring people. Furthermore, Unwin seems at times unsympathetic to labour as a background for poetry: 'Imagination, which is conditioned by a breadth of experience, is seldom very pronounced in a man whose vision is narrowed by his occupation and training.'[6] Raymond Williams, who makes judicious use of Unwin's study in *The Country and the City* (1973), takes an altogether different view of labouring-class intellectuals, including Duck: 'It is part of the insult offered to intelligence by a classsociety that this history of ordinary thought is ever found surprising.'[7] Williams's ideas on the relations of agricultural labour and literature are particularly useful.

Phyllis Mary Ashraf's *Introduction to Working Class Literature in Great Britain* (1978–9) considers a number of poets from the eighteenth century. Apart from the reservations already expressed concerning Ashraf's work, it should also be observed that she emphasizes writers from the end of the century and later, especially as they relate to Chartism and subsequent developments. H. Gustav Klaus, an admirer of Ashraf, has produced two relevant studies, the first in 1981 comparing Stephen Duck and Mary Collier, and the second in 1985 entitled *The Literature of Labour: Two Hundred Years of Working-Class Writing*.[8] The most important assertion made by Klaus is that there were two waves of labouring poets in the century, the first following Duck's success in the early 1730s, and the second in the 1770s. In support of this observation he refers first to the group of Collier, Henry Frizzle, John Bancks, Robert Tatersal, then to John Frederick Bryant, James Woodhouse, and Ann Yearsley.[9] It could be asked if Mary Leapor, Henry Jones, James Eyre Weeks,

[5] Unwin, *The Rural Muse*, 24.   [6] Ibid. 70.
[7] Raymond Williams, *The Country and the City* (London: Chatto & Windus, 1973), 101.
[8] See H. Gustav Klaus, 'Stephen Duck und Mary Collier. Plebejische Kontroverse über Frauenarbeit vor 250 Jahren', *Gulliver*, 10 (1981), 115–23; *The Literature of Labour: Two Hundred Years of Working-Class Writing* (Brighton: Harvester, 1985).   [9] Klaus, *Literature of Labour*, 6.

Joseph Lewis, and George Smith Green do not constitute a third wave, since their first works appeared around 1750. In fact, Klaus's symmetrical argument is very difficult to defend without a thorough examination of all the works published by labouring poets in the century. Such an examination would almost certainly undermine his thesis.

Critics discussing the relations between poetry and economics in the eighteenth century have in some cases made assertions which, while perfectly sound in relation to well-known figures, must be modified once labouring poets are taken into account. Irvin Ehrenpreis claims, for example, that 'Wordsworth's sympathetic, even rapt interest in common people for their own sake is hard to discover in the verse or prose of an earlier writer'. Ehrenpreis narrows his discussion to the condition of poverty in which people are dependent for subsistence on the voluntary support of strangers, and he excludes from his definition yeomen, artisans, and small merchants.[10] He goes on to consider how the distinction between deserving and undeserving poor operates in the work of a wide range of writers. Ehrenpreis's approach, while fruitful in some respects, tends to treat the poor as an object to be observed from the outside, even if it is with 'rapt interest'. What he ignores is that the poor in eighteenth-century England sometimes spoke for themselves. Jacob Viner, an economist writing on Augustan satire, manifests a similar attitude. He openly suggests that satire as a literary device was too sophisticated for the common people to use.[11] He also writes: 'I have not succeeded in finding a clear-cut English instance [excluding Swift] in which a satirist, on an economic issue, was attacking a social group clearly higher than the one he belonged to or had been hired to serve.'[12] The passage which opens this chapter is an instance of a satirist attacking a higher social class. Whether the arrogance of the rich towards intellectuals of a lower class is considered an economic issue may be argued; however, the belief that satire was almost

---

[10] Irvin Ehrenpreis, 'Poverty and Poetry: Representations of the Poor in Augustan Literature', in *Studies in Eighteenth-Century Culture*, I, Proceedings of the American Society for Eighteenth Century Studies (Cleveland and London: The Press of Case Western Reserve University, 1971), 3–4.
[11] Jacob Viner, 'Satire and Economics in the Augustan Age of Satire', in Henry Knight Miller, Eric Rothstein, and G. S. Rousseau (ed.), *The Augustan Milieu: Essays Presented to Louis A. Landa* (Oxford: Clarendon Press, 1970), 100.
[12] Ibid. 86.

always used in the service of the rich is not tenable. Among labouring poets, Mary Leapor will prove a particularly strong instance of a satirist attacking her betters.

Relatively little attention has been paid to the origins of labouring-class poetry. Stephen Duck's success under the queen's patronage is an event of some importance since it established the precedent of a labouring poet entering the mainstream of contemporary literature. Duck, however, is not the first instance of a labouring-class poet in the eighteenth century. Edward Ward (1667–1731) kept a tavern in London and was well known in literary circles early in the century. His poetry often depicts labouring-class life vividly. The following verses describe the behaviour of parish officers towards the poor, anticipating Langhorne by nearly seventy years:

> If some poor crasie Alms-man, Lame or Sick,
> Decreed to starve on Ninepence for a Week,
> Petition'd these proud Masters of the Poor,
> To make the scanty Sum but Three pence more,
> So many Tavern Consults must be held,
> Before they to the Pauper's Suit would yield,
> That Pounds in Wine of the Poor's Money flew,
> E'er the dull Sots determin'd what to do:
> At last, perhaps, 'twas gen'rously agreed,
> He should have half the Sum to serve his need;
> Three half pence Weekly added to his Store,
> To keep the Wretch still miserably Poor.
>
> . . . .
> For ev'ry one they hasten'd to the Grave,
> Themselves, not Parish, did their Pensions save.[13]

Ward is not the only figure from the labouring class in early eighteenth-century literature. Jane Holt Wiseman, a domestic servant from Oxford, had her play, *Antiochus*, produced at Lincolns Inn Fields in 1701, 1711, 1712, and 1721, and also published a volume of poems in 1717.[14] Another, more elusive contribution by labouring people to the literature of the time

---

[13] Edward Ward, 'A Journey to H——: or, A Visit Paid to the D——', in *Works*, 4 vols. (London, 1703–9), iii (1706), 99.

[14] Jane Holt (neé Wiseman), *Antiochus the Great: Or, The Fatal Relapse* (London, 1702); *A Fairy Tale* (London, 1717). See also 'Wiseman, Jane', in Todd (ed.), *A Dictionary of British and American Women Writers 1660–1800*, 329; and *ECWP* 72.

can be identified in David Foxon's *English Verse 1701–1750*; in the decades before Duck's appearance, a large number of verses were published pertaining to occupational or craft concerns. Such pieces as Henry Nelson's 'A New Poem on the Ancient and Loyal Society of Journey-Men Taylors', 'Vulcan's Speech' by an anonymous blacksmith, or 'The Taylors answer to Vulcan's speech', are all from Dublin around 1725.[15] These poems, along with many others in a similar vein, show that working people were articulating aspects of their experience in verse. Most of these compositions, however, have a narrow scope; they discuss issues of immediate concern to members of a particular occupation, although some are addressed to a wider audience. Furthermore, their literary merits are generally limited.

Scholars studying popular culture have paid close attention to crafts, recognizing occupational traditions and customs that have origins in the Middle Ages. These traditions include ceremonies of initiation, standard dress, leisure activities, music, and occupational legends and lore. Some crafts had strong traditions of literacy; a weaver, for example, could set a book on the loom and read while working.[16] The degree of self-consciousness among the weavers is notable. In 1677 a poem in three cantos was published entitled *Minerva, Or the Art of Weaving*, and reissued in 1682 as *The Triumphant Weaver*. This poem asserts the dignity of the weaver's work, and traces the skill back to Minerva in the classical myths and to the aftermath of the Fall in Genesis.[17] Peter Burke, in his influential study *Popular Culture in Early Modern Europe* (1978), judges that the two most active craft cultures were those of the weavers and the shoemakers.[18] This is directly relevant to labouring-class poetry: Robert Dodsley, later a footman, and John Bancks had both been weavers and their first works appeared at almost the same time as Stephen Duck's.

---

[15] Henry Nelson, *A New Poem on the Ancient and Loyal Society of Journey-Men Taylors* (Dublin, 1725); anon., *Vulcan's Speech* (Dublin?, 1725); anon., *The Taylors answer to Vulcan's Speech* (Dublin, 1725).

[16] Peter Burke, *Popular Culture in Early Modern Europe* (London: Temple Smith, 1978), 37.

[17] R. C., *The Triumphant Weaver; Or, The Art of Weaving Discussed and Handled* (London, 1682), 3. For a brief discussion of this poem, see Burke, *Popular Culture*, 37.

[18] Burke, *Popular Culture*, 36–42; see also E. J. Hobsbawm and Joan Wallach Scott, 'Political Shoemakers', *Past & Present*, no. 89 (Nov. 1980), 86–114.

Bancks published these lines in 1730 describing the discomforts of his work at the loom:

> In dire Machine, of quadrant Figure,
> Expos'd to all the pinching Rigour
> Of Hunger, Poverty, and Cold,
> I by my Bum and Belly hold;
> Pendant, betwixt the Earth and Skie,
> Like dying Thief—tho' not so high.[19]

Somewhat later, James Eyre Weeks, James Woodhouse, John Bennett, and Robert Bloomfield all worked as shoemakers. Woodhouse retained a sense of himself as a shoemaker long after he had gone into the book trade: the title of his most important work, 'The Life and Lucubrations of Crispinus Scriblerus' (c.1795), is an allusion to one of the patron saints of cobblers. Though less information is available about craft culture among bricklayers, this occupation produced Robert Tatersal, Henry Jones, and John Frederick Bryant, who is, perhaps, better known as a maker of clay-pipes. Most of these poets whose labour was fairly specialized were conscious of an occupational identity which could be made the subject of verse.

Poets whose work was not specialized, however, also wrote poetry. Duck himself as a thresher in Wiltshire engaged in an ordinary form of agricultural labour. While the figure of the rural swain in pastoral and georgic verse suggests immediately a poetic context for his efforts, the starkness of his account of 'The Thresher's Labour' later drew the praise of George Crabbe in the century's most vigorous counter-pastoral:

> Yes, thus the Muses sing of happy swains,
> Because the Muses never knew their pains:
> They boast their peasants' pipes, but peasants now
> Resign their pipes and plod behind the plough;
> And few amid the rural tribe have time
> To number syllables and play with rhyme;
> Save honest DUCK, what son of verse could share
> The poet's rapture and the peasant's care?[20]

---

[19] John Bancks, 'The Wish', in *The Weaver's Miscellany; Or, Poems on Several Subjects* (London, 1730), 9.
[20] George Crabbe, 'The Village', in *The Complete Poetical Works*, gen. ed. Norma Dalrymple-Champneys, ed. Norma Dalrymple-Champneys and Arthur Pollard, 3 vols. (Oxford: Clarendon Press, 1988), i. 157–8.

Indeed, pastorals and georgics in the generation before Duck's emergence had varied greatly in degrees of artificiality. The indigenous georgics of John Philips and John Gay were followed by the controversy over Pope's and Ambrose Philips's pastorals. While the details of the dispute between Pope and Tickell in *The Guardian* (1713) are well known, the most important contribution actually came from John Gay. *The Shepherd's Week* (1714), though clearly a burlesque, used images of agricultural life that would not be out of place in the work of Duck or of Mary Collier. The following passage is taken from the 'Tuesday' section in which a woman laments her false lover:

> In misling Days when I my Thresher heard,
> With nappy Beer I to the Barn repair'd;
> Lost in the Musick of the whirling Flail,
> To gaze on thee I left the smoking Pail;
> In Harvest when the Sun was mounted high,
> My Leathern Bottle did thy Drought supply;
> When-e'er you mow'd I follow'd with the Rake,
> And have full oft been Sun-burnt for thy Sake;
> . . . .
> Strait on the Fire the sooty Pot I plac't,
> To warm thy Broth I burnt my Hands for Haste.
> When hungry thou stood'st *staring, like an Oaf*,
> I slic'd the Luncheon from the Barly Loaf,
> With crumbled Bread I thicken'd well thy Mess.
> Ah, love me more, or love thy Pottage less![21]

The parodic elements of Gay's pastorals are matched by close descriptions and a genuine sympathy for rural life. The claims made for these poems, however, reveal some of the difficulties in a discussion of labouring-class poetry. Maynard Mack rather grandly pronounces Gay's pastorals 'the only lasting edifice based on country life and peasant folkways between *The Shepheardes Calendar* and *Michael*'.[22] Even if one remains within the traditional canon of the eighteenth century, it is hard to believe that a major critic could so easily dispense with Goldsmith, Crabbe, and Burns.

[21] John Gay, 'The Shepherd's Week', in *John Gay: Poetry and Prose*, ed. Vinton A. Dearing, asst. ed. Charles E. Beckwith, 2 vols. (Oxford: Clarendon Press, 1974), i. 102-3.
[22] Maynard Mack, *Alexander Pope: A Life* (New Haven, Conn. and London: Yale University Press in association with W. W. Norton & Company, 1985), 218.

If the poetry of the early part of the eighteenth century is already grappling with the problems associated with a realistic treatment of agricultural labour, it is not surprising that an agricultural labourer should eventually make an impact as a poet.[23] Raymond Williams has objected to the '"limiting" associations' which have attached to Stephen Duck's name: 'Stephen Duck... had written one fine poem before the court and the church and neo-classicism patronised and emasculated him.'[24] To have produced one important poem is rather more than the vast majority of poets could claim in any age. Yet it would be wrong to forget that Duck's fame and subsequent influence as a poet were very much a result of patronage. Joseph Spence, the Oxford professor of poetry who produced an account of Duck's life and writing in 1731, was far more interested in 'The Shunamite', a biblical piece, than in 'The Thresher's Labour' for which Duck is now remembered. Spence sees in Duck an instance of natural genius, and attempts to capture this quality in its unimproved state: 'You see I am very careful in settling the Chronology of his Poems; such a Genius is a Curiosity; and one wou'd willingly know which are his first Productions.'[25] Duck represented a demonstration of contemporary theories on the formation of intelligence. The issue of natural genius is more fully treated in Chapter 4 below; here, it is necessary to observe that his success was largely a consequence of the attention inevitably accorded to a prodigy of any description. Furthermore, Duck's popularity was not a spontaneous upper-class response to his talent or his circumstances. Rather, the queen's patronage had made interest in Duck a point of fashion. Mary Leapor is particularly perceptive in this regard. She writes, concerning the subscription for her own work: 'But as to what [the gentleman] observes concerning Stephen Duck, I am of Opinion, that it was not his Situation, but the Royal Favour, which gained the Country over to his Side; and therefore I think it needless to paint the Life of a Person, who

---

[23] For connections between the controversy over the pastoral and Stephen Duck's career, see A. J. Sambrook, 'An Essay on Eighteenth-Century Pastoral, Pope to Wordsworth (I)', *Trivium*, 5 (1970), 31–2.
[24] Williams, *The Country and the City*, 88, 134.
[25] Joseph Spence, *A Full and Authentic Account of Stephen Duck, The Wiltshire Poet* (London, 1731), 13; for a more modern examination of Duck's career, see Rose Mary Davis, *Stephen Duck, The Thresher-Poet*, University of Maine Studies, ser. 2/8 (Orono, M.: The University Press, 1926).

depends more upon the Curiosity of the World, than its Good nature' (ML ii. 314). The whole movement of labouring-class poets, including Duck, must therefore be understood against the background of a fashionable philanthropy. In reference to the number of subscriptions in Hanoverian England, Pat Rogers maintains that 'To be able to spend enough money on a leisure activity, and to be seen to do so, was an act of social definition'.[26] When the author being subscribed was poor, then the subscription was also a visible act of charity.

While patronage may have damaged Duck's talent, 'The Thresher's Labour' demonstrated that the experience of labour itself could be the basis of poetry which appealed beyond the very specific concerns of most contemporary occupational verse. As a model for labouring poets, this composition is especially important. James Sambrook observes that 'The Thresher's Labour' is 'one of the earliest eighteenth century poems to belong to no recognized literary "kind"'.[27] That Duck had opened a new avenue of literary expression is evident from the number of poems published in the 1730s, often addressed to him, in which poets assert the literary possibilities of their own labour. Robert Tatersal writes 'To Stephen Duck, The famous Threshing Poet':

> What, tho' the *Trowel* circumscribes my Muse,
> And *Bricks* and *Mortar* were my Fate to chuse;
> Beneath those servile Badges I display
> Some secret Sparks above a common Ray.[28]

Doubtless many poets envied Duck, for whom the queen had 'Enlarg'd thy Bottle, and enrich'd thy Beer'.[29] Yet, on one level, these poems mark a recognition that Stephen Duck had changed the relation of the labouring class to the literary market. Whereas prior to his success literate elements in the labouring class had been mainly consumers of literature, now they could take on somewhat more confidently the role of producers in that broader market. The growth of the book trade in the eighteenth century

---

[26] Pat Rogers, *Literature and Popular Culture in Eighteenth Century England* (Brighton: Harvester, 1985), 7.
[27] Sambrook, 'An Essay on Eighteenth-Century Pastoral, Pope to Wordsworth (I)', 32.
[28] Robert Tatersal, 'To Stephen Duck, The famous Thresher Poet', in *The Bricklayer's Miscellany: Or, Poems on Several Subjects* (2nd edn., London, 1734), 23.   [29] Ibid. 25.

was necessary for that change. Stephen Duck's poetry, for example, appeared in twelve editions before he published an authorized edition.[30] Booksellers could translate the royal favour into profit for themselves. In that sense they amplified the vogue enjoyed by Duck's verse, and exploited it further by publishing other labouring poets. In short, following Stephen Duck's appearance, the poetry of working people became saleable in a new way. During the century there were other highly successful publications, especially those of Falconer, Burns, and Bloomfield, but most, like that of Leapor, were on a smaller scale.

More important, however, than changing the relation between the labouring class and literature as a commodity, the success of Stephen Duck altered by degree the conditions of public discourse. Terry Eagleton, oddly, dismisses evidence from Daniel Defoe that in the coffee houses of London it was not uncommon for mechanicks to hold forth on issues of the day. With reference to the early part of the century, Eagleton writes: 'It does not seem that the emulsive space of the public sphere extended beyond parsons and surgeons to farm labourers or domestic servants....'.[31] This statement is certainly invalid for the years after 1730 when labouring poets became more prominent. Even before that date Eagleton's view is suspect, given the amount of occupational verse in circulation, although such material could be dismissed as ephemeral. It should, however, be observed that labouring people also produced numerous prose works during this time. Among these, a pertinent example is Claudius Rey, a weaver, who in 1719 contributed, with Defoe, to a debate relating to the importation of calico. Since by 1721 Parliament had accepted the argument of Defoe, Rey, and the weavers, and banned calico, this must surely count as significant participation in public discourse.[32] Hence, it is

[30] D. F. Foxon, *English Verse 1701–1750*, 2 vols. (Cambridge: Cambridge University Press, 1975), i. 200–1; see also Peter J. McGonigle, 'Stephen Duck and the Text of *The Thresher's Labour*', *The Library*, ser. 6/4 (1982), 288–96.

[31] Terry Eagleton, *The Function of Criticism: From* The Spectator *to Post-Structuralism* (London: Verso Editions and NLB, 1984), 14.

[32] See Claudius Rey, *The Weavers True Case* (London, 1719; 2nd edn., 1719); Daniel Defoe, *A Brief State of the Question, Between the Printed and Painted Callicoes and the Woollen and Silk Manufacture* (London, 1719); Claudius Rey, *Observations on Mr. Asgill's Brief Answer To A Brief State of the Question Between the Printed and Painted Callicoes* (London, 1719); id., *A Further Examination of the Weavers Pretences* (London, 1719). For information on this episode, see Paula R. Backscheider, *Daniel Defoe: His Life* (Baltimore and London: The Johns Hopkins University Press, 1989), 461–2.

necessary to achieve a balanced view of Duck and the poets who followed him. Prior to 1730 there had indeed been a discernible participation by labouring people in public discourse, and, more specifically, a participation in literature. Yet a significant event occurs in 1730 when a poet of the labouring class moves towards the centre of contemporary culture, eventually to be seen as a candidate for the laureateship.[33] After this it is possible for labouring poets to entertain far greater hopes of public impact.

Despite the success of Stephen Duck, the status of labouring poets was never equal to that of writers from polite society. Labouring poets carried a stigma comparable to that of women writers. Therefore, women poets from the labouring class, such as Jane Holt Wiseman, Constantia Grierson, Mary Collier, Mary Masters, Mary Leapor, Ann Yearsley, Elizabeth Bentley, Elizabeth Hands, Susannah Harrison, and Ann Candler, were doubly disabled. These poets have not been well served even by some modern critics. Unwin knows of only Collier and Yearsley; of Yearsley he makes the comment: '[We] can only judge her achievements sympathetically in the manner that Johnson judged a woman preaching.'[34] Robert Halsband writes: 'Mrs. Yearsley was not the first of those whom Robert Southey called "Our Uneducated Poets" but she was the first notable woman among them.'[35] While Yearsley is not to be disregarded, Collier, Leapor, and Hands produced better poetry, though they attracted less attention.

Negative comments on poetry written by labouring people often entailed some depreciation of labour itself. Examples from the time of Duck's appearance through the rest of the century are numerous. Jonathan Swift, for example, produced the following epigram on Stephen Duck's advancement:

> The Thresher *Duck*, could o'er the *Q——* prevail.
> The Proverb says; *No Fence against a Flayl.*

[33] See Jonathan Swift, 'Swift to John Gay and the Dutchess of Queensberry', in *The Correspondence of Jonathan Swift*, ed. Harold Williams, 5 vols. (Oxford: Oxford University Press, 1963–5), iii (1963), 421.
[34] Unwin, *The Rural Muse*, 80.
[35] Robert Halsband, 'Woman and Literature in 18th Century England', in Paul Fritz and Richard Morton (ed.), *Woman in the 18th Century and Other Essays*, Publications of the McMaster University Association for 18th-Century Studies, 4 (Toronto and Sarasota, Fla.: Samuel Stevens Hakkert, 1976), 59.

From *threshing* Corn, he turns to *thresh* his Brains;
For which Her M——y allows him *Grains*.
Though 'tis confess't that those who ever saw
His Poems, think them all not worth a *Straw*.
Thrice happy Duck, employ'd in threshing *Stubble*!
Thy Toil is lessen'd, and thy Profits double.   (Swift, ii. 521)

The mercurial Dean must have later softened his contempt, since both he and Pope subscribed to the 1736 edition of Duck's poems. In the same manner Samuel Johnson in 1763 combined a judgement against the poems of James Woodhouse with condescension towards his trade:

He spoke with much contempt of the notice taken of Woodhouse, the poetical shoemaker. He said, it was all vanity and childishness: and that such objects were, to those who patronised them, mere mirrours of their own superiority. 'They had better (said he,) furnish the man with good implements for his trade, than raise subscriptions for his poems. He may make an excellent shoemaker, but can never make a good poet. A school-boy's exercise may be a pretty thing for a school-boy; but is no treat for a man.'[36]

Johnson finds fault justifiably with Woodhouse's early verse. Woodhouse did in fact become a good poet, though there is no reason why Johnson should have foreseen this. The important aspect of Johnson's statement is that he dismisses the whole phenomenon of labouring poets as misapplied patronage. Poets like Woodhouse had best go back to their jobs. Prejudices among critics in the latter part of the century towards the labouring class manifest themselves once more in an amusing 'Proclamation' appearing in the *Monthly Review* in 1778:

Whereas it hath been represented to us, upon the oaths of several of our trusty and well-beloved booksellers, that certain journeyman taylors, shoemakers, barbers, Spitaldfields-weavers, and other handicraftsmen, and that certain apprentices, shopmen, &c. have assembled in certain clubs, called Spouting-clubs, and, having there intoxicated themselves with porter and poetry, have presumed to make rhymes, and discharge them on the Public, under the title of 'Squires and Honourables, &c. &c. to the great annoyance of said Public, and of us, the said Reviewers; WE do hereby ordain and decree that . . . [everyone] so offending in future, shall, for every such first offence, be chained to the compter, for a

[36] Boswell, *Boswell's Life of Johnson*, ii. 127; cited by Unwin, *The Rural Muse*, 71.

space, not exceeding twelve, nor less than six days; and . . . for every such second offence, be not only chained to the compter for the said space of time (more or less) but be obliged to wear bob-wigs, and flapped hats without girdle or buckle, for the space of six months.[37]

The humour of the passage argues against solemn commentary, yet the depiction of craftsmen poets as agents of mischief impersonating their superiors in society is curious indeed. Behind this passage may lie the assumption that labouring-class poets were fundamentally impostors.

The resistance to labouring-class poets is balanced in some respects by the support they received. Robert Dodsley was encouraged by Daniel Defoe and by Pope, whose gift of £100 helped him to enter the book-trade. Samuel Richardson eventually became Duck's authorized publisher, not to mention Leapor's. Jonathan Swift, despite his attitude towards Stephen Duck, had already taken an interest in Constantia Grierson, who had trained as a midwife. Chesterfield was patron to Henry Jones. William Shenstone befriended James Woodhouse. The list might be continued. The essential observation is that patronage is not simply 'emasculating', to use Raymond Williams's term. In some cases, it did produce dependence and servility. Duck, for example, by the end of his career had come to specialize in poems praising his patrons. Of the poems in the volume Henry Jones published in 1749, nearly half have in their titles the name of some eminent person, while the volume as a whole is dedicated to Chesterfield and five individual pieces to him or his wife.[38] Whatever talent Jones had was largely spent in sycophancy. Other poets, however, had the strength of mind to escape dependence. In some cases such an escape was executed only with pain, as in the case of Ann Yearsley who broke publicly with Hannah More over the right to administer a trust fund for her children.[39] The relationship of patronage was therefore complex: on the one hand, it reflected economic injustices in society as a whole, while, on the other, it was an essential means of access to the reading public for labouring poets.

Although the presence and stature of labouring poets within

---

[37] *MR* 58 (1778), 162; cited by Unwin, *The Rural Muse*, 69.
[38] Jones, *Poems on Several Occasions*.
[39] See Moira Ferguson, 'Resistance and Power in the Life and Writing of Ann Yearsley', *The Eighteenth Century: Theory and Interpretation*, 27 (1986), 247–68.

public discourse are themselves questions of considerable interest, this group of poets may be judged by their actual contribution to that discourse. Labouring poets who attempted a realistic description of work and social conditions helped to create a new literary response to social reality, a development most commonly associated with Goldsmith, Langhorne, Blake, Crabbe, and eventually Wordsworth.

The rest of this chapter will discuss Mary Leapor's poetry against the background of her economic position, and examine her experiences as a working woman. Three economic structures seem to have influenced her life and writing. Therefore, the first section will examine her responses to domestic service, the second her responses to agriculture and the use of land, and the third her attitudes towards literary patronage.

Domestic Service

Mary Leapor's treatment of her time at Edgcote House is the area of her poetry most obviously shaped by economic relations. Leapor's poetry on domestic service is part of a wide range of eighteenth-century writings concerned with this type of work. Jonathan Swift in his *Directions to Servants* takes a sceptical view of servants' moral propensities. He writes to the footman:

> The last Advice I shall give you, relates to your Behaviour when you are going to be hanged; which, either for robbing your Master, for Housebreaking, or going upon the High-way, or in a drunken Quarrel, by killing the first Man you meet, may very probably be your Lot.... Take Leave chearfully of all your Friends in *Newgate*: Mount the Cart with Courage: Fall on your Knees: Lift up your Eyes: Hold a Book in your Hands although you cannot read a Word: Deny the Fact at the Gallows: Kiss and forgive the Hangman, and so Farewel: You shall be buried in Pomp, at the Charge of the Fraternity: The Surgeon shall not touch a Limb of you; and your Fame shall continue until a Successor of equal Renown succeeds in your Place.[40]

He is, if anything, less kind to the Nurse: 'If you happen to let the Child fall, and lame it, be sure never confess it; and, if it dies, all is safe.'[41]

---
[40] Jonathan Swift, *Directions to Servants and Miscellaneous Pieces 1733–1742*, ed. Herbert Davis (Oxford: Basil Blackwell, 1964), 44–5.
[41] Ibid. 64.

Other well-known writers emphasize not the failures of servants but the tyranny of masters. Samuel Richardson's *Pamela* is predicated on the need for a servant to resist the master's will in some things. *Pamela* recounts an exchange with Mrs Jewkes, the housekeeper, whose task is to keep her captive: 'I offered to talk of a duty superior to that she mentioned, which would oblige her to help distressed innocence, and not permit her to go to the lengths enjoined by lawless tyranny; but she plainly bid me be silent on that head; for it was vain to attempt to persuade her to betray her trust.'[42] The need to define the boundaries of obedience is at the heart of Richardson's novel. Fielding's *Joseph Andrews* is another work which focuses on the hardships of the servant's life, albeit with less moral ardour than Richardson's novel. Swift, Richardson, Fielding, and others fasten upon the conflicts between domestic servants and their masters. J. J. Hecht in his study of domestic servants in the eighteenth century argues that these conflicts were common as masters pressed their authority, requiring the obedience and loyalty to which they were theoretically entitled, while servants attempted to retain independence and reduce their obligations. He argues that servants were inclined to be discontented as they observed others climb in society. That there was an increased demand for servants during the century entailed a greater independence for those dissatisfied with particular masters, hence a greater potential for conflict.[43] The magnitude of this social problem is evident in Robert Malcolmson's observation that servants, both domestic and in husbandry, constituted 13–14 per cent of the population at any time in this period.[44] Since most people left service at marriage, these conflicts affected a very large proportion of labouring-class people at some point in their lives.

In order to understand Leapor's struggle with her employers, it is necessary to consider how specific tasks made an impression on her poetry. According to the Purefoys' description of a kitchen-maid's work, Leapor was probably expected to combine basic

---

[42] Samuel Richardson, *Pamela: Or, Virtue Rewarded*, ed. Peter Sabor, introd. Margaret Anne Doody (Harmondsworth: Penguin, 1980), 205.
[43] J. Jean Hecht, *The Domestic Servant Class in Eighteenth-Century England* (London: Routledge & Kegan Paul, 1956), 77–8; for a discussion of domestic service as it related specifically to women, see Hill, 125–47.
[44] R. W. Malcolmson, *Life and Labour in England 1700–1780*, Hutchison Social History of England (London: Hutchison, 1981), 65.

cooking with extensive cleaning both in the kitchen and in other parts of the house. She may have had some outdoor work as well, such as feeding poultry. Leapor usually describes cooking in detail. In 'Crumble Hall' Urs'la addresses Roger, who is sprawled unconscious across the servants' table, in a speech reminiscent of Gay's 'Tuesday' eclogue:

> 'For you my Pigs resign their Morning Due:
> My hungry Chickens lose their Meat for you:
> And, was it not, Ah! was it not for thee,
> No goodly Pottage would be dress'd by me.
> For thee these Hands wind up the whirling Jack,
> Or place the Spit across the sloping Rack.
> I baste the Mutton with a chearful Heart,
> Because I know my *Roger* will have Part.' (ML ii. 119–20)

Leapor's descriptions of cooking often indicate hidden struggles and dissatisfactions. In 'Crumble Hall' she writes of Sophronia's rather specialized cookery. Presumably the poet was required to assist the woman and observe her methods:

> *Sophronia* sage! whose learned Knuckles know
> To form round Cheese-cakes of the pliant Dough;
> To bruise the Curd, and thro' her Fingers squeeze
> *Ambrosial* Butter with the temper'd Cheese:
> Sweet Tarts and Pudden, too, her Skill declare;
> And the soft Jellies, hid from baneful Air. (ML ii. 118)

Leapor recognizes the skill, but these lines follow hard on a suggestion that Sophronia is pretentious despite being one of the 'menial Train'. Hence, the notion of 'learned Knuckles' is an oblique satire on the woman's standards of value. Leapor's intellectual attainments are of no importance, and her poetic skills only obstruct her proper work in the kitchen. This interpretation is confirmed by another poem that compares the value of writing and cooking. 'The Epistle of Deborah Dough' describes 'Neighbour Mary':

> She throws away her precious Time
> In scrawling nothing else but Rhyme;
> Of which, they say, she's mighty proud,
> And lifts her Nose above the Croud;
> Tho' my young Daughter *Cicely*
> Is taller by a Foot than she,

> And better learnt (as People say):
> Can knit a Stocken in a Day:
> Can make a Pudden, plump and rare;
> And boil her Bacon, to an Hair:
> Will coddle Apples nice and green,
> And fry her Pancakes—like a Queen.   (ML ii. 69)

This passage does not relate directly to Leapor's employment, but it indicates what skills were desired in a young woman of the labouring class. Leapor's satire is directed against a standard of value, indeed, a division of labour, based on class and gender.

It is striking that while Leapor writes amusingly, sometimes angrily, of intellectual constraints, she rarely complains of the physical rigours of domestic service. These rigours can be associated with cleaning rather than cooking. Scrubbing pewter, for example, is described almost objectively:

> But now her Dish-kettle began
> To boil and blubber with the foaming Bran.
> The greasy Apron round her Hips she ties,
> And to each Plate the scalding Clout applies:
> The purging Bath each glowing Dish refines,
> And once again the polish'd Pewter shines.   (ML ii. 120)

According to an inventory from 1773, Weston Hall maintained a large stock of pewter (Sitwell, 38). Doubtless Edgcote House had even more. Leapor here treats the task of cleaning it as normal and manageable. Samuel Richardson, however, thought this work unusually painful. Pamela writes to her parents:

I have read of a good bishop that was to be burnt for his religion; and he tried how he could bear it, by putting his fingers into the lighted candle: so I t'other day tried, when Rachel's back was turned, if I could not scour a pewter plate she had begun. I see I could do it by degrees; it only blistered my hand in two places.[45]

Despite her questionable health, Leapor seems not to have been troubled by the physical demands of her work. This, incidentally, is not startling. The lot of domestic servants in the eighteenth century was in general less difficult than that of farm-workers. Leapor's descriptions of agricultural labour are, in fact, characterized by an awareness of the discomforts of work outdoors.

---

[45] Richardson, *Pamela*, 109.

Thus, with the recognition that her resentment was not a direct consequence of the amount or difficulty of her work, it becomes somewhat easier to isolate the conflict underlying her dismissal. Leapor's poetry records a few occasions of anger during her employment at Edgcote House. The first relates to the 'gay Vestment' ('The Disappointment', ML ii. 79) which Sophronia suggested might be given to her. The failure of this prospect causes Leapor to suspect Sophronia for her 'little Arts' (ML ii. 80). This episode has an interesting social background, since the right to 'cast clothes' or an employer's old garments was an important element in the system of rewards for servants. Low wages were supplemented by gifts of clothing, gratuities or 'vails' from guests, and surreptitious payments from tradesmen. Hecht believes that this system was a source of conflict in domestic service.[46] How much one incident, however, affected the course of Leapor's employment should not be overestimated, especially if she concealed her immediate annoyance. There is a second element in 'The Disappointment', Vido's treatment of Leapor's verses:

> when he chuses for his skilful Tongue
> A Theme so low as *Mira*'s simple Song,
> 'Tis not his Comment on the artless Lines,
> But his own Genius in the Lecture shines:
> And when he bows, 'tis that the World may see
> His own good Manners, not Respect to me.   (ML ii. 80–1)

Sophronia's behaviour, then, is linked to a belittling of Leapor's poetry. In 'The Consolation' there is no mention of the dress. The one irritation is that 'Folks will censure *Mira*'s Song' (ML ii. 82). Thus the greater problem seems to be that she is not taken seriously as a poet. If Susanna Jennens had encouraged her to read and write at Weston Hall, Leapor could not really expect the same sort of understanding and support from another employer.

Leapor's comments on the personal failings of her superiors in the Chauncy household often reflect her struggle for recognition as a poet. Sophronia's learning, for example, is in her knuckles. Vido's manipulative charm is exercised at the expense of Mira's verses. Leapor also satirizes the intellectual pretensions of a figure in Crumble Hall who can tentatively be identified as the young William Henry Chauncy who had recently gone up to Oxford:

[46] Hecht, *The Domestic Servant Class*, 77–8, 115–16.

> Here *Biron* sleeps, with Books encircled round;
> And him you'd guess a Student most Profound.
> Not so—in Form the dusty Volumes stand:
> There's few that wear the Mark of *Biron*'s Hand.   (ML ii. 116)

Biron's claim to learning resides in the possession of books that he does not read. His pretensions, it seems, are based on economic advantage.

That Leapor describes her dismissal from Edgcote House in 'An Epistle to Artemisia. On Fame' is significant. The event is seen as integral to the poet's struggle for recognition. While she doubtless simplified issues in the poem, the following passage is consistent with the pattern observed so far in her treatment of domestic service:

> Then comes *Sophronia*, like a barb'rous *Turk*:
> 'You thoughtless Baggage, when d'ye mind your Work?
> Still o'er a Table leans your bending Neck:
> Your Head will grow prepost'rous, like a Peck.
> Go, ply your Needle: you might earn your Bread;
> Or who must feed you when your Father's dead?'
> She sobbing answers, 'Sure, I need not come
> To you for Lectures; I have store at Home.
> What can I do?'
>   '—Not scribble.'
>   '—But I will.'
> 'Then get thee packing—and be aukward still.'   (ML ii. 52)

Leapor is faced with a choice between her job and her poetry. The normal eighteenth-century division of labour is on trial in this passage and, to a lesser extent, in the others quoted above. It is evident that in this instance Leapor has not allowed the meat to scorch; rather, it seems a question of how she uses her leisure, in writing or sewing. To improve her skills with the needle is judged more suitable to her economic standing: 'who must feed you when your Father's dead?' Since a servant's whole time belonged to the master or mistress, the housekeeper had a legal right to make this sort of demand, though various writers had asserted the need for servants to be allowed time to read and develop intellectually. Richard Mayo, in a book of mainly spiritual advice to servants first published in 1693, advises those who could read to teach the skill to others. To masters, he writes: 'If any of you are not able to instruct them, be deeply humbled presently, and get others to instruct them.'[47] Mayo's concern is primarily with religious instruction, but he is by no means unique in suggesting that learning was good for a servant. Samuel Johnson in *The Idler* treats the attitude of some employers that servants should not be educated. He describes the experiences of Betty Broom, one of which resembles Leapor's dismissal:

Here I was, for some time, the favourite of Mrs. Simper, my lady's woman, who could not bear the vulgar girls, and was happy in the attendance of a young woman of some education. Mrs. Simper loved a novel, tho' she could not read hard words, and therefore when her lady was abroad, we always laid hold on her books. At last, my abilities became so much celebrated, that the house-steward used to employ me in keeping his accounts. Mrs. Simper then found out that my sauciness was grown to such a height that no body could endure it, and told my lady, that there never had been a room well swept, since Betty Broom came into the house. (Johnson, ii. 91)

While it might be interesting to compare Mrs Simper's and Sophronia's reactions to lower servants better educated than themselves, the essential point is that a violation of the ordinary division of labour could easily result in a domestic servant losing his or her place.

Ann Kussmaul, a historian, observes that evidence pertaining to discipline and resentment between masters and servants in husbandry comes almost entirely from masters.[48] Kussmaul's observation is also valid for other types of work. By describing her dismissal Leapor provides a rare glimpse of eighteenth-century employment. Some labouring poets adopted a pious attitude on such issues. Robert Dodsley, for example, in his poem *Servitude* (1729), describes the various qualities required in a good servant, with emphasis on obedience: 'Submission next must an Admittance find, | The humble Liv'ry of a Servant's Mind....'.[49] Stephen Duck and Mary Collier, however, both describe reproaches from a master or mistress. Duck writes in 'The Thresher's Labour' of the 'Master's Curse':

---

[47] Richard Mayo, *A Present For Servants From their Ministers, Masters, or Other Friends, Especially in Country Parishes* (London, 1693), 46, vi.
[48] Ann Kussmaul, *Servants in Husbandry in Early Modern England* (Cambridge: Cambridge University Press, 1981), 44.
[49] Robert Dodsley, *Servitude: A Poem*, introd. and postscript Daniel Defoe (London, 1729), 20.

> He counts the Bushels, counts how much a Day;
> Then swears we've idled half our Time away:
> 'Why, look ye, Rogues, d'ye think that this will do?
> Your Neighbours thresh as much again as you.'
> Now in our Hands we wish our noisy Tools,
> To drown the hated Names of Rogues and Fools.
> But wanting these, we just like School-boys look,
> When angry Masters view the blotted Book:
> They cry, 'their Ink was faulty, and their Pen;'
> We, 'the Corn threshes bad, 'twas cut too green.'[50]

In 'The Woman's Labour', Mary Collier writes of the mistress coming to inspect the laundry:

> Then comes our Mistress to us without fail,
> And in her Hand, *perhaps*, a Mug of Ale
> To cheer our Hearts, and also to inform
> Herself, what Work is done that very Morn;
> Lays her Commands upon us, that we mind
> Her Linen well, nor *leave the Dirt behind*:
> Not this alone, but also to take care
> We don't her Cambricks nor her Ruffles tear;
> And *these* most strictly does of us require,
> *To save her Soap, and sparing be of Fire*;
> Tells us her Charge is great, nay furthermore,
> Her Cloaths are fewer than the Time before.
> Now we drive on, resolv'd our Strength to try,
> And what we can, we do most willingly;
> Until with Heat and Work, 'tis often known,
> Not only Sweat, but Blood runs trickling down
> Our Wrists and Fingers; still our Work demands
> The constant Action of our labouring Hands.[51]

In both cases there is evidence of resentment. Both poets adopt a stance of resignation in struggles with their employers. Neither

---

[50] Stephen Duck, 'The Thresher's Labour', in *Poems on Several Occasions* (London, 1736; facsimile, The Augustan Reprint Society Publication 230, Los Angeles: William Andrews Clark Memorial Library, 1985), 14.

[51] Mary Collier, *The Woman's Labour: An Epistle to Mr. Stephen Duck* (London, 1739; facsimile, The Augustan Reprint Society Publication 230, Los Angeles: William Andrews Clark Memorial Library, 1985), 13–14. See also Donna Landry, 'The Resignation of Mary Collier: Some Problems in Feminist Literary History', in Felicity Nussbaum and Laura Brown (ed.), *The New Eighteenth Century: Theory, Politics, English Literature* (New York & London: Methuen, 1987), 99–120.

does more than suggest that the employer's demands are unfair. Before comparing these poets to Leapor, it must be observed in fairness that Duck's and Collier's options in these situations were most likely obedience to an employer or destitution. Leapor, on the other hand, could leave her job and go back to her father. Furthermore, Leapor herself does not object to the amount of work required of her, the point of conflict in Duck's and Collier's verses. Yet all three poets are writing retrospectively of conflicts with superiors, and only Leapor chooses to represent her treatment as an injustice to which the correct response was not submission but resistance. Leapor's verses on her dismissal take on the force of explicit protest, whereas those of Duck and Collier, though moving and admirable, go little past complaint.

Of course, any claim made for Leapor in this respect must be qualified. There is much in her treatment of labour that tends towards resignation rather than protest, especially in relation to agriculture and husbandry, as discussed below. There are also places in her work where domestic service is described in very conventional terms. In *The Unhappy Father* the servant Plynus is corrupted because of ambition:

> Sir, without Vanity, I cannot think
> That Nature form'd me for his Lordship's Slave.
> I have a Spirit daring and ambitious:
> 'Tis fashion'd too with ev'ry little Art:
> Might serve its End in some genteel Employment.
> First for the Law a Conscience ready sear'd;
> A Soldier's Impudence; a Draper's Lye;
> Dissimulation for the Court;—and then
> Perhaps my Brains would hardly style me Poet;
> Yet by my Poverty I think I'm one.   (ML ii. 168)

The passage as a whole seems an inversion of Hamlet's Renaissance perfections. The last two lines, however, raise questions. That this character should be a servant and a poet, either by poverty or intellect, suggests a connection with Mary Leapor's own circumstances. It is possible that Plynus embodies some of Leapor's misgivings about rising from her station. Leonardo's response describes a society neither classical nor medieval but contemporary:

> Why, thou'rt the very Essence of my Wants;
> A useful Complication of Abilities.
> Here, take this purse, and with it ev'ry Wish;
> For there lies Honour, Pleasure, and Esteem,
> Nay, Friendship too; for in our Trading Age;
> That, like the rest, is hourly bought and sold.   (ML ii. 168)

Plynus's desire for advancement is seen against economic trends which entice people from their duties. There is no place for this servant's abilities within a traditional economic order. Money, however, begets social mobility. Leapor places all of these concerns in the worst possible light. Since the play was probably written before her dismissal, it is possible that she is describing a struggle against the logic of her own ambitions. In the end Plynus's aspirations come to nothing. Dr Swift would have approved of his imminent hanging, yet this minor twist in the plot suggests the moral and ideological constraints under which a servant lived. Plynus, in fact, has done nothing more than deliver a forged letter: he does not take any part in the actual slaughter. His crime is against the bond of servant and master. Dorothy Marshall describes a case in the eighteenth century which resulted in a servant being hanged: she held a candle while her lover slit the butler's throat. The lover testified against her and went free. Her crime, however, was aggravated by a breach of the employer's trust and was therefore judged the more heinous.[52] In *The Unhappy Father* Leapor opts for a highly conventional view of the domestic servant, providing a straightforward contrast between the villainy of Plynus and the loyalty of Timnus, who dives after Polonius 'to partake his Fate' (ML ii. 208), that is, to be eaten by a shark. The alternatives are extreme, perhaps absurd, and may represent Leapor's deeper struggles and resentments concerning her own employment and the frustration of her talents.

There is a further caution to be entered with respect to Leapor's treatment of domestic service. Any consideration of domestic service in the eighteenth century must avoid the danger of regarding servants as one class opposed to masters as a separate and higher class. Although he defines his terms carefully, Hecht is still somewhat confusing when he writes: 'The servant

---

[52] Dorothy Marshall, *The English Domestic Servant in History*, Historical Association Publications, gen. ser. 13 (London: George Philip & Son, 1949), 16.

class, then, was composed of recruits from social levels as diverse as the gentry and the rural proletariat....'.[53] It seems from this statement that there was not one class of domestic servants but within this type of employment people belonging to different classes. The social distinction, for example, between a land steward, who was sometimes an attorney, and a scullery maid was very great, though both might be servants in the same house. Thus a lady's companion, though a domestic servant, was often of comparable birth to her mistress and would have received appropriate treatment. On the other hand, all but the very poorest families might hire servants.[54] Thus domestic service must be seen as a type of economic relationship operating in all levels of society. Mary Leapor's struggle against a division of labour in which her poetic talents could not be developed should not be read as a repudiation of domestic service as an institution. There are two very brief references in her poetry to servants who though employed by her father were also under her control. In an invitation 'To Artemisia' she writes: 'Our *Tommy* in a Jug shall bring | Clear *Nectar* from the bubbling Spring...' (ML i. 107). 'The Sacrifice', another invitation, makes a similar comment: '... some inferior Maid shall bring | Clear Water from the bubbling Spring' (ML i. 227). Leapor, then, experienced domestic service not only as a servant but as a mistress. This observation is necessary not because the lines quoted are of great importance to her poetry, but to give a balanced view of her own conflicts as a domestic servant.

Land and Agriculture

Leapor devotes a greater part of her poetry to the description of agriculture and to questions related to the use of land than she does to domestic service. Her concerns in this area are, accordingly, more varied. The struggle against a division of intellectual and manual labour is evident, though it is less intense than in the poetry already considered. A second area of interest is the relation between labour and landscape. Here we observe tensions

---

[53] Hecht, *The Domestic Servant Class*, 19.
[54] Stone, *The Family, Sex and Marriage*, 27.

between attitudes towards land based on traditional rights and contemporary efforts at improvement.

The general exclusion of agricultural labourers from education often appears as an issue in the literature of the eighteenth century, especially after the success of Stephen Duck. Gray's 'Elegy', of course, can be read as a lament for the undeveloped mind: 'But knowledge to their eyes her ample page | Rich with the spoils of time did ne'er unroll....'.[55] This was a question particularly relevant to eighteenth-century literature and society, and it was not hard to discover contemporary instances of talent struggling against a lack of education.

Mary Leapor's treatment of the division of intellectual and manual labour in the context of agriculture is seen in 'To Lucinda'. This poem, dated August 1746, seems related to the preparations to publish her first volume. Leapor has received Lucinda's comments on her poetry:

> Like a poor Bird, who swells its little Throat,
> And warbles forth its native untaught Note:
> If chance some skilful Master tune the Reed,
> To his rough Lay melodious Sounds succeed:
> He learns th' harmonious Lesson to repeat,
> Wond'ring to hear his Music grown so sweet.   (ML ii. 58–9)

The tone of deference suggests that this person was a new acquaintance, and that Leapor respected her literary judgement. The poem is essentially a comparison between the poet's condition and that of Lucinda, the 'Fav'rite of indulgent Heav'n' (ML ii. 58). The main comparison comes in the middle of the poem:

> Fain would I to *Lucinda*'s Ear impart
> How Reason dawn'd upon my Infant Heart,
> Whilst in laborious Toils I spent my Hours,
> Employ'd to cultivate the springing Flow'rs.
> Happy, I cry'd, are those who Leisure find,
> With Care, like this, to cultivate their Mind ...   (ML ii. 59)

Leapor's intellectual ambitions are constrained by the demands of her father's garden. She goes on to complain of her exclusion from theological learning:

---

[55] Thomas Gray, 'Elegy Written in a Country Church Yard', in *The Complete Poems of Thomas Gray, English, Latin and Greek*, ed. H. W. Starr and J. R. Hendrickson (Oxford: Clarendon Press, 1966), 39.

> Th' Almighty's sacred Will's to you reveal'd;
> But from the Ignorant in Clouds conceal'd.
> The Chains of Want forbid my Heart to rise,
> When she would soar to reach her Kindred Skies. (ML ii. 60)

Leapor has specified theological learning in order to leave an escape from the logic of her complaint. A blunt statement of envy would certainly give offence: therefore, she reassumes her humility, affirms the need for different stations in life, and denies her own claim for the importance of learning:

> One little Book the mighty Sum contains:
> To all alike their Father's Will explains:
> To all who with sincere and humble Hearts
> Resolve to seek him, God his Laws imparts. (ML ii. 61)

In August 1746 Leapor looked forward to a career as a writer and perhaps felt she now had less cause to protest. There is quiet anger in this poem against a life in which her talents are wasted; yet the manner in which she disowns her own struggle at this stage in her life is surprising. That she writes boldly to Artemisia concerning her frustration, and more timorously to Lucinda, suggests partly a lingering ambivalence over the choices she has made, and, more proximately, a nervousness as she approaches the literary world. Ultimately, this poem may demonstrate not so much the frailty of Leapor's beliefs as the importance of Bridget Freemantle as her implied reader. With Freemantle Leapor could easily speak her mind; to have the same confidence with new readers would take time.

Leapor's treatment of the division of labour in this poem confirms that this was a fundamental struggle in her life and poetry, not simply a localized disagreement with Sophronia. This continuity of concern between her poems on domestic service and agricultural labour is certainly significant; however, her representation of landscape is probably the more important issue in her treatment of agriculture. It is possible that this statement commits us to a misnomer at the outset. Raymond Williams writes, 'A working country is hardly ever a landscape.'[56] The word implies an aesthetic rather than a practical relation to an environment. John Berger argues the connection between economic power and artistic perspective:

---

[56] Williams, *The Country and the City*, 120.

European means of representation refer to the experience of taking possession. Just as its perspective gathers all that is extended to render it to the individual eye, so its means of representation render all that is depicted into the hands of the individual owner-spectator. Painting becomes the metaphorical act of appropriation.[57]

Berger's term 'owner-spectator' reduces a complex formal and epistemological development to economic determinants. He is probably correct, however, in identifying the experience of taking possession as a factor in that development. John Barrell pursues a similar insight more cautiously in relation to landscape painting and poetry in the eighteenth and early nineteenth centuries. He believes that a high viewpoint 'creates a space between the landscape and the observer, similar in its effect to the space between a picture and whoever is looking at it'.[58] High perspective achieves an almost generalized view of land which can reflect an economic bias. Scant attention is paid to the 'content' of landscapes, as artists give 'little evidence of caring that the topography ... was a representation of the needs of the people who had created it'.[59] The willingness of painters and poets to improve a prospect through various techniques is related to the ideology of improvement underlying the enclosure movement. The space Barrell describes between the observer and the landscape can be sharply contrasted with the direct contact with particular topography which defines agricultural life. Thus poetry written from the perspective of the agricultural worker has a potential to reveal economic relations within particular descriptions.

Potential, of course, is not achievement. Labouring poets in the eighteenth century are able to escape literary convention only on occasion, though these occasions are of considerable interest. The temptation for rural labourer poets is not so much to write prospect poems as to treat their own labour in terms of the pastoral.

[57] John Berger, 'Past Seen from a Possible Future', in Nikos Stangos (ed), *Selected Essays and Articles: The Look of Things* (Harmondsworth: Penguin, 1972), 215; cited by Carole Fabricant, 'Binding and Dressing Nature's Loose Tresses: The Ideology of Augustan Landscape Design', in *Studies in Eighteenth-Century Culture*, 8, Proceedings of the American Society for Eighteenth Century Studies (Madison and London: University of Wisconsin Press, 1979), 114–15.

[58] John Barrell, *The Idea of Landscape and the Sense of Place 1730–1840: An Approach to the Poetry of John Clare* (Cambridge: Cambridge University Press, 1972), 21.   [59] Ibid. 59.

An idealized landscape is even more remote from reality than is a generalized landscape.

Mary Leapor is adept within the pastoral form. In places, of course, her pastorals are rather bland. This is true of 'Florimelia, the First Pastoral' rewritten from John Newton's manuscript. That she is probably dealing with a barren original only emphasizes the problems of conventionality. The following description of a shepherdess's work certainly obscures the hardships of this kind of labour:

> Her Task it was, those tender Lambs to lead,
> O'er the tall Mountain on the fertile Mead:
> Where the clear Fountains gently murmur by,
> And sounding Grottos to her Flute reply:
> Her Flute and Song delude the tedious Day,
> And her soft Hours calmly glide away.
> In Smiles the Fair One view'd the rising Sun,
> In Smiles beheld him when his Race was done:
> And when his Beams had bid the Fields adieu,
> And the damp Meadows shone with pearly Dew;
> Pent in their Fold she leaves her wanton Care,
> And to her home returns the happy Fair... (ML i. 184)

There is no question of conflict as Florimelia's 'soft Hours calmly glide away'. The images of grottoes and fountains derive from an idealized landscape rather than particular topography. The only potential for sorrow in the poem is the age of Asophus, Florimelia's father, who nonetheless sleeps easily at night since his virtue and simplicity are better than the vanities of wealth.

In sharp contrast to the Newton poems, Leapor's 'On Winter' evokes a fairly realistic landscape. Doubtless this is partly owing to echoes of the ending of *Love's Labour's Lost*, and also of Ambrose Philips's 'Winter Piece'. Leapor focuses her description on the labourers' experience of the environment:

> No joyful Choirs hail the rising Day,
> But the froze Crystal wraps the leafless Spray:
> Brown look the Meadows, that were late so fine,
> And cap'd with Ice the distant Mountains shine;
> The silent Linnet views the gloomy Sky,
> Sculks to his Hawthorn, nor attempts to fly:
> Then heavy Clouds send down the feather'd Snow;

> Through naked Trees the hollow Tempests blow;
> The Shepherd sighs, but not his Sighs prevail;
> To the soft Snow succeeds the rushing Hail;
> And these white Prospects soon resign their room
> To melting Showers or unpleasing Gloom;
> The Nymphs and Swains their aking Fingers blow,
> Shun the cold Rains and bless the kinder Snow... (ML i. 256-7)

It is interesting to compare these lines with a similar passage in Philips's poem:

> For ev'ry shrub, and ev'ry blade of grass,
> And ev'ry pointed thorn, seem'd wrought in glass;
> In pearls and rubies rich the hawthorns show,
> While through the ice the crimson berries glow.
> The thick-sprung reeds, which watry marshes yield,
> Seem'd polish'd lances in a hostile field.[60]

Philips is describing ice which has formed on trees and plants, and even, a little further, on the antlers of a stag. His interest is in the stunning visual effect. Edmund Blunden observes that Leapor has modelled her poem on Philips's, 'but the imitation glows into originality when she comes to close quarters with her subject'.[61] This is a point worth dwelling on. The traveller in Philips's poem delights in a magical illusion, a pleasing unreality, which is mourned when the ice falls away. Whereas for Philips's traveller the beauty of the landscape is the result of freezing rain, Leapor's nymphs and swains actually 'Shun the cold Rains and bless the kinder Snow'. In her poem the observing persona draws close to the nymphs and swains, even recording the effects of the cold on their fingers. While she does refer to 'white Prospects', the favoured perspective is low. Her appeal to the sense of touch entails that descriptions are organized not simply according to visual planes, but around the persons in the poem. The environment is not subjected to their observation—rather, their lives are subject to the environment. That the poem is about the people rather than the prospect is seen in the following passage:

> Poor daggled *Urs'la* stalks from Cow to Cow,
> Who to her Sighs return a mournful Low;

[60] Ambrose Philips, 'To The Earl of Dorset (The Winter Piece)', in *The Poems of Ambrose Philips*, ed. M. R. Segar, The Percy Reprints, 14 (Oxford: Basil Blackwell, 1937), 91.
[61] Blunden, 'A Northamptonshire Poetess', 65.

A Labouring Poet

> While their full Udders her broad Hands Assail,
> And her sharp Nose hangs dropping o'er the Pail.
> With Garments trickling like a shallow Spring,
> And his wet Locks all twisted in a String,
> Afflicted *Cymon* waddles through the Mire,
> And rails at *Win'fred* creeping o'er the Fire. (ML i. 257)

In these lines the environment is described almost completely in terms of its effects on people. The images of cold, wet, and heat correspond to the tactile relation between agricultural labourers and the land.

Leapor's response to the discomforts of agricultural labourers must be approached at different levels. Since there is no means of changing the weather, there is no question of protest. One must accept the griefs and misfortunes which 'scatter Thorns upon the Labourer's Pillow' (*The Unhappy Father*, ML ii. 161). Leapor writes with pity and resignation. Those two responses are difficult to distinguish since one is her response as a poet to a life which she observes; the other pertains to her own experience of that life. They are not, however, her only responses. She writes in 'An Essay on Hope':

> If trifling Hope has any room to plead,
> 'Tis that where Nature's simple Dictates lead:
> So the wet Hind, who travels o'er the Plain
> Through the cold Mire and afflicting Rain;
> Tho' his low Roofs with trickling Show'rs run,
> May hope next Morn to see the chearful Sun:
> Or when keen Hunger at the ev'ning Tide
> Drives home the Shepherd to his rustick Bride,
> His honest Reason haply might not stray,
> Tho' he should dream of Dumpling all the way. (ML i. 64)

There is something very characteristic of Mary Leapor in these lines. There is no retreat from suffering. Wet, cold, and hunger are all acknowledged. The environment is inhospitable. Yet Leapor is able to write of these things with good humour and to maintain a quiet hope.

The desire to focus on the physical experience of labourers raises a deeper issue. Since aesthetic values are informed by a range of economic, social, and cultural factors, literary choices cannot be seen as wholly separate from broader systems of value. To focus on labour in poetry must be judged an assertion of worth. Simply to describe the agricultural labourer's experience is to take a stance within a system of value which generally favours those who own the land over those who work on it. The choice of a lower perspective in itself tends towards protest. The seasons cannot be made more gentle, yet it remains possible to assert the dignity of people who have to bear their harshness. Resignation before physical evil is therefore connected with a latent struggle against social evil.

Leapor's descriptions of climate are not restricted to winter. Descriptions of winter, however, draw out most clearly the connection between labour and environment in her poetry. This is an important tendency among many labouring-class poets of the eighteenth century even if they are not themselves agricultural workers. Robert Tatersal, for example, describes winter unemployment (c.1735):

> When all the Earth in Ice and Snow is bound,
> And nought but Desolation all around,
> Then hapless me! I wander up and down,
> With half an Apron, wond'rous greasy grown!
> With anxious Looks my Countenance is clad,
> And all my Thoughts are like the Winter, sad!
> This Scene of Life corrodes my troubled Mind,
> I seek for Work; but none, alas! can find;
> Sometimes, by Chance, I have a Grate to set,
> To hang a Copper, or a Hole repleat;
> A Day or two to exercise my Skill,
> But seldom more reluctant to my Will:
> And thus I pass the tedious Winter on,
> Sometimes Repast I have, and sometimes none.[62]

The struggle of labourers against environment is depicted in the work of Stephen Duck, Mary Collier, William Falconer, Ann Yearsley, Robert Bloomfield, and others. This tendency in their poetry is not far removed from the 'incarnational' quality of some women's poetry in the century.

Working for most of her life in a nursery-garden, Leapor's own labour was particularly associated with what Barrell calls the content of landscape. *The Purefoy Letters* contain a number of lists of trees and smaller plants which Philip Leapor brought to

---

[62] Tatersal, 'The Bricklayers Labours', in *The Bricklayer's Miscellany*, 30.

their estate (an example is provided in Chapter 1). These lists are specific. One from 1735 includes pears: summer bon chretien, musk robert, jargonel, vert long and catherine; plums: white and blue perdrigon, royal, and rocha corbon; vines: white muscadine and black chester (Eland, i. 93). The gardener's idiom is distinctive, and adds vigour to Mary Leapor's poetry. In her two volumes she refers to more than eighty specific types of trees, flowers, plants, and vegetables. There were, of course, literary precedents for this. Tickell in his papers on the pastoral recommended 'this our Island as a proper Scene for Pastoral under certain Regulations'. Special attention was to be given to 'the difference of the Soil, of Fruits and Flowers'.[63] John Gay parodies the practice, including at the end of *The Shepherd's Week* 'AN ALPHABETICAL CATALOGUE OF Names, Plants, Flowers, Fruits, Birds, Beasts, Insects, and other material things mentioned in these Pastorals'.[64] The effect of such descriptions on pastorals should be considered. Leapor writes in 'The Charms of Anthony':

> Phebe.
> 'Tis *Anthony*—'tis he deserves the Lay,
> As mild as Ev'ning, and as Morning gay;
> Not the fresh Blooms on yonder Codling-tree,
> Nor the white Hawthorn half so fair as he;
> Nor the young Daisy dress'd in Morning Dew;
> Nor the Pea Blossom wears a brighter Hue.
>
> Lucy.
> None knows like him to strew the wheaten Grain,
> Or drive the Plough-share o'er the fertile Plain;
> To raise the Sheaves, or reap the waving Corn,
> Or mow brown Stubble in the early Morn. (ML i. 249–50)

Descriptions of vegetation locate the poem not in Arcadia but in England. Such images appear amid descriptions of labour which, if not minute, are certainly particular. The poem ends in a tavern, the centre of social life in a village: 'Each took his Lass, and sped 'em to the Town, | To drink cool Cider at the *Hare* and *Hound* . . .' (ML i. 252). Without making excessive claims, the emphasis on particular trees, fruits, and plants can be seen as one

---

[63] *The Guardian*, no. 30, ed. John Calhoun Stephens (Lexington: The University Press of Kentucky, 1982), 128–9.
[64] Gay, 'The Shepherd's Week', in *Poetry and Prose*, 123–6.

of several points at which this slight poem connects with physical and historical reality.

The argument that images of trees, fruits, and plants have an economic association in Leapor's verse takes on greater force with reference to 'The Month of August', a dialogue between Sylvanus, a courtier, and Phillis, a country maid. The poem works through confrontations between art and nature, between classes, and between the sexes. Sylvanus opens the poem:

> Hail, *Phillis*, brighter than a Morning Sky,
> Joy of my Heart, and Darling of my Eye;
> See the kind Year her grateful Tribute yields,
> And round-fac'd Plenty triumphs o'er the Fields.
> But to yon Gardens let me lead thy Charms,
> Where the curl'd Vine extends her willing Arms:
> Whose purple Clusters lure the longing Eye,
> And the ripe Cherries show their scarlet Dye. (ML i. 34)

The highly cultivated garden is described in a distinctly sexual manner. Carole Fabricant has discussed the ideology underlying Augustan landscape design, analysing images of sexual and economic domination. She brings forward numerous examples of nature described 'as a coy or seductive maiden, as a promiscuous or chaste consort, as a naked or overadorned damsel'.[65] Furthermore, she places landscape gardening in the context of the ideology of improvement which was used to justify the enclosure movement. She does not deny the philosophical impetus towards a Horatian retirement, but suggests that garden retreats often had less to do with spiritual delights than with 'the bodily and social pleasures of a fashionable men's club transposed to rural surroundings'.[66] Thus, Leapor's poem may be seen as a comment on the ideology of land use in her time.

Phillis's first response to Sylvanus confronts the image of the land as a young woman ripe for sexual enjoyment:

[65] Fabricant, 'Binding and Dressing Nature's Loose Tresses', 110.
[66] Ibid. 119–20; see also Fabricant's 'The Aesthetics and Politics of Landscape in the Eighteenth Century', in Ralph Cohen (ed.), *Studies in Eighteenth-Century British Art and Aesthetics* (Berkeley, Los Angeles, and London: University of California Press, 1985), 49–81; somewhat narrower is James G. Turner, 'The Sexual Politics of Landscape: Images of Venus in Eighteenth-Century English Poetry and Landscape Gardening', in *Studies in Eighteenth-Century Culture*, 11, Proceedings of the American Society for Eighteenth Century Studies (Madison: University of Wisconsin Press, 1982), 343–66.

> Not all the Sights your boasted Gardens yield,
> Are half so lovely as my Father's Field,
> Where large Increase has bless'd the fruitful Plain,
> And we with Joy behold the swelling Grain,
> Whose heavy Ears toward the Earth reclin'd,
> Wave, nod, and tremble to the whisking Wind. (ML i. 34)

The land is described according to maternal imagery. It is her father's field, and it is pregnant with the harvest. Phillis's description of land meets Sylvanus's sexual imagery with an appeal to the myth of Ceres; she sees the land within a pattern of traditional relations which Sylvanus would usurp. He continues:

> But see, to emulate those Cheeks of thine,
> On yon fair Tree the blushing Nect'rins shine:
> Beneath their Leaves the ruddy Peaches glow,
> And the plump Figs compose a gallant Show.
> With gaudy Plumbs see yonder Boughs recline,
> And ruddy Pears in yon *Espalier* twine.
> There humble Dwarves in pleasing Order stand,
> Whose golden Product seems to court thy Hand. (ML i. 35)

The fruits are 'a gallant Show', variously 'blushing', 'ruddy', 'plump', and 'gaudy'. The word 'Product' in the last line implies a similarity between Sylvanus's relation to the land and his relation to Phillis: both are to be possessed.

Phillis, as she refuses Sylvanus, identifies freedom with a certain type of orchard:

> In vain you tempt me while our Orchard bears
> Long-keeping Russets, lovely Cath'rine Pears,
> Pearmains and Codlings, wheaten Plumbs enough,
> And the black Damsons load the bending Bough.
> No Pruning-knives our fertile Branches teaze,
> While yours must grow but as their Masters please.
> The grateful Trees our Mercy well repay,
> And rain us Bushels at the rising Day. (ML i. 35)

The pruning-knife is an apt emblem of the ideology of improvement. If fruits, trees, and plants are images of labour for Mary Leapor, these lines can be taken as a criticism of owners reorganizing the land. Phillis rejects Sylvanus's world represented by an ornate landscape and a 'majestick Hall'. In the end, Phillis prefers the courtship of a yeoman, Corydon. She has made a choice not only of person, but of class. For her, social mobility is much the same as seduction, as submission to false values. Furthermore, she chooses against an improver's use of the land. In her last speech Phillis describes a harvest feast:

> Not this will lure me, for I'd have you know
> This Night to feast with *Corydon* I go:
> To Night his Reapers bring the gather'd Grain,
> Home to his Barns, and leave the naked Plain:
> Then Beef and Coleworts, Beans and Bacon too,
> And the Plumb-pudding of delicious Hue,
> Sweet-spic'd Cake, and Apple-pies good Store,
> Deck the brown Board; who can desire more?   (ML i. 37)

At harvest feasts the distinctions between the farmer and the labourers whom he hired were relaxed. The harvest feast was usually a high point of village life, and came to be regarded as a ritual of social unity. Sylvanus therefore represents a type of wealth that stands apart from labour. Furthermore, the occasion was often seen as a focus for the customary rights of agricultural workers, including the crucial right of access to common land. Customs such as the harvest feast involved, according to Robert Malcolmson, 'the assertion and recognition of a popular privilege'.[67] Thus the choice between the ornamental landscape of Sylvanus and the agricultural landscape associated with Corydon represents a problem of social and economic organization. Leapor's description of two ways of managing trees, fruits, gardens, and fields implies two possible relations between masters and labourers. Phillis's choice of Corydon is an affirmation of a traditional social order even as this imposes limits with which Leapor struggles elsewhere in her poetry:

> Let *Phillis* ne'er, ah never let her rove
> From her first Virtue and her humble Grove.
> Go seek some Nymph that equals your Degree,
> And leave Content and *Corydon* for me.   (ML i. 38)

Sylvanus is seen partly as a threat to sexual virtue, partly as a threat to social and economic structures which have traditionally guaranteed certain rights and freedoms to agricultural workers. In

---

[67] Robert W. Malcolmson, *Popular Recreations in English Society 1700–1850* (Cambridge: Cambridge University Press, 1973), 110–11.

this poem, Leapor struggles with two models of agricultural life. Sylvanus represents the rapacity of landowners seeking greater profit or 'enjoyment' from their property. Phillis takes refuge within a traditional structure of small farmers. To vindicate this position Leapor makes what is probably her most interesting use of the pastoral conventions. Agricultural workers live in a 'first Virtue', a natural order based on customary rights and usages. In this respect Leapor uses the conventions to criticize the behaviour of landowners. She is unable to define a radical alternative to agricultural improvement, yet she makes an interesting defence of the rights which are being threatened.

Enclosure in Northamptonshire was early and extensive because of the importance of sheep and cattle to the local economy.[68] The town of Brackley, however, was not enclosed until 1829. J. R. Lowerson has shown that Brackley was an exception in the area, since, of the seventeen surrounding parishes, one had been enclosed in 1634, and the rest between 1734 and 1808.[69] Leapor would have witnessed the early stages of this reorganization in agriculture. Her father's work took him at least as far as Shalstone, Buckinghamshire, and her own work took her as far as Edgcote on the Oxfordshire border. It is certain that the Leapors would have been aware of the changes going on around them, especially since Philip Leapor would have been hired for landscaping projects. Accordingly, 'The Month of August' can be seen as an early poetic response to the enclosure movement. Since the poem treats the harvest feast as the focus of a traditional way of life threatened by a landowner, it can be compared to passages from Duck and Bloomfield which, though separated by seventy years, approach conflicts in agriculture through similar imagery. Duck writes:

> In noisy Triumph the last Load moves on,
> And loud Huzza's proclaim the Harvest done.
> Our Master, joyful at the pleasing Sight,
> Invites us all to feast with him at Night.
> A Table plentifully spread we find,

---

[68] See J. M. Neeson, 'Common Right and Enclosure in Eighteenth Century Northamptonshire' (Ph.D. thesis, University of Warwick, 1978); id., 'The Opponents of Enclosure in Eighteenth-Century Northamptonshire', *Past & Present*, no. 105 (Nov. 1984), 114–39.
[69] Lowerson, 'Enclosure and Farm Holding in Brackley, 1829–51', 38.

> And Jugs of humming Ale to chear the Mind;
> Which he, too gen'rous, pushes round so fast,
> We think no Toils to come, nor mind the past.
> But the next Morning soon reveals the Cheat,
> When the same Toils we must again repeat;
> To the same Barns must back again return,
> To labour there for Room for next Year's Corn.[70]

Duck's view of the harvest feast is much harder than Leapor's. One of the chief effects of enclosure was to reduce the number of yeoman farmers and to increase the number of landless workers. Duck, as a landless worker, had none of the land-rights which the harvest feast had come to represent. For him, the ritual was already hollow. Although they describe harvest feasts in an opposed manner, Leapor and Duck are engaged in more or less the same argument. Whereas Leapor seeks to retain freedoms which are threatened with the pruning-knife, Duck belongs to a section of rural society which has already seen its rights cut away. The bitterness with which he attacks pastoral poetry implies a sense of loss: ''Tis all a gloomy, melancholy Scene, | Fit only to provoke the Muses' Spleen.'[71]

The association of customary rights and usages with a golden age of rural society is a typical response of labouring poets to the agricultural revolution. Robert Bloomfield writes in 'The Farmer's Boy' of a harvest feast in which farmers join with labourers on equal terms. Bloomfield, however, sets this feast in days long past:

> Whence comes this change, ungracious, irksome, cold?
> Whence the new grandeur that mine eyes behold?
> The wid'ning distance which I daily see,
> Has Wealth done this? . . . then wealth's a foe to me;
> Foe to our rights; that leaves a pow'rful few
> The paths of emulation to pursue.[72]

Bloomfield, writing long after 'The Deserted Village', is much more explicit in his critique of wealth than are Duck and Leapor. Yet, by appealing to the harvest feast, he too uses the chief ritual of agricultural life as the focus for social comment.

---

[70] Duck, 'The Thresher's Labours', in *Poems* 26–7.
[71] Ibid. 13.
[72] Robert Bloomfield, 'The Farmer's Boy', in *Collected Poems (1800–1822)*, ed. Jonathan N. Lawson, 5 vols. in one (Gainesville, Fl.: Scholars Facsimiles, 1971), i. 66.

That Leapor is concerned with land use in 'The Month of August' is hard to dispute; her observations, however, are oblique. Oddly, her boldest statement on landscape comes in 'Crumble Hall', a poem arising from domestic service rather than agriculture. R. A. Aubin in his well-known study of topographical poetry expresses admiration for this poem because of its humour. In the same work, he suggests that estate poems are often characterized by 'shameless bootlicking'.[73] Country house poems have, of course, been the subject of much disagreement among scholars, and 'Crumble Hall' cannot be understood except against the background of that debate. G. R. Hibbard argues that there was in the seventeenth century a tradition of country house poems written by Jonson, Herrick, Carew, and Marvell, and that these work on the contrast between useful and ostentatious ideals of architecture.[74] Raymond Williams in his discussion of country house poems, specifically those of Jonson and Carew, observes a tendency to obscure labour, and to describe as natural bounty that which is obtained by work.[75] Alastair Fowler has argued that Williams and other critics have overstated this tendency, and that the emphases on labour, hospitality, and architecture vary from poem to poem and over time.[76] The problem with placing Mary Leapor within this discussion is that it is not certain that she knew any of the poems with which these critics are primarily concerned. The only country house poem she certainly read is Pope's 'Epistle to Burlington'. There were numerous poems written about country estates in the eighteenth century, and Leapor must have read some of these, but again it is difficult to know how many.

At any rate, Leapor's use of the form is distinctive. From the passages on servants discussed above, the description of work can be judged one of the major concerns of the poem. Not only is there the close description of individual tasks such as cleaning pewter or cooking, but the whole perspective of the poem is that of the servant. Leapor describes, for example, the height of a

[73] Robert Arnold Aubin, *Topographical Poetry in XVIII-Century England*, The Modern Language Association of America Revolving Fund Series, 6 (New York: MLA, 1936; New York: Kraus Reprint Corporation, 1966), 170, 121.
[74] See G. R. Hibbard, 'The Country House Poem of the Seventeenth Century', *Journal of the Warburg and Courtauld Institutes*, 19 (1956), 159–74.
[75] Williams, *The Country and the City*, 32–3.
[76] See Alastair Fowler, 'Country House Poems: The Politics of a Genre', *The Seventeenth Century*, 1 (1986), 1–14.

ceiling: 'Here the pleas'd Spider plants her peaceful Loom: | Here weaves secure, nor dreads the hated Broom' (ML ii. 113). For the servant the height of the house is understood, however whimsically, as a problem of cleaning. Whereas in Williams's view country house poems tend to obscure labour, in this poem it is the owners who are almost unseen. Assuming that Sophronia is an upper servant, the poem draws no closer to them than a description of the room where Biron sleeps and where, Timon-like, he keeps his unread books. That the owners are not described may imply that they have withdrawn from the close relations with tenants, servants, and labourers that are called for from lords of the manor; they have grown remote in more or less the way described by Bloomfield in his discussion of the harvest feast.

Another major difference between Leapor's 'Crumble Hall' and other poems of this type is that it is not a panegyric. Howard Erskine Hill believes that both Hibbard and Williams have failed to emphasize this aspect of country house poems: 'These poems are simply panegyrical in mode, recognizable to their readers as such, and lay their chief stress on bounty and kindness: a communal sharing of the fruits of the earth.'[77] Apart from the usual salute to Artemisia at the beginning, the drift of the poem is towards criticism rather than praise. Even as Pope attacks the gaudiness of Timon's villa in his 'Epistle to Burlington', he is able to praise the alternative: 'Who then shall grace, or who improve the Soil? | Who plants like BATHURST, or who builds like BOYLE' (Pope, iii. II. 154). The absence of panegyric in itself sets Leapor's poem apart from earlier country house poems. However, its underlying values are not that far removed from the basically conservative view of society advanced in those poems:

[77] Howard Erskine-Hill, *The Social Milieu of Alexander Pope: Lives, Example and the Poetic Response* (New Haven, Conn. and London: Yale University Press, 1975), 285. For other discussions of country house poems see William A. McClung, *The Country House in English Renaissance Poetry* (Berkeley, Los Angeles, and London: University of California Press, 1977); Heather Dubrow, 'The Country-House Poem: A Study in Generic Development', *Genre*, 12 (1979), 153–79; James G. Turner, *The Politics of Landscape: Rural Scenery and Society in English Poetry 1630–1660* (Oxford: Basil Blackwell, 1979); Carole Fabricant, *Swift's Landscape* (Baltimore and London: The Johns Hopkins University Press, 1982), esp. 95–172; Virginia C. Kenny, *The Country-House Ethos in English Literature 1688–1750: Themes of Personal Retreat and National Expansion* (Brighton: Harvester, 1984).

A Labouring Poet 139

That *Crumble-Hall*, whose hospitable Door
Has fed the Stranger, and reliev'd the Poor;
Whose *Gothic* Towers, and whose rusty Spires,
Were known of old to Knights, and hungry Squires.
There powder'd Beef, and Warden-Pies, were found;
And Pudden dwelt within her spacious Bound:
Pork, Peas, and Bacon (good old *English* Fare!),
With tainted Ven'son, and with hunted Hare:
With humming Beer her Vats were wont to flow,
And ruddy *Nectar* in her Vaults to glow.
Here came the Wights, who battled for Renown,
The sable Frier, and the russet Clown:
The loaded Tables sent a sav'ry Gale,
And the brown Bowls were crown'd with simp'ring Ale;
While the Guests ravag'd on the smoking Store,
Till their stretch'd Girdles would contain no more. (ML ii. 112)

Leapor here describes the ancient duties of hospitality associated with a manor house. Strangers, the poor, knights, soldiers, friars, and ordinary rural people are provided for. Such a passage, like the harvest feast described in 'The Month of August', implies a conservative view of society organized around principles of dependence and obligation.[78] Donna Landry, however, takes a different view of this passage, which she believes is purely satirical, 'a riot of comically conspicuous consumption that wastes resources in order to satisfy human greed' (Landry, 109). For Landry, Leapor is ridiculing nostalgic ideas of the function of the country house: 'the venison is tainted, the vulnerable hare has been hunted to death to provide meat for this already groaning table, the guests gorge themselves until they are grossly bloated' (Landry, 109). This is not actually convincing. The probable sense of 'tainted', according to those in the *Oxford English Dictionary*, is 'Imbued with the scent of an animal (usually a hunted animal)'. Examples of this sense are given from Addison and Pope. Leapor is therefore unlikely to mean that the meat is rotten or poisoned, only that it smells of game.[79] As a kitchen-maid who had regularly to dress fowls, and probably to wring their necks, it is again

---

[78] For a broad examination of such issues, see Isabel Rivers, *The Poetry of Conservatism 1600–1745: A Study of Poets and Public Affairs from Jonson to Pope* (Cambridge: Rivers Press, 1973).

[79] I am indebted to Dr Jeremy Marshall and other lexicographers at the Oxford Dictionaries for advice on the various senses of this word.

doubtful that she would be squeamish about hares. Landry's last point would suggest only that the guests were taking advantage of actual hospitality. Leapor has provided a playful but none the less idealized history of the house, against which the behaviour of the current owners may be judged. Since Landry misunderstands this crucial passage, her subsequent discussion of Leapor's ironic 'disclosures' is almost entirely misguided. 'Crumble Hall' must be read not as a repudiation of established social and economic relations, but as the statement of someone who finds those relations violated or betrayed.

Beyond this historical passage the poem is divided into three sections describing the house, the servants, and the landscape. In the first section Mira climbs through the house describing various rooms and corridors. When she reaches the roof, these remarkable lines follow:

> No farther—Yes, a little higher, pray:
> At yon small Door you'll find the Beams of Day,
> While the hot Leads return the scorching Ray.
> Here a gay Prospect meets the ravish'd Eye:
> Meads, Fields, and Groves, in beauteous Order lie.
> From hence the Muse precipitant is hurl'd,
> And drags down Mira to the nether World. (ML ii. 117)

That 'nether World' is, in fact, the kitchen, where Leapor describes 'the Menial Train'. The high perspective is indulged for the space of one couplet, before Leapor's muse tumbles back into the world of work. It is interesting that she makes so little of the high perspective. The door and the leads are immediately in front of her and become particularized in the poem but, the 'Meads, Fields, and Groves' are a generalized landscape, about which she has little to say.

In the last section of the poem, Leapor again attempts to describe the landscape. This time the perspective is lower. Mira, it seems, is walking in the landscape rather than looking at it from a height:

> Now to those Meadows let frolick Fancy rove,
> Where o'er yon Waters nods a pendent Grove;
> In whose clear Waves the pictur'd Boughs are seen,
> With fairer Blossoms, and a brighter Green.
> Soft flow'ry Banks the spreading Lakes divide:
> Sharp-pointed Flags adorn each tender Side.

> See! the pleas'd Swans along the Surface play;
> Where yon cool Willows meet the scorching Ray,
> When fierce *Orion* gives too warm a Day. (ML ii. 120)

This landscape represents safety and refuge for the poet; it is a natural landscape corresponding to a natural and secure social order. All that, however, is threatened:

> And shall those Shades, where *Philomela*'s Strain
> Has oft to Slumber lull'd the hapless Swain;
> Where Turtles us'd to clap their silken Wings;
> Whose rev'rend Oaks have known a hundred Springs;
> Shall these ignobly from their Roots be torn,
> And perish shameful, as the abject Thorn;
> While the slow Carr bears off their aged Limbs,
> To clear the Way for Slopes, and modern Whims;
> Where banish'd Nature leaves a barren Gloom,
> And aukward Art supplies the vacant Room? (ML ii. 121)

Leapor's appeal to the imagery of retirement is somewhat conventional, yet she uses that ideal of landscape not as a pretext for improvement but as a defence of existing topography. The destruction of the oaks has a poignancy for her that seems to go beyond the aesthetic. Having posited a connection in Leapor's verse between images of trees, flowers, and plants, and her own habitual labour, we may judge that her conservative attitude towards landscape in this poem has an economic origin. Landowners pursue 'modern Whims' across a landscape, exposing those places which had formerly given comfort to 'the hapless swain'. The 'rev'rend Oaks' uprooted suggest the vulnerability of a traditional relation to the land. That the oaks are personified makes the association more intense. In this sense, the passage implies an aesthetic preference for an older type of landscape as well as a fear of social and economic dislocation. Within the poem's satiric vein, Leapor uses the mythological apparatus of an idealized landscape to criticize the improvements both to the hall and to the grounds:

> Yet (or the Muse for Vengeance calls in vain)
> The injur'd Nymphs shall haunt the ravag'd Plain:
> Strange Sounds and Forms shall teaze the gloomy Green;
> And Fairy-Elves by *Urs'la* shall be seen:
> Their new-built Parlour shall with Echoes ring:
> And in their Hall shall doleful Crickets sing.

> Then cease, *Diracto*, stay thy desp'rate Hand;
> And let the Grove, if not the Parlour, stand.   (ML ii. 121-2)

The curse is humorous but grim: as the landscape has been emptied so may the house be abandoned. Leapor opposes the improver's ideal of an open and clear landscape with an animistic fiction: nymphs and fairy-elves will continue to populate the 'ravag'd Plain', though there is no place for the 'hapless Swain'. Her suggestion that a house which so plainly violates the natural order will eventually be deserted recalls Pope's prediction concerning Timon's villa:

> Another age shall see the golden Ear
> Imbrown the Slope, and nod on the Parterre,
> Deep Harvests bury all his pride has plann'd,
> And laughing Ceres re-assume the land.   (Pope, iii. II. 154)

Leapor goes beyond Pope's criticism of Timon in her attitude towards changes at Crumble Hall. Pope, of course, is ready to cut down trees, as Landry rightly observes, to raise cities and build ships (Landry, 118-19). The crucial point for him is that changes in the land should be useful rather than ostentatious. Leapor, however, is less interested in colonial expansion and public works than in the defence of her own way of life.

Leapor's poems on rural landscape are among the earliest to register the conflicts associated with the enclosure movement. Her work may be compared to 'Snaith Marsh. A Yorkshire Pastoral', which appeared in 1754.[80] The author is known only as 'Ophelia'. This poem addresses the issue of enclosure directly:

> But far more waeful still that luckless day,
> Which with the commons gave *Snaith Marsh* away,
> Snaith Marsh our whole town's pride, the poor man's bread,
> Where, tho' no rent he paid, his cattle fed.

The poem describes the harshness of the new order: 'My goodly stock e'er yet they tasted food, | By cross-grain'd hinds were driv'n from their abode...' (*GM* 24 (1754), 135). The loss of common lands results in a loss of social cohesion.

---

[80] See Julia Patton, *The English Village: A Literary Study 1750-1850* (New York: Macmillan, 1919), 121-2; A. J. Sambrook, 'The English Lord and the Happy Husbandman', *Studies on Voltaire and the Eighteenth Century*, 57 (1967), 1366.

Enclosure as a subject for poetry is usually associated with Oliver Goldsmith, who touched on the question in 'The Travellers' (1764), before producing 'The Deserted Village' (1770). It is the standard criticism of Goldsmith that his treatment of rural life is distorted by the pastoral myth. Irvin Ehrenpreis claims, for example, that in 'The Deserted Village' this myth sets villagers outside the world of observation, thereby making them seem unreal.[81] A. J. Sambrook, on the other hand, sees greater efficacy in Goldsmith's protest; he suggests that this poet 'established the myth of rural catastrophe in its familiar form', and thus contributed to the development of English Utopianism among writers from Wollstonecraft to Ruskin who project a countryside humanized by fit housing and land reform. Sambrook makes the striking assertion that 'The idyll of unspoiled Auburn could be read prospectively as well as retrospectively'.[82] If Auburn is a dream of an ideal countryside, that dream need not be taken solely as a retreat from history but as an image of social possibility. While it would be wrong to deny that Goldsmith is nostalgic, Sambrook's argument certainly points towards a more generous assessment of his work.

To relate Leapor to Goldsmith on the issue of enclosure, especially in light of Sambrook's extensive claims, requires caution. It would be incongruous to see her as an influence on later writers who may never have heard of her. Yet, as one of the earliest writers to recognize the pernicious tendencies of contemporary land use, she has an importance. Her poetry does not approach a 'myth of rural catastrophe', though her description of an emptied landscape has similarities to the stance taken by Goldsmith:

> Even now the devastation is begun,
> And half the business of destruction done;
> Even now, methinks, as pondering here I stand,
> I see the rural virtues leave the land.[83]

Goldsmith's 'rural virtues' correspond to 'banished Nature' in Leapor's poem. In both cases the result of improvement is a

---

[81] Ehrenpreis, 'Poverty and Poetry', 17.
[82] Sambrook, 'The English Lord and the Happy Husbandman', 1372.
[83] Oliver Goldsmith, 'The Deserted Village', in *The Collected Works of Oliver Goldsmith*, ed. Arthur Friedman, 5 vols. (Oxford: Clarendon Press, 1966), iv. 302.

dehumanized landscape and something like a moral vacuum. The image of a golden age is central both to Leapor's and to Goldsmith's treatment of rural life. Following Sambrook's logic, though he does not use these terms, this image may be interpreted in either a descriptive or a normative sense. On a descriptive level pastoral imagery must be regarded as sentimental distortion. On a normative level, however, the possibilities are much more subtle as the following lines from one of Leapor's pastorals, 'Colinetta', demonstrate:

> Tell them if e'er I found a straggling Ewe,
> Although the Owner's Name I hardly knew;
> I fed it kindly with my Father's Hay,
> And gave it shelter at the closing Day:
> I never stole young Pigeons from their Dams,
> Nor from their Pasture drove my Neighbours Lambs:
> Nor set my Dog to hunt their Flocks away,
> That mine might graze upon the vacant Lay. (ML i. 28)

Dying Colinetta's defence of her reputation can be taken simply as an attempt to obscure conflicts relating to common pasture land. If Colinetta's sense of propriety, generosity, and fairness, is assumed to typify, in Leapor's view, the whole of rural society, then the question of a normative level in the poem is almost irrelevant since there is no difference between the descriptive and normative states of rural society. The poem would then be little more than a series of distortions, 'propaganda for the victors'.[84] The poem actually alludes to various evils in country life. The opening passage describes the fields in autumn in terms of their effect on Colinetta; her illness is the result of the 'sick Season' (ML i. 26). This treatment of physical evil is in line with Leapor's treatment of the environment in poems already discussed. Moral evil is also recognized. That Colinetta feels it necessary to defend herself against 'wayward Tongues' (ML i. 28) is characteristic of Leapor's verse. Shortly, Colinetta claims that she herself has never been envious nor has she spread scandal, although

---

[84] Roger Sales, 'The Politics of Pastoral', in Kathleen Parkinson and Martin Priestman (ed.), *Peasants and Countrymen in Literature* (Roehampton: The English Department of the Roehampton Institute of Higher Education, 1982), 98. Sales approaches the literature of the period from a staunchly ideological perspective; for a fuller statement of his ideas, see 'The Literature of Labour and "The Condition of England Question"' (Ph.D. thesis, Cambridge University, 1975).

evidently others behave in this way. Obviously, then, there is a difference between normative and descriptive elements in the poem. The passage quoted above can then be read not as a denial of conflicts over the use of common land, but as a comment on them. Whether the passage refers directly to enclosure or, more probably, to disagreements among cottagers, is not certain. In either case, Leapor maintains that common pasturage should not be turned to the sole benefit of anyone.

Pastoral myth was a dominant mode of social understanding through much of the eighteenth century.[85] It is necessary not to draw a bald distinction between pastoral and counter-pastoral. Indeed, some of Leapor's pastorals, prefiguring Goldsmith, use images of a golden age, of natural values and innate virtues, to question developments in contemporary capitalism. If this is a primitive point of reference for social criticism, it nonetheless equipped Leapor to make a brave and significant statement on rural life.

Literary Patronage

Mary Leapor enjoyed no financial benefit from her writing; however, the plan for a subscription had an impact on her writing. It represented for her the opportunity to move from a life of manual labour to a life of intellectual labour. It entailed new freedoms as well as a new form of dependence. Leapor's conflicting responses to this prospect can be traced in her poetry.

Freemantle, according to her letter, mentioned to Leapor shortly after their acquaintance (*circa* September 1745) that a subscription could be organized. This suggestion occasioned one of Leapor's longest poems, 'Mopsus; or, The Castle Builder'. In a letter 'On her Mopsus' Leapor writes: 'I am to confess, that I have drawn my own Picture in many Places where I have described this unlucky Hero' (ML ii. 316). The poem can therefore be read as Leapor's satire on her own ambitions. She writes of the hero:

> His Father plac'd him in a Country School,
> To learn *Division*, and the *Golden Rule*:

[85] See Richard Feingold, *Nature and Society: Later Eighteenth Century Uses of the Pastoral and Georgic* (Hassocks: The Harvester Press, 1978), 2.

> But when the fair aspiring Youth began
> To walk on Tiptoe to the Verge of Man;
> His discontented Thoughts began to rove
> Beyond the Prospect of his Father's Grove.
> In vain the Hawthorn spreads her snowy Pride,
> And the pale Lily gilds the Fountain-Side:
> He loaths the Country, and his Fellow Swains;
> For mighty Projects fill his working Brains... (ML ii. 11-12)

The 'mighty Projects' are, of course, a series of fantasies encouraged by a gypsy's oracle. In pursuit of these, Mopsus proposes marriage to a fine lady and is beaten by her servants; he steals his father's rent money and sets out for London, where he is robbed by a prostitute and thrown into gaol; his father sends more money, which he uses to bribe the gaoler; he is tricked into marrying an aristocrat's mistress who promptly gives birth; the woman leaves and the baby dies; the prodigal returns to his father. The poem ends with an affirmation of pastoral values:

> Here with calm Virtue, and a peaceful Mind,
> In rural Plenty, dwells the sober Hind:
> His equal Days in one smooth Tenor run;
> The same at rising as declining Sun:
> No more Delusions in his Fancy rise,
> Grown grave by Sorrow; by Experience wise. (ML ii. 42)

Whereas in poems considered in the preceding section pastoral conventions allow Leapor room to criticize changes in rural society, in 'Mopsus' the same conventions appear almost repressive. A labouring person who aspires to a better and more rewarding life is judged to be grossly deceived. It seems that pastoral conventions are useful in defending traditional rights, but that the idea of an immediate economic advance is much harder for Leapor to accommodate. However, that is not to repudiate the idea of a serious normative function for the pastoral conventions in her work, even with respect to 'Mopsus'. Allowing that the countryside is the locus of virtue, Leapor makes sweeping though defensible observations on the attitudes of the rich and the power of money. When, for example, Mopsus receives an infusion of money from his parents, his relation to the law changes:

> Now struts the Youth—His Suff'rings at an End;
> The Prince of *Bridewel*, and the Ruler's Friend.

> A pow'rful Guinea brib'd the Keeper's Will:
> He gain'd his Freedom; and the Law was still. (ML ii. 31)

Leapor's assessment is certainly not naïve, though it might be conventional. To connect 'Mopsus' with the question of literary patronage it is necessary to observe the differences in economic structures between the countryside and the city as they are portrayed in the poem. Mopsus's father pursues an ordered and predictable way of life: 'His Calves and Oxen were his only Care, | His homely Servants, and his smiling Heir' (ML ii. 11). In contrast to the stability of ancient usages, Mopsus in the city is obliged to place his trust first in oracles, then merely in promises. A chain of deceptions and disappointments culminates in his marriage. Viscount Simper's emissary, Sir Sidrophel, communicates the peer's intention:

> This noble Lord, the Axle of your Fate,
> 'Tis he must raise you from your humble State.
> But stay—methinks I see a double Cause:
> O, now I find; there's Marriage in the Clause:
> His Lordship's Sister—Yes, it must be She.
> When this shall come to pass—remember me. (ML ii. 33)

Each of Mopsus's disappointments is caused by misplaced trust. As his pursuit of fortune becomes a search for a wealthy bride or patron, so he enters an economic world defined by favours. His father, a small farmer, lives simply within a set of economic relations which are, at least in theory, secure. Mopsus, however, puts himself in the power of would-be benefactors, and his vulnerability is ruthlessly exploited.

'Mopsus' can be taken as a comic piece. Leapor's willingness to make jokes at her own expense is one of the admirable qualities of her work. Still, in this poem she is examining a condition into which she would enter by seeking patrons for her verse. A subscription would make her economically dependent upon the goodwill of the wealthy. After her experience at Edgcote she may have doubted this prospect. Poems which show no trace of a late composition, however, are also deeply sceptical of wealthy patrons. 'The Friend in Disgrace' is a dialogue in which one friend fails to recognize another who has suffered misfortune:

> Sure the Court is mighty lulling,
> (Not the Streams of *Lethe* more)
> E'en the Groom and dirty Scullion
> Know not those they lov'd before.
> So on that fatal Day you did
> The Levee of his Grace attend;
> You of your Memory was rid,
> I of my Fortune and my Friend. (ML i. 11-12)

In this poem patronage is seen as corrupting; those who strive for it must sacrifice essential human values. In another poem, 'The Way of the World', dependence is seen not as corrupting but as hopeless. Virginius, a wealthy man, receives 'starv'd Dependents' (ML i. 94) with hints of favour. He tells one man that if he returns on Tuesday, he may receive hundreds of pounds:

> But *Tuesday* see, the joyful Day is come;
> Now to his Patron—'But he's not at home.'
> 'Alas! But then to-morrow Morn will do,
> And I'll be early.—Gentlemen, adieu.'
> Next Day at Six before the Gate appears,
> The Wretch divided by his Hopes and Fears.
> The haughty Servants meet him with a Frown.
> 'I'd see his Honour.'—'But he's not come down;'
> 'Your Servant, Sir—I'll stay then in the Hall:'
> 'But he is sick and can't be spoke withal.'
> 'I'll wait with Patience till another Day,
> And for his Honour and his Health shall pray.'
> At last the Knight (his Fate had ordered so)
> Was seiz'd and boarded by the lurking Foe;
> And wisely thinking 'twas in vain to fly,
> Smooth'd up his Face and with a leering Eye
> Began. 'Oh Mr. What-d'ye-call, Is't you?
> I'm glad to see you: Yet I'm sorry too,
> Sure some ill Stars presided o'er your Fate,
> I cou'd have serv'd you, but you're come too late.' (ML i. 95-6)

In light of these passages from other poems, 'Mopsus' can be seen not only as a pastoral retreat from ambition but also a firm recognition of the hazards of patronage.

In his celebrated letter to Chesterfield, Samuel Johnson asks: 'Is not a Patron, My Lord, one who looks with unconcern on a Man struggling for Life in the water and when he has reached ground encumbers him with help.'[86] Other writers also complained of their treatment at the hands of benefactors, even when this had nothing to do with dedications. Joseph Lewis, an ivory turner, suffered excruciating poverty. At times he was reduced to publishing acrostics in newspapers begging money for his wife and children. In 1758 he published the following 'Verses occasion'd by a barbarous Disappointment that the Author lately met with; wrote extempore, and left for a certain Gentleman, at his House':

> Sir,
> I Call'd at the House, where you said I shou'd dine,
> But was damnably plagu'd for to find out the Sign
> What's worse—when I travelled all over the lane,
> A pox o' the Journey—my Labour was vain.
> No Mutton, nor Lamb, was there roasting or broiling,
> And the Devil a Pea on the Fire was boiling.
> You say, that you're moving, 'tis true what you say;
> But my Belly can witness you move the wrong Way.[87]

It could be argued that Lewis's poem refers only to a failure of etiquette. For a person in this poet's position, however, such a failure has immediate economic implications: he has lost his supper. Examples of Grub Street poverty could be multiplied endlessly. Depending on favours for a substantial part of one's livelihood was the vulnerability that Mary Leapor was reluctant to assume.

The literary implications of economic dependence must be

[86] Samuel Johnson, Letter 61, in *The Letters of Samuel Johnson with Mrs. Thrale's Genuine Letters to Him*, ed. R. W. Chapman, 3 vols. (Oxford: Clarendon Press, 1952), i. 65.

[87] Joseph Lewis [Lancelot Poverty-struck], 'Verses occasion'd by a barbarous Disappointment that the Author lately met with; wrote extempore, and left for a certain Gentleman, at his House', in *The Miscellaneous and Whimsical Lucubrations of Lancelot Poverty-struck* (London, 1758), 79–80. For discussion of this poet, see Arthur Sherbo, 'The Case for Internal Evidence (I): Can *Mother Midnight's Comical Pocket-Book* be Attributed to Christopher Smart?', *Bulletin of the New York Public Library* [*BNYPL*], 61 (1957), 373–82; Betty Rizzo, 'Found: Joseph Lewis, Elusive Author of *Mother Midnight's Comical Pocket-Book*', *BNYPL* 77 (1974), 281–7; Arthur Sherbo, 'Another Reply, This Time to Betty Rizzo', *BNYPL* 77 (1974), 288; David Erdman, 'Editor's Epigraph', *BNYPL* 77 (1974), 289; Karina Williamson, 'Joseph Lewis, "our Doggrel Author"', *Bulletin of Research in the Humanities*, 81 (Spring 1978), 74–83; Betty Rizzo, 'Joseph Lewis in REAL CALAMITY', *Bulletin of Research in the Humanities*, 81 (Spring 1978), 84–9.

observed. W. B. Coley has written that depending on wealthy patrons presented writers of the period with two difficulties: 'ideological inconstancy and the threat of the loss of the dependency itself'.[88] Coley argues that writers in the eighteenth century form a class which is generally dependent on another, higher class for economic support.[89] Paul Korshin argues, on the other hand, that very few writers could have been supported by patronage to such an extent that they actually lost their independence. He draws a clear line between individual patronage, which had declined by this time, and the subscription method, which, while it left authors obliged especially to those who solicited for them, reduced individual dependence:

the subscription method democratized literary patronage, and made it possible for a community of wealthy people to contribute to the support of many authors. The sense of obligation which pervades and often exacerbates the traditional patron–client relationship is usually diminished or wholly absent in the author–subscriber relationship.[90]

Korshin's argument does not absolutely exclude Coley's, though their emphases are different. The opportunities of individual patronage may have been reduced, but few major writers from the time of Gay and Swift to that of George Crabbe did not look for such patronage or shape some composition towards the expectations of a patron. In the case of labouring poets this is particularly true, since the usual path to publication lay through 'discovery' by a learned or wealthy person. Leapor was, of course, discovered by Freemantle who, though relatively learned, had to bring her friend to the attention of others who had the social connections to promote her work: 'Some of her Papers, a little time before her Death were communicated to several Persons of Rank and of distinguished Taste and Judgement, who were pleased to express a great Satisfaction in the View they had of promoting a Subscription...' (ML i. 4). While Leapor could

---

[88] W. B. Coley, 'Notes toward a "Class Theory" of Augustan Literature: The Example of Fielding', in Frank Brady, John Palmer, and Martin Price (ed.), *Literary Theory and Structure: Essays in Honor of William K. Wimsatt* (New Haven, Conn. and London: Yale University Press, 1973), 138.

[89] Ibid. 132–3.

[90] Paul J. Korshin, 'Types of Eighteenth-Century Literary Patronage', *Eighteenth Century Studies*, 7 (Summer 1974), 464; see also Michael Foss, *The Age of Patronage: The Arts in Society 1660–1750* (London: Hamish Hamilton, 1971).

never have been published without some support of this kind, patronage introduced a new influence on her writing. In some respects she resisted that influence and in others succumbed to it. It seems that Leapor absolutely rejected the idea of seeking a patron through a dedication. Freemantle suggested that they find 'some great Lady'. Leapor, however, was not convinced:

'But, Madam, I am not acquainted with any great Lady, nor like to be.'
'No matter for that; 'tis but your supposing your Patroness to have as many Virtues as other Peoples always have: You need not fear saying too much; and I must insist upon it.'
She really seemed shock'd, and said, 'But, Dear Madam, could you in good Earnest approve of my sitting down to write an Encomium upon a Person I know nothing of, only because I might hope to get something by it?—No, Myra!' (ML ii, pp. xxvi–xxvii).

Leapor also expresses her distaste for flattery in 'Advice to Myrtillo'. In this poem one Leapor persona advises another on the means to literary success:

> Do you the Levee of his Grace attend,
> And (like most Poets) shou'd you want a Friend,
> Make not his Worth the Measure of your Song;
> But learn his Humour, and you can't be wrong:
> Perhaps this Maxim may offend the wise;
> But you must flatter, if you mean to rise... (ML i. 169)

The usual reward for a dedication at the time, according to Korshin, was about £10, the amount Chesterfield gave Johnson on the proposals for his dictionary.[91] The benefit Leapor sacrificed can therefore be valued rather precisely at this figure. Indeed, in 'The Penitent' the same amount is suggested by Parthenissa as the whole profit to be expected from the poems (see ML i. 118). The sum, though substantial, would have been paid just once by the patron—consequently, one cannot claim that there was any potential for real dependence, although in the circumstances Leapor might easily have exchanged flattery for profit. Johnson wrote in *The Rambler* (no. 136) of the dangers of 'promiscuous dedication' (Johnson iv. 356). It is a measure of Leapor's resolve that she refused to dedicate.

There are other problems associated with both individual patronage and subscriptions. It was common, especially with

---

[91] Korshin, 'Types of Eighteenth-Century Literary Patronage', 467.

labouring poets, to make an appeal to readers' charitable instincts; therefore, it was necessary to present the author as one of the deserving poor. An extreme instance is Hannah More's depiction of Ann Yearsley. She writes concerning the subscription for Yearsley's first volume (1785):

> It is not intended to place her in such a state of independence as might seduce her to devote her time to the idleness of Poetry... Pressing, as her distresses are, if I did not think her heart was rightly turned, I should be afraid of proposing such a measure, lest it should unsettle the sobriety of her mind, and, by exciting her vanity, indispose her for the laborious employments of her humble condition; but it would be cruel to imagine that we cannot mend her fortune without impairing her virtue.[92]

Cruel indeed. Not many patrons wrote with such pomposity, though it was usual in subscription proposals or prefaces to volumes by labouring poets to include a description of the author as hard-working, moral, and content within his or her station. In Leapor's first volume we read:

> in Justice to the Memory of the Author, as well as for the Satisfaction of all those who have so chearfully and generously contributed to improve the best Legacy she could bequeath to her Father, we beg leave to inform them, that her Conduct and Behaviour entirely corresponded with those virtuous and pious Sentiments which are conspicuous in her Poems. She was courteous and obliging to all, chearful, good-natured, and contented in the Station of Life in which Providence had placed her. The generous and charitable Spirit that appeared in her was exerted upon all Occasions to the utmost of her Ability, and was such as would have been ornamental in a much higher Sphere, to which in all Probability, if it had pleased God to spare her Life, her own Merit would have raised her.   (ML i. 4)

This description is not nearly as condescending as that produced by Hannah More. Still, it was thought necessary to present Leapor as one of the deserving poor, and to deny any rebelliousness in her character. This could be taken as a minor concession to advertising, except that the explicit statement at the beginning of the book seems related to an exclusion from the first volume of almost all the poems embodying Leapor's sharpest social criticism. According to the proposal, only one volume was to be printed. Therefore, 'The Disappointment', 'The

---

[92] Hannah More, 'A Prefatory Letter to Mrs. Montague', in Ann Yearsley, *Poems, on Several Occasions* (London, 1785), p. xi.

Consolation', 'Epistle to Artemisia. On Fame', 'Crumble Hall', 'An Essay on Woman', 'Advice to Sophronia', 'The Visit', and 'Man the Monarch', were likely to have been denied publication. While 'The Month of August' and a number of other poems which pursue sexual and economic questions do appear in the first volume, Leapor's most angry works were left out. An interesting example of the choices made for this first volume is between the two poems to Octavia on the subject of marriage. The poem which advocates marriage so long as the partner is chosen reasonably is included, but not the second poem, which examines the dangers of marriage *per se*. While this editorial choice may have had partly to do with the length of the two poems, it seems none the less that there was limited scope for rebellious thought in Leapor's first volume.

The facts behind the selection of poems for the first volume may prove elusive. Leapor communicated with a 'Gentleman' about the choice of a specimen to be printed with the proposals, about revisions, and about the total number of lines she had written (see ML ii. 314–15). Therefore, she may have had a considerable influence on the choice of poems to be printed. Her death, however, preceded the publication by almost eighteen months. In that time plans may have changed. One point is probable: Freemantle, not to mention Susanna Jennens, would have been reluctant to offend the Chauncys and other subscribers among the local gentry by putting forward the poems about Edgcote House. It is likely that these were not sent for publication until Edwards and Richardson decided on a second volume. If so, this seems a substantial concession to patronage. Without those pieces Leapor appears relatively innocuous; she is talented, perhaps tragic, but rarely challenging.

Other factors may also have been at work. It is known that Freemantle criticized 'An Essay on Woman' when it was written; apart from concern with Leapor's penmanship, it seems that she objected to the description of a miser and the reflections on wealth which follow. Leapor responds: 'Now to the Muses: I don't call them to fortify my Walls against Wealth itself, but against Wealth in such a Shape as we had then described; and you are not to think, that Poets, who love Ease and Pleasure, and the most gay Delights of Life, should hate the only Means of obtaining it' (ML ii. 309). This passage shows Leapor enthusiastic about the prospect of financial success while critical of certain attitudes towards money. It also shows that Freemantle sometimes misunderstood or disapproved of the social content in her friend's verses. If the exclusion of much social criticism from the first volume is to be understood, the strongest possibility is that Freemantle strove to present her friend to the publisher and to potential subscribers as talented, pious, and humble. Her desire to defend Leapor's posthumous reputation has already been discussed in relation to 'Mira's Picture'. It seems that she was uneasy about poems which even in the most literal sense made the poet look bad. If Freemantle portrayed Leapor as relatively docile, it must be said that the poet occasionally adopted obsequious postures herself. 'To Lucinda', because of its date, is an important indication that she saw a need to tone down her protests as she approached a polite readership. If there is ultimately too little information to determine precisely who decided to exclude much of Leapor's best work from the first volume, it is still very likely that this exclusion was related to the subscription.

Raymond Williams's assessment of Stephen Duck's collapse as a poet once he entered polite society has already been commented upon. Rayner Unwin has also touched upon the problem of patronage with relation to labouring poets:

When a figure such as Duck, amenable, respectful and flattering in his gratitude came to be transplanted from his native Wiltshire to mingle with the best society of the land, his mentors no longer questioned his right to such an elevation, but were immediately at pains to educate him to become an inconspicuous unit in his new social caste. As Duck had not solicited these changes, nor had struggled into this new society unaided, it was gratifying and philanthropic to assist him . . .[93]

Unwin is describing a real difficulty for labouring poets who could not pursue a career without some form of patronage. It is, however, a mistake to see Duck's experience as typical. Few labouring poets received so much patronage, either from individuals or by subscription. Furthermore, it must be recognized that Duck was psychologically fragile and might have collapsed even in ideal circumstances. Finally, that a poet has written a good poem does not always mean he or she is capable of another,

[93] Unwin, *The Rural Muse*, 53.

A Labouring Poet

and to read Duck's career as an arrested development may be sentimental. A 'paradigm' in this matter is hard to establish. While many labouring poets are almost servile towards their patrons, others move towards independence. Ann Yearsley is one example, though her talent was never pronounced. More valuable is James Woodhouse, who reversed the pattern of Duck's career. Born fourteen years after Mary Leapor, Woodhouse lived to the age of 85. His first volume of poems, published in 1764, is essentially a tribute to the gardening skills of his patron, William Shenstone. As he grew older he adopted more radical views, which at one point cost him a job. Poets were more likely to hold radical opinions towards the end of the century than in Stephen Duck's time; however, the following passage (c.1795) reveals a political consciousness which developed despite early patronage. He addresses landowners:

> Your Horses—Hounds—Yes Hogs— at board, and bed,
> Are better clothed—skreen'd, fenc'd, and lodg'd, and fed—
> Ev'n Farmer's Hog may fill his hungry maw,
> Well shelter'd take his rest on wholesome straw,
> Whilst labouring Boors may find more scanty draff,
> And lay tired limbs on stinking straw, or chaff!
> Princes and Peers, for Horses, or for Hounds,
> Expend, in mansions, twice ten thousand pounds;
> While those that furnish all, yield all defence,
> Crowd kraals that ne'er cost half ten thousand pence![94]

How a poet might respond to patronage was subject to a number of variables, including the character of the patron, the degree of support, the intellectual and political climate, and, above all, the psychological hardiness of the poet.[95]

As an economic structure, patronage had an effect on Leapor's poetry. Certainly, she was not inclined to trust herself to a system based on gifts and favours. While her social views were sometimes inconsistent, there is a real sense in which she made compromises

---

[94] James Woodhouse, 'The Life and Lucubrations of Crispinus Scriblerus', in *The Life and Poetical Works of James Woodhouse (1735–1820)*, ed. R. I. Woodhouse, 2 vols. (London, 1896), i. 58.

[95] See Betty Rizzo, 'The Patron as Poet Maker: The Politics of Benefaction', in *Studies in Eighteenth-Century Culture*, 20, Proceedings of the American Society for Eighteenth Century Studies, East Lansing, Mich.: Colleagues Press, (1990), 241–66. Rizzo makes a number of striking suggestions as to the possible motives of patrons of natural poets, and also examines the lot of the patronized poet.

for the sake of the subscription. How important these compromises were, and to what degree they were amplified by Freemantle or her editors and publishers, cannot be judged precisely on the evidence available. Had Leapor survived she might have burned some of her unpublished verses as she did her juvenilia. Alternatively, she might have published that material at a more propitious time. Her attitude towards individual patrons sets her beyond most of her contemporaries in defending the integrity of her work. The subscription provided an alternative to flattery and must surely have seemed to her the most manageable form of dependence.

CHAPTER 4

PRIMITIVISM AND EDUCATION

The cult of the primitive in eighteenth-century England had numerous manifestations: the Gothic fashion in literature, architecture, and landscape; ballad collecting, archaeology, and other forms of antiquarianism; an interest in undeveloped societies such as those of the South Sea Islanders, the American Indians, and the Eskimos; the peculiar fascination with people who had lived outside normal society, such as Peter the Wild Boy, who was found in a wood near Hanover and learned no more than a score of words in his lifetime, or Mlle Le Blanc, who was captured near the Marne living in a tree;[1] and, of course, Lord Monboddo's quest for a human being with a tail.

Oddities notwithstanding, this cult contributed substantially to the development of new attitudes towards originality, nature, and emotion in literature. Although the gap between primitivist

[1] See Chauncey Brewster Tinker, *Nature's Simple Plan: A Phase of Radical Thought in the Mid-Eighteenth Century* (Princeton, NJ: Princeton University Press, 1922; London: Humphrey Milford, Oxford University Press, 1922), 6–7. For standard works on primitivism, see A. O. Lovejoy, 'Monboddo and Rousseau', in *Essays in the History of Ideas* (Baltimore: The Johns Hopkins Press, 1948), 38–61; René Wellek, *A History of Modern Criticism 1750–1950*, 6 vols. (London: Jonathan Cape, 1955–86), vol. i: *The Later Eighteenth Century* (1955), esp. 105–32; M. H. Abrams, *The Mirror and the Lamp: Romantic Theory and the Critical Tradition* (Oxford: Oxford University Press, 1953), esp. 78–84; James M. Osborn, 'Spence, Natural Genius and Pope', *Philological Quarterly*, 45 (1966), 123–44; Walter Jackson Bate, *The Burden of the Past and the English Poet* (London: Chatto & Windus, 1971), esp. 47–54. See also Lois Whitney, *Primitivism and the Idea of Progress in English Popular Literature of the Eighteenth Century* (Baltimore: The Johns Hopkins Press, 1934); A. O. Lovejoy, Gilbert Chinard, George Boas, and Ronald S. Crane, gen. eds., *A Documentary History of Primitivism and Related Ideas*, 1 vol. only: A. O. Lovejoy and George Boas, *Primitivism and Related Ideas in Antiquity* (Baltimore: The Johns Hopkins Press, 1935); Samuel H. Monk, *The Sublime: A Study of Critical Theories in XVIII-Century England* (New York: Modern Language Association of America, 1935); Basil Willey, *The Eighteenth Century Background: Studies on the Idea of Nature in the Thought of the Period* (London: Chatto & Windus, 1940); Ernest Lee Tuveson, *The Imagination as a Means of Grace: Locke and the Aesthetics of Romanticism* (Berkeley and Los Angeles: University of California Press, 1960); Patricia Phillips, *The Adventurous Muse: Theories of Originality in English Poetics 1650–1760*, Studia Anglistica Upsaliensia, 53 (Uppsala: Uppsala University, 1984), esp. 66–106.

theory and actual literary practice was great, it became possible through claims of natural genius for labouring-class poets to command the interest of readers and critics of a higher class. Such claims, of course, usually distorted and, in some cases, entirely misrepresented, the efforts of these poets. This chapter will show that Mary Leapor's education, though haphazard and incomplete, was considerably greater than was admitted at the time of her publication. To describe her as a primitive or a natural genius is, in the final analysis, a mistake.

The primitive poet was thought to compose directly from nature, hence spontaneously, artlessly, and without forethought either of design or of audience.[2] The primitive poet was therefore unencumbered by tradition or textuality. Such a talent was already complete and could undergo no education or development. William Duff writes in *An Essay on Original Genius* (1767):

The truth is, a Poet of original Genius has very little occasion for the weak aid of Literature: he is self-taught. He comes into the world as it were completely accomplished. Nature supplies the materials of his compositions; his senses are the under-workmen, while Imagination, like a masterly Architect, superintends and directs the whole.[3]

That a natural poet had no need of books was a common claim. One critic, Thomas Blackwell, went so far as to argue that in the case of poets like Homer or Hesiod, the fewer books read the better. Blackwell's *An Enquiry into the Life and Writings of Homer* (1735) gives a fascinating description of the qualities associated with natural poetry:

But what marvellous Things happen in a well ordered State? We can hardly be surprised; We know the Springs and Method of acting; Every thing happens in Order, and according to Custom or Law. But in a wide Country, not under a regular Government, or split into many, whose Inhabitants live scattered, and ignorant of Laws and Discipline; In such a Country, the Manners are simple, and Accidents will happen every Day: Exposition and loss of Infants, Encounters, Escapes, Rescues, and every other thing that can inflame the human Passions while acting, or awake them when described, and recalled by Imitation.[4]

[2] Abrams, *The Mirror and the Lamp*, 83.
[3] William Duff, *An Essay on Original Genius* (London, 1767), 281–2.
[4] Thomas Blackwell, *An Enquiry into the Life and Writings of Homer* (London, 1735), 26–7.

Blackwell appears well insulated from the violence of his own time. The England which produced *Moll Flanders* or even *The Dunciad* ought to have satisfied any desire for extreme experience. A self-congratulating sense of modernity is fairly common in the early eighteenth century; what is thought lacking in emotional, cultural, and artistic experience is attributed to an expertise in living. René Wellek identifies among critics of the time a biological or organic view of history, according to which humanity develops from the childhood of earlier times to eventual old age and death.[5] According to such a view, the vigour of ancient times has given way to a less exuberant though more orderly and mature way of life. A writer such as Blackwell seems, on the one hand, ideologically assured about his own society: 'We know the Springs and Method of Acting'. On the other hand, he recognizes a narrowness and constraint in that culture.

Theories of primitivism, it could be argued, allowed writers, thinkers, and artists to deal with problems of disorder without seriously questioning their society. Primitivism explained and even sentimentalized those who lacked education or economic security. As with the pastoral myth, it could either obscure or bring into focus problems of social disadvantage. Even in its most blinkered forms, however, primitivism concentrated attention on people outside the élite, and made possible in some quarters a gradual increase in understanding.

The idea of inspired poets had a venerable history, but the primitivists of the eighteenth century were keen to find contemporary instances of natural genius. The great model in English was Shakespeare warbling 'his native wood-notes wild'. In 1767 Richard Farmer produced *An Essay on the Learning of Shakespeare*, by which he hoped to see the poet 'acquitted... of all piratical depredations on the Ancients:... his *Studies* were most demonstratively confined to *Nature* and *his own Language*'.[6] Mrs Montagu, who along with Hannah More later promoted Ann Yearsley, wrote of Shakespeare in 1769: 'Heaven-born genius acts from something superior to rules, and antecedent to rules;

---

[5] Wellek, *History of Modern Criticism*, 127–32; also useful is the discussion of Wellek's argument in Rizzo, 329–31.
[6] Richard Farmer, *An Essay on the Learning of Shakespeare* (Cambridge, 1767), 49.

and has a right of appeal to nature herself.'[7] Even where commentators avoid comparisons with Shakespeare and are generally more restrained, interest in a primitive poetic impulse is sometimes intense. Mark Akenside writes in *The Pleasures of the Imagination*:

> Ask the swain
> Who journeys homeward from a summer day's
> Long labour, why, forgetful of his toils
> And due repose, he loiters to behold
> The sunshine gleaming as thro' amber clouds,
> O'er all the western sky; full soon, I ween,
> His rude expression and untutor'd airs,
> Beyond the pow'r of language, will unfold
> The form of beauty smiling at his heart.[8]

Akenside hopes for great poetry from labourers, though he also sees a need for raw talent to be improved by culture. In view of such expectations, labouring poets were able to present themselves, or, at least, be presented to the public as natural geniuses.

Some labouring poets understood their own work in primitivist terms. Ann Yearsley writes 'To Mr. ****, an Unlettered Poet, on Genius Unimproved':

> FLORUS, canst thou define that innate spark
> Which blazes but for glory? Canst thou paint
> The trembling rapture in its infant dawn,
> Ere young Ideas spring; to local Thought
> Arrange the busy phantoms of the mind,
> And drag the distant timid shadows forth,
> Which, still retiring, glide unform'd away,
> Nor rush into expression? No; the pen,
> Tho' dipp'd in awful Wisdom's deepest tint,
> Can *never* paint the wild extatic mood.[9]

There is something strange about one supposedly natural poet writing to another in epistemological terms. It is difficult to believe that Yearsley has produced this self-conscious poem purely through inspiration rather than as a result of reading

---

[7] Elizabeth Montagu, *An Essay on the Writings and Genius of Shakespeare* (London, 1769), 7–8.

[8] Mark Akenside, *The Pleasures of the Imagination* (London, 1744), 119–20.

[9] Ann Yearsley, 'To Mr. ****, an Unlettered Poet, on Genius Unimproved', in *Poems, on Various Subjects*, (London, 1787), 77–8.

contemporary authors chosen by Hannah More. Yearsley wishes to appear learned, even as she boasts of the 'extatic mood'. James Woodhouse recalled with some resentment the role of natural genius:

> As tutor'd Bears are led from place, to place,
> Displaying biped gait, and burlesque grace;
> Their action clumsey, and their shape uncouth,
> While grunting bagpipe greets the gaping youth;
> And, with most solemn phiz, and upright air,
> Make witlings titter, whilst the ignorant stare—
> As dancing Dogs make Oafs and Children, swarm;
> Dress—mien—demeanour—all in human form—
> As Monkeys, rear'd erect, on paws, or breech,
> Well mimic Man in all but laugh, and speech—
> Or as, from street to street, queer Camel's shown,
> From other beasts, by pipe and tabor, known;
> Tho' seldom eye perceives a bungling brute
> Whose make, and motion, less with music suit;
> So was he sent the twofold City through,
> For Cits, like Swains, are pleas'd with something new,
> That each Subscriber's eyes might freely range,
> O'er Clown, so clever! Spectacle, so strange![10]

That an intelligent labouring person should be portrayed as a prodigy or a marvel is plain snobbery, yet it was a necessary part of the subscription process for the poet to face this humiliation. The primitivist movement increased the chances of publication for a poet of the labouring class, but it also obliged such a poet to assume a public identity which was not only humiliating but often deceptive.

Not all critics believed primitivist ideas. Samuel Johnson's amusing treatment of the subject in Chapter XXII of *Rasselas* is well known. Lord Kames in his *Elements of Criticism* (1762) argues for a universal standard of taste; however, he excludes from true taste the people for whom other commentators claimed natural genius: 'Those who depend for food on bodily labour, are totally void of taste; of such a taste at least as can be of use in the fine arts.'[11] Thus, the pose of natural genius, even where it was

[10] Woodhouse, ' The Life and Lucubrations of Crispinus Scriblerus', in *Life and Poetical Works*, i. 71–2.
[11] Henry Home, Lord Kames, *Elements of Criticism*, 2 vols. (9th edn., Edinburgh, 1817), ii. 446; cited by Wellek, *History of Modern Criticism*, 109.

assumed without deceit, was likely to impress only a part of the literary establishment.

Mary Leapor made it plain that she did not wish to be described in the subscription proposal, since that would excite the world's curiosity rather than its good nature (ML ii. 314). When that proposal appeared after her death there was strong emphasis on the defects in her education:

[She] had no other Education than in common with those of her own Station; could borrow no Helps from the Converse of her Country Companions; yet, by the Strength of her own Parts, the Vivacity of her own Genius, and a perpetual Pursuit after Knowledge, not only acquired a Taste for the most exalted and refined Authors in our Language, but aspired to imitate 'em.[12]

There is no deception here, except perhaps on the point of her 'Country Companions'. Evidently, this term refers to acquaintances of her own class, and not to the Jennens family or Bridget Freemantle from whose converse she certainly borrowed helps. The proposal, however, indicates that she read something beyond Alexander Pope and the Bible, for it combines a primitivist appeal to genius with an assertion that her natural parts had been improved by a knowledge of the best writers. Joseph Spence had provided Stephen Duck with a reading list of good authors, as Shenstone was to do for Woodhouse, and More for Yearsley. It seems that, despite the more extreme theoretical claims concerning natural genius, few of those who promoted such geniuses actually subscribed to a pure primitivism. It was common to attempt some reconciliation of those theories with a more neo-classical conception of literature. Nonetheless, the note to Leapor's first volume attempts to minimize her reading: 'Mrs. *Leapor* from a Child delighted in reading, and particularly Poetry, but had few Opportunities of procuring any Books of that kind' (ML i. 3). Freemantle compounds this impression when she observes that Leapor's whole library consisted of sixteen or seventeen volumes (ML ii, p. xxxii). In 1754 John Duncombe, though not an extreme primitivist, provided the obligatory comparison between Leapor, the natural poet, and Shakespeare, in his *Feminiad*.[13] In his letter

---

[12] *Proposals For Printing by Subscription The Poetical Works, Serious and Humorous, Of Mrs. Leapor, lately Deceased.*

[13] Duncombe, *The Feminiad*, 20–1.

to the *Gentleman's Magazine*, he implied the same comparison: 'Molly Leapor . . . was a most extraordinary uncultivated genius, who "warbled her native wood-notes wild".' As apologists for her work, Freemantle, Duncombe, and, to a lesser degree, the author of the proposals (presumably Garrick), portray Leapor in terms which minimize her opportunities of learning. This, obviously, is not a literary fraud on the scale of the 'Rowley' poems or *Ossian*, yet it is a distortion that must be corrected.

That Mary Leapor had few of the characteristics of the natural poet envisaged by literary theorists of the day is certain. Betty Rizzo argues this point vigorously:

But the truth about Leapor is that though she was different from those educated poets suffering from the anxiety Bate expresses as 'What is there left to do?' the difference is not what the public supposed. In fact, Leapor, like the other primitives, knew exactly what was left to do: she had to catch up, make up for lost time, follow Pope and learn to write like him. She was overwhelmed with an anxiety, not the anxiety of influence but the anxiety *for* influence. (Rizzo, 332)

This point is absolutely essential for an understanding of Leapor. From 'To Lucinda', 'Mopsus', and 'A Summer's Wish', Rizzo demonstrates that Leapor was unhappy with her lack of education, and that she used her poetry to moderate her ambitions and her emotional excesses. Rizzo's argument opens another issue that is crucial to Leapor's poetry: whereas Leapor is a formidable social critic, she none the less affirms many of the central values of her culture. As an intellectual, she recognized that Pope, Swift, Gay, Addison, Steele, and other leading writers of her time embodied a tradition of learning. Her attitude towards that tradition was fundamentally respectful. She wished to put on the mind of her culture, and that could only be achieved by extensive reading.

There is an aspect of Leapor's poetry that Rizzo overlooks. Following Freemantle, Duncombe, and others, Rizzo asserts that 'she was probably as primitive a poet as one could find: uneducated, without free access to many books, without much conversation, consigned to a station designed to be unacquainted with such things' (Rizzo, 338). From 'Epistle to Artemisia. On Fame', it is evident that Leapor knew a number of aspiring poets, and discussed writing with them. The folder of manuscript poems preserved at Weston Hall only confirms the internal evidence that she was not deprived of literary acquaintances, even if their attainments were limited. More importantly, there is a large number of references in her poetry to books she has read. Indeed, there is solid internal evidence, supported by some small pieces of external evidence, that Leapor had read some works of classical literature, and many contemporary authors.

Bridget Freemantle's letter contains a curious defence of Leapor's originality:

Since the Publication of her Poems, I hear she has been accused of stealing from other Authors; but I believe very unjustly, and imagine the Censure proceeds rather from a random Conjecture that it must be so, than any just Foundation. I don't find that the Particulars are pointed out; and if there are really any Lines in her Book that bear so near a Resemblance to what has been wrote by other Authors, as to give room for such a Conjecture, I, that was so well acquainted with her Way of Thinking, dare venture to answer for her, that it proceeded from the Impression the Reading those Passages some time before happen'd to make upon her Mind, without her remembring from whence they came; and therefore she can no more be reckon'd a Plagiary on that Account, than a Person could justly be accused of being a Thief, for making use of a Shilling or two of another's Money that happen'd to be mix'd with his own, without his knowing it.

Besides, I don't believe it impossible for two People to think exactly alike upon a Subject, and even to express themselves almost in the very same Words for a Line or two, without ever having been acquainted with one another's Thoughts; tho' I don't know that this was the Case of *Myra*. (ML ii, pp. xxiii–xxiv)

Freemantle takes the charge of plagiarism seriously. It was, of course, a common occurrence in the eighteenth century for a new author to be accused of some imposture. Indeed, according to Janet Todd, women writers were the particular object of this kind of scepticism.[14] Many women produced poems defending themselves against the charge that they could not have written their own works. Mary Masters, for example, attempted to answer doubts about a psalm she had versified:

> But still the Poem, howsoe'er design'd,
> Is a true Picture of the Author's Mind.

[14] Todd, Preface and Acknowledgements, in *A Dictionary of British and American Women Writers 1660–1800*, p. xx.

> Whate'er I write, whatever I impart,
> Is simple Nature unimprov'd by Art.
> Search but those Strains, you think so much excel,
> Scan ev'ry Verse, and try the Numbers well:
> You'll plainly see, in almost ev'ry Line,
> Distinguishing Defects to prove them Mine.[15]

Masters often apologizes for her incapacity as a poet. Here she gives voice to a sense of inferiority underlying the work of many natural poets. She claims that the poem must be hers since it is basically incompetent.

The accusation of plagiarism against Leapor should not be dismissed out of hand. Whoever made the charge was probably aware of the number of echoes and allusions in her writing. To describe this as plagiarism is, as Freemantle observes, unjust. Leapor often refers to major writers in order to disagree with them. Moreover, it is a long-established strategy among poets to rework passages by other authors. What Leapor borrows she usually changes. She does little for which she could not have found a sanction in Pope's 'An Essay on Criticism'. Nevertheless, the accusation is interesting since it suggests that some readers found Leapor's credentials as a natural poet or original genius suspect even at the time of publication. Defending Leapor, Freemantle implies that the poet read widely enough to forget where particular lines or passages came from. Had Leapor lived and allowed herself to be described as an original genius, she might have faced the sort of embarrassment that overtook Burns as the extent of his reading became known. In 'To Lucinda' she does in fact assume the role of the uncultivated poet; therefore, her humility about her education could easily have been taken as an attempt to deceive, even if that was not her intention. Given what now seems the fragility of primitivist thinking, it is surprising that there were not even more scandals associated with the movement.

Leapor's Education and Reading

To assess Leapor's early education is difficult. It is probable, as Betty Rizzo observes, that she attended the school in Brackley

---

[15] Mary Masters, 'To the Gentleman who questioned my being the Author of the foregoing Verses', in *Poems on Several Occasions* (London, 1733), 45.

run by a Mr Cooper (Rizzo, 314–15), that is, the Magdalen Free School. This establishment may have resembled the one attended by Mopsus: 'His father plac'd him in a Country School, | To learn *Division*, and the *Golden Rule*...' (ML ii. 11). Victor E. Neuburg describes a typical school in the eighteenth century: 'For the children of the poor who could pay a trifling weekly fee, some sort of education could be acquired at the random, private-venture establishments set up by, perhaps, a "dame" or an old soldier —almost anyone, in fact, who was unsuccessful or incapable in any other sphere of activity.'[16] A private-venture school would have followed the same method as the charity schools in which, according to M. G. Jones, children were taught first to read and later to write; they were taught arithmetic only when the other skills had been perfected.[17] Keith Thomas argues that even in the eighteenth century it was not uncommon for people to read print, sometimes only black letter, without learning to write.[18] Leapor herself had poor handwriting, probably as a result of this emphasis on teaching students above all to read. Richard Cooper was, however, an able and committed teacher (Clarke, 146–7). Leapor was doubtless better than most pupils. It is conceivable that she received extra attention. Cooper was not only a teacher but a bookbinder, and may have allowed her to read the books in his possession. Her interest in the law, a point which will be returned to, may also have originated with him, since he supplemented his income by taking wills (Eland, ii. 288).

Cooper did not run the only school in Brackley. There was also the public school run by Magdalen College, Oxford, and a small academy operated by the vicar, Thomas Bowles. Betty Rizzo considers the possibility that Elizabeth Lisle Bowles, the vicar's wife, took an interest in Mary Leapor (Rizzo, 322). A close connection between Leapor and the Bowles family would be particularly interesting with respect to her education. One of the

---

[16] Victor E. Neuburg, *Popular Literature: A History and Guide from the Beginning of Printing to the Year 1897* (Harmondsworth: Penguin, 1977), 106; see also Neuburg's *Popular Education in Eighteenth Century England* (London: Woburn Press, 1971).

[17] M. G. Jones, *The Charity School Movement: A Study of Eighteenth Century Puritanism in Action* (Cambridge: Cambridge University Press, 1938), 80.

[18] Keith Thomas, 'The Meaning of Literacy in Early Modern England', in Gerd Baumann (ed.), *The Written Word: Literacy in Transition*, The Wolfson College Lectures, 1985 (Oxford: Clarendon Press, 1986), 99–102.

vicar's main scholarly projects was to replace Lily's Latin grammar, which had been in use since 1548: 'that the Roman Dialect may be no longer the slow and ungrateful Production of Force, Drudgery, and servile Punishments, the long-prevailing Obscurities of former Ages are clear'd'.[19] Bowles appears a humane teacher. The first edition of his grammar, *A Compendious and Rational Institution of the Latin Tongue*, was published in 1740. Since Leapor would have seen Bowles at least every Sunday, it is hard to imagine that she would not have known he had published this book, or that she would not have gone out of her way to obtain a copy and read it. If she was a friend, or even a protégée, of Elizabeth Lisle Bowles, then she would certainly have read the book.

There is not much evidence that Leapor actually learned Latin. As Betty Rizzo argues, however, she did feel the need to catch up, to fill the gaps in her learning. That she did not know Latin or Greek would have seemed an important gap, as Chesterfield wrote to his son: 'the word *illiterate* in its common acceptation means a man who is ignorant of those two languages'.[20] Whether Leapor learned Latin or, as is likely, read the major authors in translation, Bowles's grammar would have been an excellent guide. At the end of the volume there is a short, lucid essay on each important Roman author. For example, he writes of Virgil:

His Pastorals describe that innocent Simplicity which was the Blessing of the first Ages of the World, and which he has supported by rural Scenes, Songs and Music, Omens of Birds, Comparisons, and all such Ideas as are common to a pastoral Life. His Georgics reconcile the most lively and ornamental Parts of Poetry with the Simplicity of the plain and common Precepts of Agriculture; and not only instruct in rural Affairs, but furnish the attentive Mind with many excellent Improvements in Arts and Sciences. Industry and Sobriety, the Love of one's Country, and a Religious Frame of Mind, are every where inculcated . . .[21]

What Edmund Blunden calls Leapor's sense of completeness of form when she varies from the standard couplet may owe

---

[19] Thomas Bowles, Preface, *Aristarchus: Or, A Compendious and Rational Institution of the Latin Tongue* (Oxford, 1740; rev. edn., 1748), p. iv. The earlier edition did not include the preface from which the quotation is taken.

[20] Philip Dormer Stanhope, *The Letters of the Earl of Chesterfield to his Son*, ed. Charles Strachey, 2 vols. (London, 1901), i. 230; cited by Thomas, 'The Meaning of Literacy', 101.

[21] Bowles, *A Compendious and Rational Institution of the Latin Tongue*, 105.

something to Bowles's book, since it also contains chapters on versification and scanning. The grammar is, however, a very brief affair, and it is most likely that it would have provided Leapor with no more than a smattering of Latin, and an over-view of the literature.

Leapor's reading of the classics cannot have been systematic. For example, she writes to Bridget Freemantle about her preference for the Apocrypha, especially the prayer of Manasses, over some classical authors:

> The style is pleasant, and has something in it of modern Eloquence; and those agreeable Repetitions awaken the Readers Attention, and leave a pleasing Anguish on the Mind. In the Whole, it is the perfect Picture of a wounded Soul: And *Manasses* in his Chains and Afflictions, is a greater Favourite of mine, than all the *Caesars*, *Cicero*, or *Cato* himself.
>
> I would beg of you, if you please, to send me the rest of the *Odyssey*; for I long to know the End of the Fable; and I have Leisure To-day from dirty Work. (ML ii. 320)

Although it is remarkable that by the last year of her life Leapor had not yet read through Homer, this letter suggests that she was indeed accustomed to wide reading. Freemantle appears to have been worried that she would borrow time from her other responsibilities to read Homer. A letter that follows the one quoted above, and was probably written on the same day, though the two are separated by the editor or printer, responds to Freemantle's misgivings: 'I thank you for your kind Admonition: Yet I believe you mistook my Intention; which was not to meditate upon *Homer*, but, out of an excessive Curiosity (peculiar to my Temper), to know the latter End; tho' I intend to read and digest him at a more proper time' (ML ii. 313).

This letter reveals something of Freemantle's position regarding the poet. On the one hand, she supplies books and encourages her friend's intellectual development. On the other hand, she is intent that Leapor should fulfil her obligations. Other references suggest that these letters were written around August 1746, the busiest month for farmers and their families. It is likely that Freemantle did not wish to be the cause of the poet annoying her father. A basic point confirmed by these letters is that Leapor was able to borrow books from Freemantle. It appears that she had read the *Iliad* some time earlier, for there are several brief references to that epic in her poetry. The most substantial occurs in 'Soto', a character of a drunk. Soto disgorges two gallons of beer and falls asleep:

> Down drops the Youth, his giddy Head
> Falls easy on the liquid Bed:
> So swam *Achilles* fierce and brave,
> On angry *Xanthus*'s swelling Wave;
> And 'scap'd with being wet to th' Skin;
> For *Pallas* held him up by th' Chin:
> So *Bacchus* saves, by mighty Charms,
> His helpless Devotee from Harms . . .   (ML i. 177)

Roger Lonsdale notes that these lines allude to the eleventh book of the *Iliad* (*ECWP*, 526 n).

Homer was not the only Greek poet whom Leapor read. In the last stanza of 'An Hymn to the Morning' there is, of course, the reference to Sappho's sweeter song (ML i. 25). Leapor might have encountered some of Sappho's verse in several translations. Pope's version of 'Sappho to Phaon' is a strong possibility. Ambrose Philips also translated some of Sappho's poems, and his version of 'A Hymn to Venus' appeared in *The Spectator*, no. 223, while no. 229 compared translations of the 'Ode to Lesbia', by Catullus, Boileau, and Philips. Edmund Blunden sees in 'The Month of August' evidence that Leapor may have read Theòcritus, perhaps in 'the hearty, homely translation by Creech'.[22] While there are no direct references to Theocritus, and no obvious allusions or echoes in Leapor's text, there are enough similarities in tone for Blunden's observation to be at least plausible.

Leapor alludes to Roman poets in several places. In 'The Proclamation of Apollo' she describes a feast which makes repast of Homer's song, and 'Next *Virgil* on the Table Shines, I And then smooth *Ovid*'s tender Lines' (ML i. 46). There is another reference to Virgil in 'An Epistle to Artemisia. On Fame'. Leapor alludes to the personification of fame in the fourth book of the *Aeneid*:

> Bold *Maro* paints her of gigantic Size,
> And makes her Forehead prop the lofty Skies;
> With Eyes and Ears he hung the Lady round,
> And her shrill Clarion shook the Heavens around . . .   (ML ii. 43)

---

[22] Blunden, 'A Northamptonshire Poetess', 65; see also Thomas Creech, *The Idylliums of Theocritus* (Oxford, 1684).

Leapor probably knew Ovid and Virgil from a volume of Dryden's translations (1701) in the library at Weston Hall (see Appendix). She refers to one other Roman poet, albeit indirectly: 'Upon her Play being returned to her, stained with Claret' is based on Horace's familiar poem 'To his Book'. There was, of course, a long tradition of poets addressing their books in the manner of Horace, and it cannot be assumed that she had actually read this or any other of Horace's works. As a reader of Alexander Pope, however, she must have known something about Horace. Her own interest in the epistle form if not a result of reading Horace, would surely have led her to seek out this author.

Leapor shows some knowledge of classical prose writers. In 'An Imperfect Scene', which was to be included in *The Unhappy Father*, Lucy describes how Lycander took advantage of her: 'He first seduc'd me from my native Home, | With Vows of Friendship, and *Platonic* Love...' (ML ii. 223). In 'The Mistaken Lover', the story of deception in love is seen as a lesson for young men and women:

> ''Twill help to make our *Strephons* wise,
> And stop the Growth of tender Lies:
> And more than *Plato*'s moral Page
> Instruct the *Celia*'s of the Age.'   (ML i. 89)

In the letter quoted above, Leapor mentions three Roman prose writers whom she has read. The standard translation of Caesar's writings at the time was that of Martin Bladen.[23] Cicero's works could be had in a number of translations. Cato the Censor's writings, however, were not widely available in translation, and Leapor may only be referring to Addison's play about Cato of Utica. In 'The Sow and the Peacock' she humorously describes the intellectual attainments of the pig: 'Philosophy she had good Store, | Had ponder'd *Seneca* all o'er...' (ML i. 180). Her knowledge of Seneca probably came from Roger L'Estrange's book, *Seneca's Morals By Way of Abstract & Discourse*, a volume which is in the library of Weston Hall.

Leapor's knowledge of the classics was probably patchy, at best. Discounting the possibility that she knew Latin or, even less likely, Greek, her experience of classical writers would have been

---

[23] Martin Bladen, trans., *Julius Caesar's Commentaries* (London, 1705).

filtered through the sensibilities of their translators, and reworked according to contemporary tastes in literature. Indeed, a very significant part of what she read would have been translated by Pope, Dryden, and, to a lesser extent, Philips, authors whose English works were among the main influences on her own verse. Her reading of the classics may not have provided a sharp contrast to the literature of her own time. Still, her reading was not necessarily limited to those authors mentioned in her poems. The library at Weston Hall contains English versions of Josephus, Plutarch, Juvenal, and Lucretius, which Leapor may have read even though she makes no allusion to them in her poetry. She may have wanted to make a show of erudition in her poetry, but she probably did not drop every name she knew.

Leapor's knowledge of English writers is much wider than her knowledge of the classics, as we would expect. Here, again, it is possible to trace a pattern of allusions and echoes. Her reading concentrated on authors from the Restoration to her own time, doubtless because these books were more easily obtained than earlier ones. There are, naturally, references to Chaucer and Shakespeare. 'The Fox and the Hen' is a rewriting of 'The Nun's Priest's Tale', complete with a fox named Reynard and a hen called Partlet (ML i. 97–100). There is also a reference to Chanticleer in 'Mopsus' (ML ii. 24). It is likely that Leapor knew this tale from the translation by Dryden at Weston Hall, although she may simply have read it from a chap-book. If this is so, she seems aware also of the antiquity of the tale. The hen addresses the fox:

> 'From long ago, (or Record lies)
> You Foxes have been counted wise:
> But sure this Story don't agree
> With your Device of eating me.'   (ML i. 99)

Leapor knows that Reynard's hen-house depredations have been going on for a very long time.

She may have read a great deal of Shakespeare. *The Unhappy Father*, for example, is indebted to *Othello*, with Leonardo, cast in the role of Iago, provoking Eustathius to a rage of jealousy in which he kills his wife, who is called Emilia like Iago's wife in Shakespeare's play. The names of Lycander and Polonius are borrowed respectively from *A Midsummer Night's Dream* and *Hamlet*. As noted in Chapter 3, 'On Winter' echoes the closing lines of *Love's Labour's Lost*. The library at Weston Hall contains a full set of Pope's edition of Shakespeare.

Leapor certainly read *Paradise Lost*. In *The Unhappy Father*, Leonardo speaks the following lines:

> So the grand Foe of human Kind, like me,
> Arriv' d within fair *Eden*'s blissful Bounds;
> There felt, like me, the keen alternate Pangs
> Of Admiration, Hatred, and Despair.
> Alike our Aim; both Mischief, his and mine.
> No Matter; I have lost the Sense of Joy,
> Excepting this,—To breed Dissension here.   (ML ii. 164)

This is an unmistakable reference to the fourth book of the epic. Since Milton's works enjoyed a huge circulation after the subscribed edition of 1688, it would be surprising if Leapor had not read them. The copy of *Paradise Lost* at Weston Hall is the first edition, second issue; it seems that the literary tastes of the Blencowe and Jennens families were something more than middle-brow. Outside her plays Leapor uses blank verse only in 'The Fields of Melancholy and Chearfulness' (ML i. 145–53); her preference for rhyme, especially the heroic couplet, indicates that influence from *Paradise Lost* in terms of technique was limited. Interestingly, almost two-thirds of 'The Fields of Melancholy and Chearfulness' is a meditation on death:

> Complaining Sounds were heard on ev'ry Side,
> And each bewail'd the loss of something dear:
> Some mourn'd a Child that in its Bloom expir'd,
> And some a Brother's or a Parent's Fate:
> Lost Wealth and Honours many Tongues deplor'd,
> And some were wretched, tho' they knew not why.   (ML i. 146–7)

The use of blank verse as well as the basic gloominess of the poem points not so much to Milton as to a reading of Edward Young or Robert Blair.

Among the volumes which Leapor herself owned was a copy of Dryden's *Fables*. It is perhaps superfluous to observe that a number of her poems are also fables, and in large measure indebted to Dryden and Gay. Her probable debt to Dryden's translations has already been observed. Among the volumes of plays in her possession, it is likely that some were by Dryden, though there is no indication of which ones. At Weston Hall there is a six-volume set of Dryden's *Miscellany Poems*, another six-volume set of his *Dramatic Works*, and a copy of his *Fables*. Congreve would have been an obvious choice of reading for an aspiring playwright, and it could be argued that the closing scene of *The Unhappy Father* is based on *The Mourning Bride*, in which Almeria attempts to poison herself, having heard that her suitor, Alphonso, has been killed. In Leapor's play Terentia likewise considers drinking a cup of poison after hearing that Polonius has been devoured by a shark. In both plays the heroines are prevented from killing themselves at the last moment by the return of the man supposedly dead. While cups of poison are not uncommon in seventeenth- and eighteenth-century drama, the parallels between the two plays are sufficient to suggest that Leapor had read Congreve. It should also be noted that Leapor gave one of her poems the title 'The Way of the World'. There is a copy of *The Works of Congreve* (1719) at Weston Hall. Leapor's plays show similarities also to the works of Nicholas Rowe. Betty Rizzo notes the resemblances between her treatment of women and this playwright's domestic tragedies.[24] Apart from a passage from 'The Fair Penitent' which seems to be echoed in Emilia's speech on the lot of women, Leapor writes an entire poem, 'The Temple of Love', about a dream which follows a reading of 'Jane Shore'. Although it is possible that she knew the story in chapbook form, the phrase 'I read the Scenes of *Shore*'s deluded Wife' (ML i. 162), indicates that she was reading the play. There is an edition of Rowe's *Dramatick Works* (1720) at Weston Hall. The plot of *The Unhappy Father* owes something also to Otway's 'The Orphan', in which a young woman, Monimia, lives in a country house under the care of an ageing guardian whose two sons compete for her love. Although Leapor does not follow Otway in allowing the young woman to be tricked into a loss of virginity, Terentia's circumstances at the beginning of the play are very likely modelled on those of Monimia. There is a set of *The Works of Mr. Otway* (1722) at Weston.

Finally, Leapor's unfinished play about the Saxon king Edwy may be partly modelled on Thomson's and Mallet's *Alfred* or Thomson's *Edward and Eleonora*. Leapor's play, however, does

---

[24] Rizzo, 'Leapor, Mary', in Todd. (ed.), *A Dictionary of British and American Women Writers 1660–1800*, 192.

not share the topicality of these works. It also contains references to Addison's *Cato*. At one point Elgiva cries, 'O! for the Constancy of *Cato*'s Daughter!' (ML ii. 238) When the soldier Dusterandus speaks of ravishing Emmel, he echoes Sempronius, who has designs upon Marcia, Cato's daughter:

> How will my Bosom swell with anxious Joy,
> When I behold her strugling in my Arms,
> With glowing Beauty, and disorder'd Charms,
> While Fear and Anger, with alternate Grace,
> Pant in her Breast, and vary in her Face![25]

If there is any truth in the claim of Corydon in 'Mira's Picture' that Mira 'sits whole Ev'nings, reading wicked Plays' (ML ii. 297), Leapor must have read a great number. Those that can be identified by allusions, echoes, or parallels, may be the ones she most admired and strove to imitate. Since she wrote only tragedies, her reading of comedies is difficult to pursue, yet comedies are surely the more 'wicked' form, and may, if Corydon is believed, have constituted a large part of her reading.

Leapor refers to a number of minor poets from the Restoration and the early part of her own century. She writes in 'An Epistle to Artemisia. On Fame' of one of her visitors:

> Comes *Codrus* next, with Talents to offend;
> A simple Tutor, and a saucy Friend,
> Who pour'd thick Sonnets like a troubled Spring,
> And such as *Butler*'s wide-mouth'd Mortals sing:
> In shocking Rhimes a Nymph's Perfections tells,
> Like the harsh Ting-Tong of some Village-Bells.   (ML ii. 51)

This is an allusion to Whachum, who serves as versifier to the cunning man Sidrophel in *Hudibras*:

> He serv' d his *Master*,
> In quality of *Poetaster*:
> And *Rimes* appropriate could make,
> To ev'ry month in th' *Almanack*,
> When *Termes* begin, and end, could tell,
> With their *Returns*, in Doggerel.
>   . . . . . .
> His *Sonnets* charm'd th'attentive Crowd,
> By wide-mouth'd Mortal trol'd aloud,

---

[25] Joseph Addison, *Cato: A Tragedy* (London, 1713), 43-4.

> That, circled with his long ear'd Guests,
> Like *Orpheus* look'd, among the Beasts...²⁶

Leapor's debt to Samuel Butler bears further attention. Her poem 'Mopsus' depicts a comic knight-errantry which recalls *Hudibras*. Leapor's poem is written in heroic couplets rather than octosyllabics, yet she draws directly from *Hudibras* in the figure of Sir Sidrophel, an astrologer hired by Viscount Simper:

> A sage he *hir'd*, whose deeply-thoughtful Skull
> Could teach the Vulgar when the Moon was full;
> Who scatter'd Hate among the friendly Stars,
> And made e'en *Venus* retrograde to *Mars*.   (ML ii. 32)

Sidrophel offers Mopsus advice supposedly garnered from the stars, on his prospects in marriage. In Butler's poem, Sidrophel offers similar counsel to the hero:

> You are in *Love*, Sir, with a *Widdow*,
> Quoth he, that does not greatly heed you;
> And for three years has rid your *Wit*
> And *Passion* without drawing *Bit*:
> And now your bus'ness is, to know
> If you shall carry her, or no.²⁷

Leapor was somewhat uneasy about Hudibrastics. In a letter to Freemantle she describes 'Mopsus' as 'a kind of popular Piece' (ML ii. 316); evidently she saw this poem as something less than 'polite'. Certainly, to mock astrologers and almanacs is to dismiss a great deal of popular literature—but even to parody astrologers and chap-book romances in the manner of Butler is, in Leapor's view, to be writing at a popular level. Still, it may be judged that Leapor understood her own role as a poet partly in terms drawn from Samuel Butler. In an octosyllabic piece, 'The Epistle of Deborah Dough', she compares herself to a local cunning man: 'But there's a Man that keeps a Dairy, | Will clip the Wings of Neighbour *Mary*...' (ML ii. 69). This man is a writer of verses, but more like Whachum than Mira:

> some People would infer
> That this good Man's a Conjurer.

---

²⁶ Samuel Butler, 'The Second Part: Canto III', in *Hudibras*, ed. John Wilders (Oxford: Clarendon Press, 1967), 162–3.   ²⁷ Ibid. 168.

> But I believe it is a Lye;
> I never thought him so; not I:
> Tho' *Win'fred Hobble*, who, you know,
> Is plagu'd with Corns on ev'ry Toe,
> Sticks on his Verse with fast'ning Spittle,
> And says it helps her Feet a little.
> Old *Frances* too his Paper tears,
> And tucks it close behind her Ears;
> And (as she told me t'other Day)
> It charm'd her Tooth-ach quite away. (ML ii. 70–1)

Leapor, in this poem, considers the role of the poet in popular culture. If in relation to landscape improvement Leapor makes a stand within popular culture, here, despite the humour, she shows herself to be alienated from that culture. Indeed, it appears that a reading of Samuel Butler has helped her to define herself as a poet.

Leapor refers to another supposedly popular writer in 'The Proposal'. The muse addresses Mira about the plan for her to publish in magazines, where her verses will not be appreciated by 'drowsy Swains | . . . Protesting with a Critick's Spite, | That none since *Durfey* knew to write' (ML i. 174). Thomas D'Urfey (1653–1723), author of many dramatic and poetic works, was often the butt of literary jokes, and Leapor's reference to him shows her own desire to identify with refined authors. Her knowledge of him may have come from the volume of his *Tales* (1704) at Weston Hall, though his works were very widely circulated and she may have known him from many sources.

Another poem suggesting the extent of Leapor's reading is 'Proserpine's Ragout', which, as a descent into the underworld, follows a long tradition of poems based on Lucian. One possible model is Edward Ward's 'A Journey to Hell', which examines dozens of social problems, many of which Leapor summarizes in the last section of her poem. That Leapor may have read Ward's poem is suggested by another possible echo; she writes in 'The Penitent' concerning the sale of her poems: 'Now, could you find an honest Dealer, | As an Attorney or a Taylor . . .' (ML i. 120). In 'The Inspir'd Quill' she again refers to lawyers:

> To some Attorney let me go,
> For there my Talents suit (you know)

> Heroicks I shall write but ill;
> But I'm a Doctor at a Bill... (ML i. 118)

There were two lawyers in Brackley, a father and son named John Welchman; their reputations were dubious, especially the father's, though they were certainly not tailors. More likely, Leapor is thinking of these lines from 'A Journey to Hell', describing tailors who

> After long Troubles did themselves withdraw,
> From making Sutes of Cloaths, to manage Suits of Law:
> Well knowing it requires an equal Skill,
> To make a Lawyer's or a Taylor's Bill.[28]

Though not conclusive, the similar rhymes and the association of lawyers and tailors suggest that Leapor was thinking of Ward's poem.

Another poet who used the device of a satirical descent into Hell was William King. That Leapor knew some of King's poems is probable; one of her own invitation verses is entitled 'To Artemisia. Dr. King's Invitation to Bellvill: imitated'. Unfortunately, this poem has proved difficult to trace, as it does not appear in William King's collections, or among the works of the younger William King of Oxford, or those of Henry King. Leapor's descriptions of cooking, although drawn from her own immediate experience, probably owe something to King's 'The Art of Cookery'. It is worth noting that Margaret Doody believes Leapor's kitchen imagery derives from Swift.[29] That does not exclude a reading of King. Indeed, 'Proserpine's Ragout', which is both a descent into the underworld and a cooking poem, at least suggests a reading of this poet.

An author Leapor obviously admires is mentioned along with Pope in 'The Muses Embassy':

> The Muses, as some Authors say,
> Who found their Empire much Decay,
> Since *Prior*'s Lute was stopp'd by Death,
> And *Pope* resign'd his tuneful Breath... (ML ii. 276)

In her letters Leapor refers to two contemporary authors, Colley Cibber (ML ii. 312), to whom she sent her play, and Stephen

---

[28] Ward, 'A Journey to H——: Or, A Visit Paid to the D——', in *Works*, iii. 25.
[29] Doody, 'Swift among the Women', 82.

Duck, whose career she discusses in relation to her own subscription (ML ii. 314). There are two volumes of *Plays Written by Mr. Cibber* (1721) at Weston, but no volume of Stephen Duck. It is probable nonetheless that she had read both authors. Betty Rizzo observes the connection between Leapor's 'Colinetta', and the pastorals of Ambrose Philips.[30] Philips's shepherd Colinet appears in his second and fourth pastorals; Leapor alters the name to Colinetta for her shepherdess, and follows Philips in the use of images from English rural life. Leapor's poem 'On Winter' is, of course, modelled on Philips's 'Winter Piece' (see Chapter 3 above).

The folder of manuscript poems at Weston Hall contains transcripts of poems by Mary Wortley Montagu and Mary Astell on the death of Mrs Bowles. This is interesting, since it indicates that both authors were known to Susanna Jennens and probably to Mary Leapor, although there are no copies of their works in the library. Since Leapor does not name any female writers in her own works, it is valuable to know where she might have derived her views on issues of gender. That she should have developed her arguments on the rights of women, as well as a rhetoric to articulate those ideas, suggests that she read other women writers as well, though there is no easy way of proving this. One possibility is that she read the pamphlets of 'Sophia', but the only support for this is that the passage from Nicholas Rowe which lies behind Emilia's long speech in *The Unhappy Father* also appears on the title-page of *Woman Not Inferior to Man* (1739). Since it is almost certain that Leapor read Rowe's works for herself, the connection with 'Sophia' is no more than tenuous.

A poet of the mid-eighteenth century with limited access to books would be expected to read Swift before most other authors. Margaret Anne Doody has made a very reasonable case for Swift as a major influence on Leapor's work, particularly on 'The Mistaken Lover'. A reading of Swift presumably also lies behind poems like 'On Patience. To Stella' and 'On Discontent. To Stella'. Even without direct allusions, it may be taken for granted that Leapor read *Gulliver's Travels*, if only in chap-book form, since it was one of the most widely circulated books of the time.

Leapor makes no direct reference to John Gay. Yet her own

---

[30] Rizzo, 'Christopher Smart, The "C.S." Poems, and Molly Leapor's Epitaph', 26.

Primitivism and Education 179

taste for fables makes it more than probable that she read his fables as well as those of Dryden. None of her own fables is closely based on Gay's. That she read some part of his works, however, is beyond question. The following passage from 'The Mistaken Lover' has a strong resemblance to a passage in 'The Fan'. Leapor describes the behaviour of an amorous beau:

>He purchas'd all the Songs of Note,
>And got the Lover's Cant by rote:
>He brib'd her Footmen and her Maids,
>And with his nightly Serenades
>Her vaulted Roofs and Gardens rung:
>For her he ogled, danc'd and sung;
>Was often at her Toilet seen,
>With Sonnets to the *Paphian* Queen:
>Then at her Feet dejected lying,
>Praying, weeping, sighing, dying.   (ML i. 82–3)

Gay's Strephon does much the same:

>*Strephon* had long confess'd his am'rous Pain,
>Which gay *Corinna* rally'd with Disdain:
>Sometimes in broken Words he sigh'd his Care,
>Look'd pale, and trembled when he view'd the Fair;
>With bolder Freedoms now the Youth advanc'd,
>He dress'd, he laugh'd, he sung, he rhim'd, he danc'd;
>Now call'd more pow'rful Presents to his Aid,
>And to seduce the Mistress, brib'd the Maid;
>Smooth Flatt'ry in her softer Hours apply'd,
>The surest Charm to bind the force of Pride:
>But still unmov'd remains the scornful Dame,
>Insults her Captive, and derides his Flame.[31]

The lines which follow this contain a lengthy appeal to Venus. Evidently Leapor has rewritten the passage in a different metre to suit the purposes of her own poem.

As might be expected, the essays of Addison and Steele had an important influence on Leapor's writing. In fact, she based entire poems on periodical essays. In 'An Enquiry' she writes of worlds too minute to be seen:

>Pluck off yon Acorn from its Parent Bough,
>Divide that Acorn in the midst—and now

[31] Gay, 'The Fan', in *Poetry and Prose*, i. 59–60.

> In its firm Kernal a fair Oak is seen
> With spreading Branches of a sprightly Green:
> From this young Tree a Kernal might we rend,
> There wou'd another its small Boughs extend. (ML i. 199)

This is based on *The Tatler*, no. 119, in which Addison describes a 'good Genius' speaking to him about microscopes:

> I have been shown a Forrest of numberless Trees, which has been picked out of an Acorn. Your Microscope can show you in it a compleat Oak in Miniature; and could you suit all your Organs as we do [in our spiritual state], you might pluck an Acorn from this little Oak, which contains another Tree; and so proceed from Tree to Tree, as long as you would think fit to continue your Disquisitions.[32]

Another of Leapor's poems drawn from a periodical is 'The Inspir'd Quill'. She writes:

> The sage *Pythagoras*, you know,
> Asserted many Years ago,
> That when or Man or Woman dies,
> The Soul to some new Mansion flies? (ML i. 112)

The quill describes how in previous lives it has been a usurer, a beau, a lap-dog, a lawyer, and a crow. This follows the pattern of *The Spectator* no. 343, in which a monkey writes a letter describing his own career of transmigration: he has been variously a brahmin, a tax-collector, a flying fish, an emmet, a miser, a bee, a rake, a bay-gelding, and a beau. It is a distinct possibility that Leapor knew Pythagoras not only from this source but from Dryden's translation of Ovid, which is discussed above, although plainly the humour of her poem is modelled on *The Spectator*. Leapor's reading of periodicals included *The Guardian*, according to one of her letters (ML ii. 311). At Weston Hall there is a collection of the writings of Addison and Steele in various editions.

The influence of Alexander Pope is evident throughout Leapor's verses, though in her plays that influence tends to be submerged. It is not certain that she read all of Pope. According to Freemantle, she owned 'Part of Mr. *Pope*'s Works' (ML ii, p. xxxii). This means little, since Freemantle lent Leapor the

---

[32] Donald F. Bond, ed., *The Tatler*, 3 vols. (Oxford: Clarendon Press, 1987), ii. 208.

translation of the *Odyssey*, and probably owned his other works. At Weston Hall, apart from his edition of Shakespeare, there is only a volume of Pope's prose. This is surprising, since there were a number of aspiring poets in the house at different times, all of whom would have wanted to read his verse. Leapor, at any rate, read most of his works. The evidence is not far to seek. Titles such as 'An Essay on Woman' or 'An Epistle to a Lady' are borrowed directly from Pope. 'The Proclamation of Apollo', according to one of the letters, springs from a reading of the *Dunciad*:

The Occasion of this Whim was the reading of that list prefixed to Mr. *Pope*'s *Dunciad*, which tells us the Number of his Enemies.—After having fretted at their Impudence, who durst scribble against my favourite Author, I began to reflect on the Stupidity of Goose-quill Wars, and these Knight-Errants of *Apollo*. (ML ii. 309)

Another poem is entitled 'On Mr. Pope's Universal Prayer', and, like its original, asserts the need for religious tolerance. In other places she quotes Pope directly, as in 'Dorinda at her Glass': 'Thus Pope has sung, thus let Dorinda sing; | "Virtue, brave Boys, —'tis Virtue makes a King:"' (ML i. 7), lines taken from 'The First Epistle of the First Book of Horace Imitated' (Pope, iv. 285, l. 92). In one of her letters she quotes from memory Pope's desire to 'Maintain a Poet's Dignity and Ease, | And see what Friends, and read what Books I please'. Here she is drawing from the 'Epistle to Dr Arbuthnot' (Pope, iv. 114, ll. 263–4). This poem is likely also to be the model for her 'Epistle to Artemisia. On Fame' (see *ECWP*, 526 n). Although she makes no direct reference to it, there is no doubt that Leapor read 'The Rape of the Lock'. 'Dorinda at her Glass' is about a woman at her toilet; Leapor is not, however, simply re-creating Belinda's youthful folly, since Dorinda is an older woman attempting to deny the imminence of death. Still, the poem is a response to Pope's work. 'Crumble Hall', similarly, is partly a response to the 'Epistle to Burlington'.

In some areas of her work, it must be observed, Leapor moves away from Pope—her pastorals, for example, use images from actual rural life. As a reader of the *Guardian*, she must have known about the controversy on this point, and chosen to follow Philips rather than Pope. In Chapter 2 we saw how Leapor questions Pope's views of women, and in Chapter 3 we saw her present a far less enthusiastic view of landscape improvement than that in the 'Epistle to Burlington'. Leapor's regard for Pope, however, surpassed by a very long way her feelings for any other writer. 'Celadon to Mira', a poem in which the shade of Pope appears to Mira, ends with this remarkable couplet: 'Still look to Heav'n and its Laws attend, I And next the Lines of thy aerial Friend' (ML i. 142). Pope's verse has for Leapor a significance second only to scripture. Of course, Leapor's enthusiasm for Pope was shared by many poets of the time. The impression that Leapor read Pope and little else is understandable though false. Leapor's identification with Pope can be seen in the grief of her poem 'On the Death of a justly admir'd Author', and in the anger against his critics expressed here in 'The Libyan Hunter':

>   Old Story tells us, on an earthly Plain
>   Once *Jove* descended wrap'd in golden Rain:
>   Now Fate permits no such familiar Powers,
>   But Shoals of Criticks fall in leaden Showers:
>   These gaze at Wit, as Owls behold the Sun,
>   And curse the Lustre which they fain wou'd shun;
>   These Beasts of Prey no living worth endure,
>   Nor are the Regions of the Dead secure ...   (ML i. 153)

Repeatedly through her work Leapor asserts her allegiance to Pope; she sees in him a genius thoroughly misunderstood. Doubtless, she projects on to him her own resentment against those who belittle her writing. Pope, for Leapor as for many others in her time, is the apogee of literary achievement, the ultimate model of good writing. Leapor may rightly be described as an imitator of Pope, yet her willingness to depart from his procedures or argue against some of his ideas shows that there is nothing slavish in her imitation. Indeed, Leapor's attitude towards Pope very much reflects her tendency to respect the intellectual, social, and religious traditions of her society while arguing bravely against specific ideas or practices which she believes are oppressive. Leapor's passionate admiration of Pope's work is matched by a robust independence of mind.

There is no simple equation between authors named, quoted, or echoed by Leapor and the full extent of her reading. In some cases she may simply be dropping names of authors she has not read, yet it is most likely that she read more authors than can be identified simply from her poetry. Her references to other writers indicate a substantial amount of reading, yet she makes no discernible reference to Thomson's poetry, or to the novels of Defoe, Richardson, and Fielding. Since these authors had a huge circulation, it is hard to imagine that she did not read some of their works.

Leapor's reading included some learned works which are not in the narrow sense literary. Chapter 5 below discusses her knowledge of some theological and spiritual works. The library at Weston Hall contains a number of such books. 'To Lucinda' records her feeling that theology was the most important gap in her reading, though at the end of her life she was reading philosophy or theology, as she indicates in 'An Epistle to a Lady':

> But tho' these Eyes the learned Page explore,
> And turn the pond'rous Volumes o'er and o'er,
> I find no Comfort from their Systems flow,
> But am dejected more as more I know.   (ML i. 38–9)

These volumes were doubtless borrowed from Freemantle, but it is difficult to know what they were. As discussed in Chapter 2 above, Leapor at some point became acquainted with at least part of John Locke's writings. The expression 'pond'rous Volumes' suggests that she was reading substantial works by a number of authors.

In several poems Leapor displays a knowledge of the law. Apart from her comments on lawyers' bills, there is evidence of a knowledge of documents. One of her best poems, 'Mira's Will', opens with the word 'Imprimis', and closes with the direction:

> All this let my Executors fulfil,
> And rest assur'd that this is Mira's Will,
> Who was, when she these Legacies design'd,
> In Body healthy, and compos'd in Mind.   (ML i. 10)

The schoolteacher in Brackley, Richard Cooper, was both a bookbinder and a scrivener of sorts. In the smallpox epidemic of 1742 he took down a will for Henry Purefoy which was executed by John Welchman, senior. It is very probable that Leapor's comments on attorneys would have originated through her contact with Cooper, who in turn would have witnessed any sharp dealing by Welchman (see Clarke, 105–9). Her knowledge of the law suggests an association with Cooper that went beyond the ordinary curriculum; he may have put her to some use in relation to his legal work or his book business. Her grasp of legal nomenclature is evident in 'The Inspir'd Quill':

> Once more to gain a human Face,
> I step'd into a Lawyer's Case:
> This Station pleas'd me wond'rous well,
> And in a trice I learn'd to spell,
> Cou'd read old *Coke* with prying Eyes,
> Explain, distinguish, and advise,
> Talk *Latin* to a good degree;
> As *Admittendo Custode*,
> *Eject*, *Extendi*: and my Fee:
> 'Tis true I scorn'd to rob or kill,
> But not to cheat or forge a Will:
> In Jointures I cou'd split a Hair,
> And make it turn against the Heir:
> I spar'd no Widow for her Tears,
> No Orphan for his tender Years:
> My Maxim was get Money, Man,
> Get Money, where and how you can ...   (ML i. 115)

Leapor uses a few Latinisms, indicating at least an acquaintance with the language, that is, enough to recognize pretence in a lawyer. Sir Edward Coke was a byword for legal knowledge in her time, and the reference does not imply that she had read his works. Leapor does have a grasp of legal jargon, none the less, and that suggests some knowledge of law books.

It can be established that Leapor had read at least a fair selection of literary works, and a more modest number of works in other areas. Although Leapor's reading constituted something less than a full education, she cannot be considered a primitive. Indeed, there is a great difference between a person who educated herself and a primitive as conceived by eighteenth-century theorists. Leapor worked hard to repair the gaps in her learning, and would have continued to do so. It is interesting that in 'An Epistle to a Lady' she actually calls herself learned (see ML i. 39). While 'To Lucinda' does portray Mira as a primitive, it is likely that 'An Epistle to a Lady' represents Leapor's true judgement of the depth of her own education. Donna Landry accurately describes her as the 'most writerly' of women poets of the labouring class (Landry, 119). Leapor had some grasp of literary tradition and a reasonable knowledge of contemporary authors; therefore, she was to some extent also a 'readerly' poet.

CHAPTER 5

POETRY AND THE LAST THINGS

Romantic myth makes much of the early death of a gifted poet. Chatterton, Keats, Shelley, Wilfred Owen, and many others have been understood as doomed prodigies. Obviously, such notions appear innocent in the context of modern criticism. It is nonetheless reasonable to see the expectation of death bringing an artist's work to sudden maturity and focus. Sacheverell Sitwell, for example, speaking of Aubrey Beardsley, refers to illness as 'the hot house and forcing place of talent', transforming rather ordinary gifts into something exceptional.[1] It is very probable that Mary Leapor's experience of her mother's death, her fears for her father, and ultimately her own expectation of an early death, caused her to approach her writing with greater urgency than might be expected in a young poet. A strong sense of human limitation may be detected in Leapor's considerations of death and in her treatment of theological subjects. This chapter will examine her view of death against the background of beliefs and attitudes prevalent in the eighteenth century.

Many historians have examined attitudes towards death and cultural practices surrounding bereavement.[2] The material which they have uncovered is vast, and emphasizes at almost all points the desire in earlier times for a good death. These historians also

---

[1] Sacheverell Sitwell, *For Want of the Golden City* (London: Thames and Hudson, 1973), 73.
[2] Philippe Ariès, *The Hour of Our Death*, trans. Helen Weaver (London: Allen Lane, 1981); John McManners, *Death and the Enlightenment: Changing Attitudes to Death among Christians and Unbelievers in Eighteenth-Century France* (Oxford: Oxford University Press, 1981); Clare Gittings, *Death, Burial and the Individual in Early Modern England* (London and Sydney: Croom Helm, 1984); Ruth Richardson, *Death, Dissection and the Destitute* (London and New York: Routledge & Kegan Paul, 1987); Ralph Houlbrooke, ed., *Death, Ritual and Bereavement* (London and New York: Routledge in association with The Social History Society of the United Kingdom, 1989); James C. Riley, *Sickness, Recovery and Death: A History and Forecast of Ill Health* (London: Macmillan, 1989); Roy Porter and Dorothy Porter, *In Sickness and in Health: The British Experience 1650–1850* (London: Fourth Estate, 1988), esp. 245–57; for a literary perspective, see Paul Henry Moore, 'Death in the Eighteenth-Century Novel 1740–1800', D.Phil. thesis (Oxford, 1986).

emphasize the enormous importance that was placed on the correct and decent burial of loved ones. Ruth Richardson's study, *Death, Dissection and the Destitute*, is particularly interesting in that it shows how anatomical experiments in the eighteenth and nineteenth centuries offended basic sensibilities even at the lowest levels of society, or, rather, precisely at the lowest levels of society since it was the dead of prisons and workhouses who were made available to anatomists. This sort of scholarship makes clear that the human body, alive or dead, was viewed with a deeper sense of mystery in earlier times.

Whereas in the twentieth century sickness is often regarded in objective or even mechanical terms, previous centuries tended to see mind and body in a closer unity. Roy Porter writes: 'For the early modern mind, the condition of the body, registering the ups and downs of health and sickness, meshed with wider ideas of identity and destiny, of social, moral and spiritual well-being.'[3] Sickness was not usually conceived of in purely material terms, but was seen in close relation to other crucial human experiences. Sickness was often thought an intervention of the divine will, especially as punishment for sin. Since eighteenth-century physiology was relatively primitive, it is not uncommon to find contagion written about with terror. Benjamin Grosvenor, for example, writes in a pamphlet entitled *Observations on Sudden Death* (1720):

> Diseases and *Death* are secretly lurking for us every where. It is in our Bosoms, in our Bowels; in every thing we Taste, in every thing we enjoy. Sleeping or waking, abroad or at home, at the Table, in the Church; in Company or alone; in the Street or the Closet. The great wonder is, that it is no more frequent and common . . .[4]

The image of death as a personified attacker is common in the century. Samuel Johnson writes in *The Rambler* (no. 78): 'To neglect at any time preparation for death, is to sleep on our post at a siege, but to omit it in old age, is to sleep at an attack' (Johnson, iii. 49). Sudden unexplained illness was a danger at all times, even to a person who was perfectly healthy. This entailed a deep cultural awareness of the insecurity of life. Porter goes so far as to speak of a 'sickness culture', in which the omnipresent threat to health and survival is embedded in the general consciousness.

---

[3] Roy Porter, *Disease, Medicine and Society in England 1550–1860* (London: Macmillan, 1987), p. 24.
[4] Benjamin Grosvenor, *Observations on Sudden Death* (London, 1720), 18.

The first half of the eighteenth century produced many writers, including Edward Young, Elizabeth Rowe, Robert Blair, and Thomas Gray, whose meditations on death touched a chord among contemporary readers. Although readers now find the general run of graveyard poetry difficult to enjoy, it must be recognized that this type of poetry confronted an important aspect of contemporary life. Edward Young writes:

> Yet why *complain*? or why complain for One!
> Hangs out the Sun his Lustre but for me?
> The single Man? are Angels all beside?
> I mourn for Millions: 'tis the common Lot...[5]

Whereas twentieth-century medicine has extended lifespans, and to an extent sanitized illness, pain, and death, the eighteenth-century mind had to face these realities with greater frequency and intensity. Apart from grasping at a generalized statement, Young's claim to mourn for millions suggests how a poet might feel utterly surrounded by death. Although Mary Leapor is less lugubrious than Edward Young, her sense of mortality is evident throughout her poetry. Indeed, without recognizing Leapor's struggle to come to terms with death, it is not possible to arrive at a full assessment of her work.

Mary Leapor's adult life can be said to begin with the death of her mother. The stage at which one was normally thought to have become an adult in the eighteenth century was marriage. Patricia Meyer Spacks assesses the dominant attitudes towards adolescence: 'In one way or another [moralists] suggest that the young should be thought of, should think of themselves, as children until the very moment at which they assume full adult responsibility.'[6] When Anne Leapor died, around Christmas 1741, her daughter was almost certainly employed already as a domestic servant, yet her mother's death was likely to have impressed on her the need to take responsibility for her own life. Upon her eventual return to Brackley after leaving Edgcote House, she took over her father's domestic affairs and participated in his business. She thus seems to have assumed full adult responsibility

[5] Edward Young, 'Night the First', in *Night Thoughts*, ed. Stephen Cornford (Cambridge: Cambridge University Press, 1989), 43.
[6] Patricia Meyer Spacks, '"Always at Variance": Politics of Eighteenth-Century Adolescence', in Patricia Meyer Spacks and W. B. Carnochan, *A Distant Prospect: Eighteenth-Century Views of Childhood* (Los Angeles, 1982), 6.

rather earlier than usual. After her mother's death, Leapor may have enjoyed certain freedoms as mistress of even a small household. She enjoyed a surprising range of social connections with some of the leading women in the area, who apparently regarded her, if not as their equal, as considerably more than a child.

Apart from changes in the pattern of Mary Leapor's life following her mother's death, it is evident that the experience left a mark on the poet's mind. It must be observed, however, that she does not write about it specifically until several months before her own death. In a letter to Freemantle, whose mother was then seriously ill, she recalls the death of her own mother but attempts to play down the actual grief:

> I, who cannot boast of a Heart so susceptible and delicate as yours, have at least felt the Strength of Nature in the parting Pang; and can assure you from Experience, that (to a Soul capable of strong Ideas) the Apprehension of this formidable Evil is more terrible than its real Approach; tho' I hope there is no immediate Danger... (ML ii. 321)

Since the letter is intended to console her friend for the imminent loss of her mother, it is difficult to know exactly what this reveals about Leapor's bereavement in 1741. 'An Epistle to a Lady', written no more than a few months later than the letter, contains the following lines:

> Yet did these Eyes a dying Parent see,
> Loos'd from all Cares except a Thought for me,
> Without a Tear resign her short'ning Breath,
> And dauntless meet the ling'ring Stroke of Death. (ML i. 40)

Evidently Leapor found her mother's death a time of difficulty for herself, although her mother's dignity in her last moments seems to have been reassuring. Her description of her mother's death, though deeply felt, is restrained by the standards of the time. Thomas Turner, the Sussex diarist, wrote in 1761 of his wife's death: 'Oh, may her agonizing pains and dying groans have such a constant impression on my mind that (through the assistance [of] God's grace) I may ever have the thought of death in my mind, and that by a truly religious course of life may be prepared to meet that King of Terrors...'.[7] Turner was, of course, writing soon after the event, yet the idea of bearing in mind the horrors

---

[7] David Vaisey, ed., *The Diary of Thomas Turner 1754–1765* (Oxford: Oxford University Press, 1984), 228.

of death as an inducement to morality is very common among writers at the time, as it had been for centuries.

Direct references to her mother's death do not occur in Leapor's writing until more than four years after the event. This may be because she continued to find her memories painful, or because much of her earliest writing was burned. It is possible none the less to discern the impact of the experience in *The Unhappy Father*, which was completed some time before Leapor's friendship with Freemantle began. Since 'Epistle to Artemisia. On Fame' indicates that Leapor wrote little between her return to Brackley and her meeting with Freemantle, it is probable that the tragedy was finished before she left Edgcote, and that it had been started some time earlier, perhaps in the latter half of 1744 or even before that. *The Unhappy Father* is a decidedly morbid work. The world of the play is centred in the patriarch, Dycarbas, who nourishes his children:

> Methinks I flourish like the spreading Vine,
> Whose curling Branches are with Clusters hung,
> That draw their Juices from its friendly Stem.   (ML ii. 140)

Such images of nurture curiously emphasize the absence of a mother in the play. Dycarbas is a widower, and the other leading character, Terentia, is an orphan under his guardianship. It is not difficult to see a connection between Leapor's own circumstances and the dramatic world which she creates. Even if this situation is based partly on Otway's *The Orphan*, Leapor none the less chooses that particular model for her own play. Indeed, *The Unhappy Father* seems to reflect Leapor's experience on a somewhat deeper level. The basic concern of the play is expressed in Terentia's first speech; she asks Polonius: 'are we truly happy, or deceiv'd?' (ML ii. 130). She goes on to speak of changing fortune:

> In this strange World, made up of Sun and Show'rs,
> Who e'er was plac'd beyond the Reach of Woe?
> The Cheek, that late was dimpled o'er with Smiles,
> Pleas'd with the Farce of transitory Joy,
> Grows pale and languid, if the Curtain falls,
> Till the next Scene exhibits something gay...   (ML ii. 130)

The events of the play are intended to expose 'the Farce of transitory Joy', as Terentia's world is shattered by a series of unexpected deaths. The eventual report that Polonius has been swallowed by a shark is absurd and suggests that the universe of the play is random; that the shark actually swallows the carcass of a dead sailor barely softens this suggestion. Paulus, one of the servants, speaks, near the end:

> Now, who shall bid Polonius welcome here?
> For this ill-fated Mansion is become
> The gloomy Seat of arbitrary Death;
> And the pale Tyrant keeps a Revel here... (ML ii. 213)

Death has swept over the house in a manner that cannot be explained. Terentia, of course, can see no grounds for hope and is prevented from killing herself only by the fortuitous return of Polonius. Even so, the two foresee a bleak future: 'Let frequent Sighs employ the lonely Hours, | And Grief be all the Bus'ness of our Lives' (ML ii. 218). The play ends with a vision of loss:

> So two kind Friends in some toss'd Vessel ride,
> Where a black Tempest swells the raging Tide:
> Trembling they stand, and weep their native Shore,
> While the Sky thunders, and the Waters roar;
> Till unawares some envious Billow sweeps
> One lov'd Companion in the frothy Deeps.
> His wretched Fellow rends the Air with Cries,
> Calls on his Name, and rolls his ghastly Eyes
> Round the vex'd Ocean, and the dismal Skies:
> His frantic Hands tear off his scatter'd Hairs;
> Now calls on Heav'n, yet of its Help despairs;
> Till the kind Waves his short-liv'd Sorrows end,
> And wash the Mourner to his sinking Friend. (ML ii. 219)

That the play should end with images of bereavement again suggests that it is, at some level, a response to the death of the poet's mother. Although the play contains suggestions of ultimate hope, those suggestions are few. Terentia recovers her will to live with the return of Polonius, yet the course of events suggests that the human condition is profoundly insecure.

The Unhappy Father can be seen as typical of attitudes in its time. Death is 'a pale Tyrant' who strikes without explanation. Five important characters are wiped out in quick succession. While it is well to remember that tragedies typically end in cadaverous heaps, *The Unhappy Father* may have been shaped by the poet's experiences during the winter of 1741–2, when the *Purefoy*

Letters record, with near-panic, a smallpox epidemic in Brackley (Eland, ii. 288). The cause of Anne Leapor's death is not recorded; it is possible that she was a victim of this outbreak. Although the disease primarily affected children, it could be contracted by adults. Up to 50 per cent of smallpox cases would end in death.[8] The parish register records a substantial number of deaths in Brackley that winter.[9] The time in which the poet was mourning for her mother would have been darkened by fears of further deaths, and probably by the actual loss of people known to her. Epidemics were frequent in Leapor's time, and a series of arbitrary deaths in a play would have seemed less like melodrama than plain verisimilitude.

Leapor's loss of one parent doubtless entailed concern for the other. Philip Leapor would have been almost 48 when his wife died. According to Keith Thomas, 50 was at the time generally considered the beginning of old age, and some almshouses admitted people as young as 40 so long as they were unable to work.[10] It is, then, easy to recognize the barb in Sophronia's comment: 'Go, ply your Needle: You might earn your Bread; I Or who must feed you when your Father's dead?' (ML ii. 52). In the letter to Freemantle quoted above, Leapor goes on to observe that with the death of her father she would lose not only a bond of affection but 'all the Necessaries of Life: Left naked and defenceless, without Friend, and without Dependence; with a weak and indolent Body to provide for its own Subsistence' (ML ii. 323). Leapor's welfare was dependent on her father's ability to earn. If he died his estate would probably be negligible and the poet destitute. It is little wonder that she tried not to dwell on the subject. Repeatedly in her poems she utters prayers for her father, as in 'A Prayer for the Year, 1745':

> Preserve my Parent and my Friend
> From Danger, Guilt or Shame:
> In Peace their chearful Days extend
> To praise thy holy Name.   (ML i. 71)

---

[8] Riley, *Sickness, Recovery and Death*, 111.

[9] See 'Brackley Parish Register 1727-1756', Northamptonshire Record Office, Delapré Abbey, Northampton.

[10] Keith Thomas, 'Age and Authority in Early Modern England', *Proceedings of the British Academy*, 62 (1976), 240.

In addition to such evidence there is, of course, Freemantle's report that Leapor expressed concern for her father on her deathbed: 'He is growing into Years.—My Heart bleeds to see the Concern he is in...' (ML ii, p. xxviii). This report is at least consistent with statements in Leapor's poems and letters. Even if the poet's relationship with her father was stormy, there is evidence that she held him in some regard, and that his death would have meant not only a loss of pounds and shillings, but a genuine sorrow.

Leapor was uneasy about her own health and seems to have expected an early death. This expectation is manifested throughout her poetry, though at times she writes with a remarkable hard-headedness. In 'The Consolation', written at Edgcote House, she imagines her own headstone:

> Inscrib'd with—'*Natus Anno Dom*'
> 'Here lies *Mary* in this Tomb.'
> . And there's no odds, that I can spy,
> 'Twixt *Mary* Queen of *Scots* and *I*.   (ML ii. 83)

This is graveyard poetry, but with an edge. Leapor's willingness to make the thought of impending death the occasion of satire is very much in the spirit of 'Verses on the Death of Dr. Swift'. That poem, of course, describes Swift's bequest to the madhouse:

> 'O, may we all for Death prepare!'
> 'What has he left? And who's his Heir?'
> 'I know no more than what the News is,
> 'Tis all bequeath'd to publick Uses.'   (Swift, ii. 558)

Leapor may have taken the idea for another poem, 'Mira's Will', from Swift. Certainly the black humour of Leapor's poem is Swiftian. It has already been observed that 'Mira's Will' suggests that Leapor had a knowledge of documents. It is, in fact, one of her most sophisticated compositions. Unlike Swift, Leapor has no estate *per se*, and so she distributes her various personal qualities:

> IMPRIMIS—My departed Shade I trust
> To Heav'n—My Body to the silent Dust;
> My Name to publick Censure I submit,
> To be dispos'd of as the World thinks fit;
> My Vice and Folly let Oblivion close,
> The World already is o'erstock'd with those;

> My Wit I give, as Misers give their Store,
> To those who think they had enough before. (ML i. 8)

Leapor goes on to grant patience to 'slighted Virgins and neglected Wives', truth to modish lovers, reflection to youth, good-nature to husbands, and her pen to the 'small poets'. At this point in the poem the distribution of her estate is complete and she gives directions for the order of her funeral. This was, of course, an essential function of wills in the past. She writes:

> Let a small Sprig (true Emblem of my Rhyme)
> Of blasted Laurel on my Hearse recline;
> Let some grave Wight, that Struggles for Renown,
> By chanting Dirges through a Market-Town,
> With gentle Step precede the solemn Train;
> A broken Flute upon his Arm shall lean.
> Six comick Poets may the Corse surround,
> And All Free-holders if they can be found... (ML i. 9)

In describing the mock-procession, Leapor remains close to actual customs. Henry Bourne's *Antiquitates Vulgares* (1725) is generally hostile to popular culture, yet approves of funeral processions since they are an emblem of 'our dying shortly after our Friend'. The carrying of ivy, rosemary, laurel, or another evergreen, is thought to signify the immortality of the soul. Such processions would usually sing psalms.[11]

Processions are found repeatedly in Restoration and eighteenth-century literature. Leapor produces a crowd scene, but there is no physical disorder or violence. It would, then, be stretching the point to describe her poem in terms of charivari. There is a sense of formality implied first by casting the poem as a legal document and second by fixing a strict pattern of movement for the procession. This sense of order, however, is undercut in various ways. The legatees named near the beginning of the poem are figures of folly or contradiction. Leapor's poetry is then represented by nothing more than 'blasted Laurel'. The dirge-singer will find no renown in market-towns like Brackley. A poet who is also a freeholder is a rarity, though that idea has its own significance for Leapor (see Chapter 1 above). The 'melancholy

---

[11] Henry Bourne, *Antiquitates Vulgares; Or, The Antiquities of the Common People* (Newcastle, 1725), 19–23.

Throng' who bring up the rear of the procession is composed of yet more paradoxical creatures:

> Then follow next the melancholy Throng,
> As shrewd Instructors, who themselves are wrong.
> The Virtuoso, rich in Sun-dry'd Weeds,
> The Politician, whom no Mortal heeds,
> The silent Lawyer, chamber'd all the Day,
> And the stern Soldier that receives no Pay.
> But stay—the Mourners shou'd be first our Care,
> Let the freed Prentice lead the Miser's Heir;
> Let the young Relict wipe her mournful Eye,
> And widow'd Husbands o'er their Garlick cry. (ML i. 9–10)

To catalogue objects of satire is a common technique in eighteenth-century poetry, yet in this context the effect is forceful nonetheless, ironically undermining a sense of order. The greatest challenge, however, to the ostensible solidity and formality of the poem is the basic presumption of the persona's death. Mira will simply not be present to the events she describes. Indeed, the sense of reality in the poem is predicated on this absence. A will is opened only when the testator is dead. It takes a rather hard-headed poet to make jests which go so close to the bone, or at least a student of Swift who has mastered one of the Dean's most disturbing conceits.

Elsewhere in her poetry, Leapor is less satiric, and reveals a fear of death. In 'Celadon to Mira', the shade of Alexander Pope speaks:

> Say, why thy Features lose their healthful Dye,
> And the Tears tremble in the languid Eye?
> The mighty Conflict I with pity see,
> When thy rude Passions struggle to be free,
> And rack thy Breast—the incoherent Stage,
> Where grave and comick jar like Youth and Age;
> Now Death appears all horrible and grim:
> But the next Moment none so fair as him,
> And now you sigh—Ah, let me calmly die:
> Then shrinking, trembling from the Grave you fly,
> Such jarring Tumults in your Bosom roll;
> (Ah, what so various as a Woman's Soul!)
> But thou, beware, and if thy Fate has join'd
> A sickly Body to a roving Mind;

> Be calm nor mourn at the Supreme Decree,
> Nor think the Mandate shall be chang'd for thee,
> But meet with Patience what thou canst not flee.   (ML i. 138-9)

That Leapor should speak of a 'mighty Conflict' suggests that for some time she anticipated death and attempted to adopt a patient and resigned attitude. Of particular interest are the lines: 'But thou, beware, and if thy Fate has join'd | A sickly Body to a roving Mind ... '. Given that in her time it was usual to see mind and body in a closer unity than we do now, Leapor finds a deep inadequacy in her own response to illness. Indeed, the unsettled mind is linked to the unhealthy body as though both were dimensions of a more general failure in her life. Her attitudes here are linked to the assumption underlying physiognomy that the body reflects mental and moral worth. Roy and Dorothy Porter describe the sense of shame that could accompany illness in earlier times:

> Every disease, every pain, had its meaning, and meanings typically had their moral. Generally implicitly, sometimes explicitly, most stories of sickness were exemplary of correct and incorrect attitudes and actions. On the grand scale, the idle, the feckless, and the debauched were those who were expected to succumb to disease—perhaps including the idle rich no less than the improvident poor.[12]

Her frequent illnesses caused Leapor to doubt her own maturity, and even her moral and spiritual stature. In 'The Moral Vision' she describes a personal ideal of 'a lively but a guiltless Mind, | A Body healthful and a Soul resign'd' (ML i. 68). Well-being is defined in terms which are at once physical, intellectual, moral, and spiritual.

Leapor's sense that she did not have long to live is an important factor in the struggle for 'content' which is so prominent in her poems. Indeed, she sometimes treats her hopes of improving her life in this world as a distraction from the true business of soul-making. Leapor desires a calm mind undisturbed by fancy or ambition. She writes 'On Patience. To Stella':

> When *Stella*'s Spirit shall be taught to know
> Joy's proper Medium, and to smile in Woe;
> When her still Passions know their due Degree;

---

[12] Porter and Porter, *In Sickness and in Health*, 72.

> Then teach! O teach the happy Art to me!
> Me, who from Thought to frolic Fancy skim,
> Now wrapt in Morals, and now lost in Whim;
> While a strange Group of Passions sway,
> That rule by Changing, and by Turns obey... (ML ii. 4)

Leapor believes that true religion should be cheerful; however, emotions tend towards disorder and must be disciplined. In Leapor's view, the soul must at all times embrace the will of God and rejoice in it, even though this may run against natural inclinations. Earthly desires must be submerged in the divine purpose. This was very much in line with most writings on spirituality at the time. Jeremy Taylor, for example, writes of contentment:

> For since all the evil in the World consists in the disagreeing between the object and the appetite, as when a man hath what he desires not, or desires what he hath not, or desires amisse; he that composes his spirit to the present accident, hath variety of instances for his vertue, but none to trouble him, because his desires enlarge not beyond his present fortune: and a wise man is placed in the variety of chances like the Nave or Centre of a wheel, in the midst of all the circumvolutions and changes of posture, without violence or change, save that it turns gently in complyance with its changed parts, and is indifferent which part is up and which is down; for there is some vertue or other to be exercised, whatever happens...[13]

Isaac Barrow describes stark alternatives: contentedness constitutes 'a kind of temporal heaven; which he that hath, is thereby *ipso facto* in good measure happy, whatever other things he may seem to want; which he that wanteth, doth, however otherwise he be furnished, become miserable, and carrieth a kind of hell within him'.[14] Leapor accepted the need for contentment as a central part of her own beliefs. She writes in 'Essay on Happiness':

> NOTHING, dear Madam, nothing is more true,
> Than a short Maxim much approv'd by you;
> The Lines are these: 'We by Experience know
> Within ourselves exists our Bliss or Woe.'
> Tho' round our Heads the Goods of Fortune roll,
> Dazzle they may, but cannot chear the Soul.

---

[13] Jeremy Taylor, *The Rule and Exercises of Holy Living* (London, 1650), 128.
[14] Isaac Barrow, 'Of Contentment. The First Sermon', in *Of Contentment, Patience and Resignation to the Will of God* (London, 1685), 2.

Content, the Fountain of eternal Joy,
Can Riches purchase, or can Want destroy?
No. Born of Heav'n, its Birth it will maintain,
No Slave to Power nor the Prize of Gain:
Say, who can buy what never yet was sold?
No Wealth can bribe her, nor no Bonds can hold:
Sometimes she deigns to shine in lofty Halls,
But found more frequent in a Cottage Walls;
Her Flight from thence too often is decreed,
Then Poverty is doubly curs'd indeed. (ML i. 54-5)

As we have seen in other chapters, Leapor has considerable difficulty reconciling the need to be contented with the need to stand up for her rights. There is in Leapor's work an uncertainty concerning the value of action in the world. In poems of social protest she is grappling with a form of historical engagement, while in her religious poems she is looking towards the next world. How these impulses are reconciled is an important question in Leapor's work, and one which is inseparable from her sense of impending death.

Mary Leapor understood death in religious terms. Her poems reproduce many images and ideas which are found in the writings on death which proliferated in her time.[15] The need for spiritual vigilance at life's end was generally considered essential, since the soul was about to be judged and, as Samuel Johnson believed, 'no man can be sure of his acceptance with GOD'.[16] Most writers on death argued strongly against hoping for an opportunity to reform

---

[15] For examples of seventeenth- and eighteenth-century *ars moriendi*, see Jeremy Taylor, *The Rule and Exercises of Holy Dying* (London, 1651); William Sherlock, *A Practical Discourse Concerning Death* (London, 1689); John Kettlewell, *Death Made Comfortable: Or The Way to Dye Well* (London, 1695); William Assheton, *A Method of Devotion for Sick and Dying Persons* (London, 1706); Charles Drelincourt, *The Christian's Defence Against the Fears of Death*, trans. M. D'Assigny (London, 1675); Thomas Ken, 'Preparatives for Death', in *The Works of Thomas Ken*, 4 vols. (London, 1721); i. 3-160; Thomas Uvedale, *The Death-Bed Display'd* (London, 1727). See also Sister Mary Catherine O'Connor, *The Art of Dying: The Development of the Ars Moriendi*, Columbia University Studies in English and Comparative Literature, 156 (New York: Columbia University Press, 1942); Nancy Lee Beaty, *The Craft of Dying, A Study in the Literary Tradition of the Ars Moriendi in England*, Yale Studies in English, 175 (New Haven, Conn. and London: Yale University Press, 1970).

[16] Boswell, *Boswell's Life of Johnson*, iv. 123; cited by Isobel Grundy, 'Samuel Johnson: A Writer of Lives Looks at Death', *Modern Language Review*, 79 (1984), 257.

one's life at the very last. One of Isaac Barrow's works, for example, bore the title *Practical Discourses Upon The Consideration of our Latter End; and The Danger and Mischief of Delaying Repentance* (1694). William Sherlock wrote in his enormously influential work, *A Practical Discourse Concerning Death* (1689): 'Some Men talk of preparing for Death, as if it were a thing that could be done in two or three days, and that the proper time of doing it, were a little before they die: but I know no other Preparation for Death, but living well...'[17] In another passage he writes, 'It is very proper to leave the World, before we are removed out of it,'[18] and in *A Practical Discourse Concerning a Future Judgement* (1692), Sherlock recommends that his readers imbue their souls with a 'strong, and vigorous, and constant Sence of Judgement' as a means of governing their lives.[19] Some writers attempted to impress on their readers a sense of physical horror. Thomas Uvedale writes in *The Death-Bed Display'd* (1727):

> The ghastly Face, of BEAUTY once the Seat,
> Is all besmear'd with a cold clammy Sweat,
> Tenacious, slimy, and in Substance thick,
> Most apt to make it to the Coffin stick
> Now Stinks and Odours equally delight,
> The Nose grown cold, pinch'd in, and senseless quite.[20]

Sherlock, however, advised the dying person not to think of the body's dissolution, but to go with Moses up the mountain to 'take a prospect of the heavenly *Canaan*, whither he is going'.[21] In a society where the dead were laid out in their own homes by members of their family, it is unlikely that death could have been imagined simply as a spiritual transition. Leapor, like most people of her time, would have been accustomed to the sight of corpses. In 'The Third Chapter of the Wisdom of Solomon', she departs from the passage she is paraphrasing to describe a body at the moment of death:

> When thoughtless Mortals by constraint attend
> On the last Moments of their parting Friend,
> See the chang'd Features wear a deathful Hue,

---

[17] Sherlock, *A Practical Discourse Concerning Death*, 353.
[18] Ibid. 160.
[19] William Sherlock, *A Practical Discourse Concerning a Future Judgement* (London, 1692), 189.   [20] Uvedale, *The Death Bed Display'd*, 4.
[21] Sherlock, *A Practical Discourse Concerning Death*, 157.

> The Temples water'd with a fainting Dew,
> The Limbs that tremble with convulsive Pain:
> Then stand agast the ignorant and vain ...   (ML i. 53)

Leapor is fully aware of the changes which come over a body at death. Yet in her poetry the important point is what happens to the soul, which, as in this poem, 'glides unobserv'd away' (ML i. 53).

Leapor repeatedly attempts in her poetry to focus her mind on the moment of her own death, and to find strength for the ordeal. She often describes the moment as an encounter with a spectre:

> Death drives us to the horrid Steep;
>   And while we vainly mourn,
> He pointing shews th'unmeasur'd Deep,
>   From whence we ne'er return.
>
> There the grim Spectre, with a Smile,
>   His panting Victim sees:
> Who fain wou'd linger here a while,
>   To swallow nauseous Lees.   (ML i. 265)

This personification of death is essentially the same image as the 'pale Tyrant' in *The Unhappy Father*, arbitrary and apparently brutal. Death comes as an attacker, in the face of which the only hope is God's mercy. In 'A Request to the Divine Being', she writes:

> May my still Days obscurely pass,
>   Without Remorse or Care;
> And let me for the parting Hour,
>   My trembling Ghost prepare.   (ML i. 282)

The only critic who has given any attention to this area of Leapor's writing, Hoxie Neale Fairchild, unfortunately misses the point badly. Commenting on this passage, he writes: 'Until that hour approaches, however, her sensible spirit will tremble very little.'[22] Although it is fair to speak of Leapor as a sensible spirit, the passages examined so far indicate that she was genuinely troubled by the prospect of an early death.

'An Epistle to a Lady' was probably written near the end of Leapor's life, and brings to a conclusion, at least in terms of her

---

[22] Fairchild, *Religious Trends in English Poetry*, vol. ii: *1740–1780: Religious Sentimentalism in the Age of Johnson*, 54.

poetry, the whole struggle to confront death. It draws together the strands of protest and resignation in her poetry. In a sense, this poem is the last stage in the 'mighty conflict' referred to in 'Celadon to Mira'. It describes in one passage a physical decline which is matched by a dulling of the senses:

> But see pale Sickness with her languid Eyes,
> At whose Appearance all Delusion flies:
> The World recedes, its Vanities decline,
> *Clorinda*'s Features seem as faint as mine:
> Gay Robes no more the aking Sight admires,
> Wit grates the Ear, and melting Musick tires:
> Its wonted Pleasures with each Sense decay,
> Books please no more, and Paintings fade away:
> The sliding Joys in misty Vapours end:
> Yet let me still, Ah! let me grasp a Friend:
> And when each Joy, when each lov'd Object flies,
> Be you the last that leaves my closing Eyes. (ML i. 40)

Leapor expects death shortly. The comfort she most desires is friendship. In this she anticipates Thomas Gray, who would describe a similar consolation in his 'Elegy':

> For who to dumb Forgetfulness a prey,
> This pleasing anxious being e'er resign'd,
> Left the warm precincts of the chearful day,
> Nor cast one longing ling'ring look behind?
>
> On some fond breast the parting soul relies,
> Some pious drops the closing eye requires;
> Ev'n from the tomb the voice of Nature cries,
> Ev'n in our Ashes live their wonted Fires.[23]

These stanzas come from that section of the 'Elegy' Johnson most admired: 'I have never seen the notions in any other place; yet he that reads them here persuades himself that he has always felt them.'[24] Leapor is, however, less concerned with remembrance than with the mystery that lies before her:

> But how will this dismantl'd Soul appear,
> When strip'd of all it lately held so dear,
> Forc'd from its Prison of expiring Clay,
> Afraid and shiv'ring at the doubtful Way. (ML i. 40)

---

[23] Gray, 'Elegy Written in a Country Church Yard', in *Complete Poems*, 41.
[24] Samuel Johnson, 'Gray', in *Lives of the English Poets*, ed. George Birkbeck Hill, 3 vols. (Oxford: Clarendon Press, 1905), iii. 442.

Leapor's images here evoke Isaac Watts's hymns. For example, in 'Death and immediate Glory' he writes:

> Shortly this Prison of my Clay
> Must be dissolv'd and fall
> Then, O my Soul, with Joy obey
> Thy heav'nly Father's Call.[25]

In another hymn, 'A Prospect of Heaven makes Death easy', Watts writes:

> But timorous Mortals start and shrink
> To cross this narrow Sea,
> And linger shivering on the Brink,
> And fear to launch away.[26]

Leapor's images of the body as a prison of clay and of the soul's trepidation before making its journey to God can be seen as fairly standard. Yet when she speaks of the soul as dismantled or stripped, there are political or social overtones which must be recognized. John Tillotson writes in one of his sermons:

While we are upon the Stage of this World, we sustain several Persons; one is a Prince and a great Man, another is a Captain and a mighty Man; and whilst this Life lasts, these Differences are considerable: But when we retire and go off the Stage, we shall then be undress'd, we shall be strip'd of all our Titles, and of all our Glory, and go out of the World as naked as we came into it. Death and Judgement level all Mankind, and when we come to appear before the Judgement Seat of Christ, we shall all stand upon equal Terms.[27]

Earlier in 'An Epistle to a Lady', Leapor had complained of poverty: 'You see I'm learned, and I shew't the more, | That none may wonder when they find me poor' (ML i. 39). The poem seems to embody a disillusionment: 'The World recedes, its Vanities decline . . .'. In 'The Consolation' Leapor uses the image of death as leveller to conclude her protest against a specific injustice. She has a strong sense of a Judgement after death. Since all must ultimately come to God on equal terms, she is generally unwilling in life to be cowed by her superiors. Yet when she

---

[25] Isaac Watts, *Hymns and Spiritual Songs 1707–1748*, ed. Selma L. Bishop (London: The Faith Press, 1962), 104.   [26] Ibid. 231.
[27] John Tillotson, 'Sermon CXXVI', in *The Works of the Most Reverend Dr. John Tillotson*, 2 vols. (London, 1712), ii. 155.

speaks of being stripped herself of all she 'lately held so dear', she is little comforted by the thought of getting even with those who have injured her or patronized her. Rather she fears losing the little she has. Death is genuinely a 'doubtful Way'. In her attempt to find courage, she considers first her mother's death in the passage quoted above; her mother's calm submission provides an example of how one might 'dauntless meet the ling'ring Stroke of Death'. Leapor goes on to consider the possibility of actually surviving her illness, but concludes that this would only be 'To share the Follies of succeeding Times l With more Vexations and with deeper Crimes...' (ML i. 41). Leapor's view of human endeavour is deeply pessimistic: although she has struggled to improve her circumstances, she sees little to be achieved by a longer life. Indeed, her final resignation to death can be seen as a social statement:

> Ah no—tho' Heav'n brings near the final Day,
> For such a Life I will not, dare not pray;
> But let the Tear for future Mercy flow,
> And fall resign'd beneath the mighty Blow.
> Nor I alone—for through the spacious Ball,
> With me will Numbers of all Ages fall:
> And the same Day that *Mira* yields her Breath,
> Thousands may enter through the Gates of Death. (ML i. 41)

These lines, some of Leapor's best, are very close to statements made by others who wrote about death. Her emphasis on the sheer number of people who might die with her recalls immediately the passage from *Night Thoughts* quoted above. Even more interesting is a passage from Jeremy Taylor's *The Rule and Exercises of Holy Dying*, under the heading 'Remedies Against Fear of Death':

[Death] is a thing that every one suffers, even persons of the lowest resolution, of the meanest vertue, of no breeding, of no discourse. Take away but the pomps of death, the disguises and solemn bug-bears, the tinsell, and the actings by candle-light, and proper and phantastic ceremonies, the minstrels and the noise-makers, the women and the weepers, the swoonings and the shrikings, the Nurses and the Physicians, the dark room and the Ministers, the Kindred and the Watchers, and then to die is easie, ready and quitted from its troublesome circumstances. It is the same harmless thing, that a poor shepherd suffered yesterday, or a maid-servant to day; and at the same time in which you die, in that very night, a thousand creatures die with you, some wise men, and many fools; and the wisdom of the first will not quit him, and the folly of the latter does not make him unable to die.[28]

Given that Taylor's works had a very wide circulation in the eighteenth century, there is a strong possibility that Leapor had this passage specifically in mind. In 'An Epistle to a Lady' Leapor accepts that her own struggle for a better life will fail. Rather than continue that struggle against injustice she prefers to trust in 'future Mercy'. The vision of thousands dying with her suggests that death will draw human beings together in an essential unity.

Leapor's vision of equality in death would not have been universally shared. Although lip-service might be paid to the notion that God is no respecter of persons, funeral practices sometimes declared bluntly that the reverse was true. In the Magdalen College Chapel in Brackley there is the following inscription: 'Underneath (in the same vault with his Father) lieth the Body of John Welchman Esq. who died OPULENT.' (Clarke, 110). The Welchmans knew their worth. For a woman of Leapor's class to look forward to the levelling of such distinctions can be seen as a last poignant act of resistance.

---

[28] Taylor, *The Rule and Exercises of Holy Dying*, 131–2.

CONCLUSION

'For many a genius being lost at the plough is a false thought —the divine providence is a better manager.'[1] Christopher Smart is the great instance of a powerful poet of the eighteenth century being rediscovered in our own century. Smart, for a time anyway, entertained an enthusiasm for Mary Leapor's poetry. Perhaps he would be pleased to see that her gifts were not ultimately forgotten, and that her quiet achievement would hold an interest for readers in another time. Among the many 'submerged' poets of the period whose works came to light in the 1980s, there is no talent larger than that of Mary Leapor, if none so large as Christopher Smart. Still, an examination of Leapor's poetry leads inevitably to a consideration of literary canon.

The reasons for studying poetry are always disputed. Recent scholarship, however, has revealed that a more pertinent question for eighteenth-century studies now is why certain kinds of poetry have never been studied. Roger Lonsdale has shown how anthologies assembled at the turn of the nineteenth century systematically excluded living authors, women, and the poor.[2] That this occurred is perhaps a tragedy for literature, yet it was also the culmination of a tendency in the eighteenth century for the literary establishment to undervalue poets who stood outside the élite in terms of class, gender, or education. The present challenge to the canon of polite eighteenth-century verse obliges scholars to undertake a task for which modern critical theory, despite its sophistication, leaves them ill-equipped.

To alter the canon of eighteenth-century poetry requires that scholars be willing to judge aesthetic value. This is perhaps an old-fashioned way to conceive of the critic's task, but to claim that a poet is worth reading is to make a qualitative assertion. Judgement must, however, be linked to historical criteria, since it

---

[1] Christopher Smart, *The Poetical Works of Christopher Smart*, vol. i: *Jubilate Agno*, ed. Karina Williamson (1980), B:571, p. 79.
[2] ECV, p. xxxvi; see also Thomas F. Bonnell, 'Bookselling and Canon-Making: The Trade Rivalry over The English Poets, 1776–1783', Studies in *Eighteenth-Century Culture*, 19, Proceedings of the American Society for Eighteenth-Century Studies (East Lansing, Mich.: Colleagues Press, 1989), 53–69.

is impossible to recognize a poet's intelligence without understanding the issues with which he or she is concerned. Moreover, critics must judge whether a poet is competent. In the broadest sense, critics must judge whether a poet is significant. These are the traditional tasks of the literary scholar, but in relation to the large number of poets whose works have recently been recovered, they must be undertaken with a new resolve. It is, of course, possible to take the view that the literary judgements of the past are generally sound, and that it is only self-congratulatory to propose a broad reconsideration of the canon. Sadly, if there is anything less helpful than received opinion, it is received scepticism. Not all submerged poets are good poets, and not all poets who write a poem worth including in an anthology ever write another. Some, like Mary Leapor, actually produce work of sustained quality. Yet, unless poets are read, researched, and understood, much that is valuable will remain somewhere below the water-line.

How a reconsideration of the canon would affect the status of poets who have generally been accepted as major figures is a crucial question. Lonsdale describes his intention as 'less to subvert traditional accounts of the nature and development of eighteenth-century poetry than to supplement them' (ECV, p. xxxvii). To lose sight of, or wilfully to ignore, the achievements of, for example, Pope, Swift, Johnson, Gray, or Smart, would be an egregious error. The object, as Karina Williamson puts it, is 'not to dislodge the canonical writers, but to lodge them in a broader and more heterogeneous context'.[3] While the merits of minor poets ought to be recognized for their own sake, an understanding of their work is also essential for any real appreciation of major poets. Marilyn Butler has discussed the danger of narrowing our sense of literature to a few great authors:

The questions that can be asked of major figures dwindle in number and importance with the fading of minor ones. . . . Keats now communes too often with Shakespeare, Wordsworth with St. Augustine, everyone with the Bible. However much an artist is indebted to the mighty dead, he or she almost certainly borrows more from the living—that is, from writers no longer available for reading except in libraries. In the end, evaluation

---

[3] Karina Williamson, review of *Eighteenth-Century Women Poets: An Oxford Anthology*, ed. Roger Lonsdale, *Essays in Criticism*, forthcoming.

itself is threatened: how can you operate the techniques for telling who a major writer is, if you do not know what a minor one looks like?[4]

This is essentially an argument for a historical approach to criticism, and for the evaluative function of the critic.

Mary Leapor, of all the submerged poets, has been the one most warmly received by scholars and reviewers in the past few years. Accordingly, an examination of her work has implications for the study of eighteenth-century poetry. She may be seen as a test case for poets outside the canon.

This book argues that Leapor's poetry reveals a deep intelligence exercised especially upon issues of gender and class. She is accustomed to reading and is conscious of participating within a literary tradition. She is also a religious poet whose treatment of imminent death is at times distinguished. Her poetry deals subtly and competently with a large number of issues. Her work is personal, in that she communicates often painful concerns within the context of female friendship, yet as a social critic she confronts the dominant culture of her time. Her poetry achieves a remarkable range of feeling; it is at times a vehicle of comedy, of pathos, or of rage. Her language is usually forceful and her handling of forms can rarely be faulted. Although she is not inventive in terms of technique, she brings to poetry a perspective and a tone of voice that are truly individual. In all of this, it is possible to recognize a poet of substance.

To establish that at least one of the submerged poets can bear close examination is an encouragement to further research. It is unlikely that a poet will be found whose accomplishment goes beyond that of Mary Leapor; however, George Farewell, Mary Barber, Mary Jones, Esther Lewis, Mary Whateley, James Woodhouse, Susanna Blamire, Joanna Baillie, and a number of others produced enough work of genuine quality to merit serious attention from literary scholars. An understanding of such poets is likely to change our sense of the literature of the period.

It is a cliché of literary history that Alexander Pope exhausted the couplet, that once he was finished there was nothing else to be done with twenty syllables and a rhyme. If this were true

---

[4] Marilyn Butler, *Literature as a Heritage: Or, Reading Other Ways*, Inaugural Lecture delivered 10 Nov. 1987 (Cambridge: Cambridge University Press, 1988), 6.

his influence could only be seen as oppressive, a weight bearing down on hundreds of minor talents. There were important poets, such as Johnson, Churchill, or Crabbe, whose use of the couplet and whose intense social observation, though often admired, have sometimes been looked upon as reactionary or even antediluvian in terms of poetic practice and temperament. They seem rather lonely adherents to an older literary tradition. Mary Leapor certainly belongs to that Scriblerian tradition. It has been shown repeatedly through this book that though her work is profoundly influenced by Pope and Swift, she often disputes their opinions, and within the procedures she has learned from them develops ideas of her own. Her work shows very clearly that their influence, even as it was deeply imbibed, left room for the individual talent to define itself.

Leapor was not the only submerged poet to write successfully and individually in this manner after the deaths of Swift and Pope. Lonsdale has observed a strain of old-fashioned but accomplished verse being written by women through to the end of the century. There were also men who produced good poetry in this way, though it too might have seemed old-fashioned. If this is so, it is perhaps time to overturn the notion that by writing so well Pope unwittingly did damage to poetry. He and Swift certainly had legions of imitators whose works are entirely without value. Yet their influence on gifted poets through the rest of the century was often decidedly beneficial. Thus, to raise the status of a poet like Mary Leapor has the interesting and desirable effect of revealing something new about established figures, and may even raise the value of those who have been most valued.

Literary historians, anxious to account for the appearance of Romanticism, have ignored the continued vitality of a Scriblerian tradition in the mid-century and beyond. The standard division of the period into phases of neo-classicism, sensibility, and Romanticism, makes it difficult to place the proper value on poetry arising out of that tradition after about 1740. To see each phase in terms of a single dominant fashion is simplistic, since it associates innovation and development first only with sensibility and later only with Romanticism. A more reasonable approach to the literary history of the century would begin with the firm recognition that not all good poets moved in a single direction. Leapor, as well as many others, realized new possibilities within a Scriblerian tradition or mode. Recognizing their accomplishment allows us to understand a particular pattern of growth and continuity through several generations of poets.

Mary Leapor did not live long enough to become a writer of the first rank. Indeed, if she had lived she might have developed no further. Still, her accomplishment is by no means negligible. She is one of the leading women poets of her century. She is also arguably the most gifted labouring poet. She is one of the few poets of the mid-century, male or female, actually to produce a substantial amount of accomplished work. She is not the outstanding poet of her generation, a distinction belonging to Gray or Smart, but she certainly stands among the next rank as a poet of originality, wit, and an unvanquished humanity.

APPENDIX

The Weston Hall Library

Susanna Jennens did not leave a list of the books she owned. What follows is an inventory of works in English at Weston Hall published before Mary Leapor's death. Some books from this period have been excluded since they appear to have been added to the library by subsequent owners of the house. Not all of the books in this inventory were certainly in the library during Leapor's employment in the house or during her subsequent friendship with Jennens. Moreover, it is believed that some of Jennens's books were removed from the house after her death. There is no reason to doubt, however, that most of these books did belong to Jennens, and that Leapor had access to them.

ADDISON, JOSEPH. *Remarks on Several Parts of Italy.* 2nd edn. London, 1718.
—— *The Works of the Right Honourable Joseph Addison.* Edited by Thomas Tickell. 4 vols. London, 1721.
AUBERT DE VERTOT D'AUBEUF, RENÉ. *The Revolutions of Portugal.* Translated by G. Rousillon. London, 1724.
BACON, FRANCIS. *Sylva Sylvarum: Or, Natural History.* 7th edn. London, 1658.
BAILEY, NATHAN. *An Universal Etymological Dictionary.* 2nd edn. London, 1724.
BARROW, ISAAC. *Euclides Elements.* London, 1722.
—— *Of Contentment, Patience and Resignation to the Will of God.* Edited by Thomas Barrow. 2nd edn. London, 1714.
—— *The Works of the Learned Isaac Barrow, D.D.* 3 vols. London, 1700.
BURNET, GILBERT. *Bishop Gilbert's History of his Own Time.* Edited by Gilbert Burnet the younger and Thomas Burnet. Vol. i of 2. London, 1724.
BURNET, THOMAS. *The Theory of the Earth.* 2 vols. London, 1684.
BUTLER, JOSEPH. *The Analogy of Religion.* London, 1736.
BUTLER, SAMUEL. *Hudibras.* London, 1710.
—— *Posthumous Works.* 3 vols. 3rd edn. London, 1715–17.
CHAMBERLAYNE, EDWARD, and CHAMBERLAYNE, JOHN. *The Present State of England.* 21st edn. London, 1704.
CHARNOCK, STEPHEN. *Discourse upon the Existence and Attributes of God.* 3rd edn. London, 1699.
The Christian's Duty. London, 1730.

Appendix: The Weston Hall Library 211

CIBBER, COLLEY. *Plays Written by Mr Cibber.* 2 vols. London, 1721.
CLARENDON, EDWARD HYDE, first earl of. *The History of the Rebellion and Civil Wars in England.* 3 vols. Oxford, 1720-1.
CLARKE, JOHN. *An Enquiry into the Cause and Origin of Evil.* London, 1720.
—— *An Enquiry into the Cause and Origin of Moral Evil.* London, 1721.
CLARKE, SAMUEL. *An Exposition of the Church Catechism.* 2nd edn. London, 1730.
CONGREVE, WILLIAM. *The Works of Congreve.* 2 vols. 3rd edn. London, 1719.
[COURT, PIETER CORNELIS DE LA]. *The True Interest and Political Maxims of the Republick of Holland and West Friesland.* London, 1702.
CROXALL, SAMUEL, trans., *A Select Collection of Novels.* 6 vols. London, 1720-2.
DEFOE, DANIEL. *The History of the Union.* London, 1736.
—— *Robinson Crusoe.* 2 vols. London, 1722.
DENNIS, JOHN. *The Select Works of Mr John Dennis.* 2 vols. London, 1718.
DRYDEN, JOHN. *The Dramatick Works of John Dryden.* Edited by William Congreve. 6 vols. London, 1717.
—— *Fables.* London, 1721.
—— *Miscellany Poems.* 6 vols. 4th edn. London, 1716.
—— *The Works of the Late Famous Mr. John Dryden.* Vol. iii: *Poems on Various Occasions and Translations from Several Authors.* London, 1701.
D'URFEY, THOMAS. *Tales Tragical and Comical.* London, 1704.
EVELYN, JOHN. *Kalendarium Hortense: Or, The Gard'ner's Almanac.* 9th edn. London, 1699.
The Evening Post. Nos. 105-229 (13-15 Apr. 1710-27-30, Jan. 1711).
FARQUHAR, GEORGE. *The Works.* 2 vols. 5th edn. London, 1721.
FÉNELON, FRANÇOIS. *Instructions for the Education of a Daughter.* Translated by George Hickes. 2nd edn. London, 1708.
FROWDE, PHILIP. *Philotas.* London, 1731.
GONDI, JEAN FRANÇOIS PAUL DE. *Memoirs of the Cardinal De Retz.* Translated by P. Davall. Vols. i-iii of 4. London, 1723.
GORDON, THOMAS, and TRENCHARD, JOHN. *Cato's Letters.* 4 vols. London, 1724.
HARRINGTON, JAMES. *The Oceana of James Harrington.* London, 1700.
The High German Doctor. London, 1720.
The History of the Catiline's Conspiracy. London, 1683.
HORNECK, ANTHONY. *The Great Law of Consideration.* 6th edn. London, 1694.
JONES, DAVID. *A Continuation of the Secret History of White-Hall.* London, 1697.

Appendix: The Weston Hall Library

JOSEPHUS, FLAVIUS. *The Works of Flavius Josephus*. Translated by Roger L'Estrange. 3 vols. 2nd edn. London, 1709.
JUVENALIS, DECIMUS JUNIUS. *The Satires of Decimus Junius Juvenalis*. Translated by John Dryden. 5th edn. London, 1713.
KER, JOHN. *The Memoirs of John Ker*. London, 1726.
LEE, NATHANIEL. *The Works of Mr Nathaniel Lee*. 3 vols. London, 1722.
LE SAGE, ALAIN RENÉ. *Le Diable Boiteux Or, The Devil Upon Two Sticks*. 2 vols. 6th edn. London, 1729.
LOCKE, JOHN. *An Essay Concerning Human Understanding*. Vol. i of 2. 8th edn. London, 1721.
LUCRETIUS. *Of the Nature of Things*. Translated by Thomas Creech. 2 vols. London, 1714.
MANLEY, MARY de la RIVIÈRE. *Secret Memoirs and Manners*. 2 vols. London, 1716.
Memoirs of the Royal House of Savoy. London, 1707.
MILLER, PHILIP. *The Gardener's Dictionary*. 3 vols. 2nd abridged edn. London, 1741.
MILTON, JOHN. *Paradise Lost*. London, 1668.
MONTESQUIEU, CHARLES DE SECONDAT, baron de. *Persian Letters*. Translated by M. Ozell. Vol. ii of 2. London, 1722.
NELSON, ROBERT. *An Address to Persons of Quality and Estate*. London, 1715.
—— *The Christian's Exercise*. London, 1715.
OTWAY, THOMAS. *The Works of Mr Thomas Otway*. 2 vols. London, 1722.
PÉTIS DE LA CROIX, FRANÇOIS. *The Persian and Turkish Tales Complete*. Translated by Dr King. Vol. ii of 2. 3rd edn. London, 1729.
PLUCHE, ANTOINE. *Spectacle de la Nature: Or, Nature Display'd*. Translated by Mr Humphreys. 4 vols. 4th edn. London, 1739.
PLUTARCH. *Plutarch's Morals*. Translated by M. Morgan, S. Ford, W. Dillingham, and T. Hoy. Vol. ii of 5. 2nd edn. London, 1691.
POPE, ALEXANDER. *The Works of Mr Alexander Pope in Prose*. Vol. ii of 2. London, 1741.
PRIDEAUX, HUMPHREY. *The Old and New Testament Connected in the History of the Jews*. Vol. i of 2. 3rd edn. London, 1717.
PUFFENDORF, SAMUEL. *The History of Popedom*. Translated by J. C. London, 1691.
—— *An Introduction to the History of the Principal Kingdoms and States of Europe*. Translated by J. Crull. 8th edn. London, 1719.
RAPIN, RENÉ. *Of Gardens*. Translated by J. Gardiner. London, n.d.
ROWE, NICHOLAS. *The Dramatick Works of Nicholas Rowe*. 2 vols. London, 1720.
The Rule of Life. London, 1742.

Appendix: The Weston Hall Library

SAINT-EVREMOND, CHARLES MARGUETEL DE SAINT DENIS, seigneur de. *The Works of Monsieur de St Evremond.* 3 vols. London, 1714.
SCARRON, PAUL. *Scarron's Novels.* Translated by John Davies. London, 1694.
SENECA, LUCIUS ANNAEUS. *Seneca's Morals by Way of Abstract and Discourse.* London, 1735.
SEVIGNÉ, MARIE DE RABUTIN CHANTAL, marchioness de. *Letters of Madame de Rabutin Chantal.* 2 vols. London, 1732.
SHAFTESBURY, ANTHONY ASHLEY COOPER, first earl of. *Characteristicks of Men, Manners, Opinions, Times.* 3 vols. 3rd edn. London, 1723.
SHAKESPEARE, WILLIAM. *The Works of Shakespear.* Edited by Alexander Pope. 6 vols. London, 1725.
SHERLOCK, WILLIAM. *A Practical Discourse Concerning Death.* 20th edn. London, 1726.
STANHOPE, GEORGE. *A Paraphrase and Comment upon the Epistles and Gospels.* 3rd edn. London, 1714–15.
STEELE, RICHARD. *The Englishman.* London, 1714.
—— *A Letter to a Member of Parliament.* London, 1714.
——, ed. *Poetical Miscellanies.* London, 1714.
—— *The Political Writings of Sir Richard Steele.* London, 1715.
UVEDALE, THOMAS. *The Death-Bed Display'd.* London, 1727.
VANBRUGH, JOHN. *The Provok'd Wife.* London, 1735.

Bibliography

Manuscripts

'Bishop's Transcripts of the Parish Register of Marston St. Lawrence 1706-1812.' Northamptonshire Record Office, Delapré Abbey, Northampton.

Blencowe, Anne. Manuscript poems. Weston Hall, Weston, Northamptonshire.

'Brackley Corporation 1729-1753: Register of Oaths and Declarations.' Ellesmere Collection. Northamptonshire Record Office, Delapré Abbey, Northampton.

'Brackley Parish Register 1687-1702.' Northamptonshire Record Office, Delapré Abbey, Northampton.

'Brackley Parish Register 1727-1756.' Northamptonshire Record Office, Delapré Abbey, Northampton.

'Brackley Parish Register: Burials 1771-1812.' Northamptonshire Record Office, Delapré Abbey, Northampton.

Eland, George. 'List of Brackley Tradesmen from Eland's *Purefoy Letters*, 1931.' Northampton Record Office, Delapré Abbey, Northampton.

'Hinton-in-the-Hedges Parish Register 1559-1812.' Northamptonshire Record Office, Delapré Abbey, Northampton.

Jennens, Susanna, Barnardiston, Mary, and others (unidentified). Manuscript poems and papers. Weston Hall, Weston, Northamptonshire.

'Plan of Brackley 1760.' Map 2985. Northamptonshire Record Office, Delapré Abbey, Northampton.

Richardson, Samuel. 'Letter to Isaac Hawkins Browne, December 10, 1750.' Hyde Collection, Somerville, New Jersey.

'Weston Poll-Book 1695.' Northamptonshire Record Office, Delapré Abbey, Northampton.

Reviews

AMIS, KINGSLEY. Rev. of *The New Oxford Book of Eighteenth-Century Verse*, ed. Roger Lonsdale. *The Listener* (6 Dec. 1984), 27.

BARRON, JANET. 'They Kept Scribbling', rev. of *Eighteenth-Century Women Poets: An Oxford Anthology*, ed. Roger Lonsdale. *Literary Review*, no. 136 (Jan. 1990), 57-8.

CASTLE, TERRY. 'Unruly and Unresigned', rev. of *Eighteenth-Century Women Poets: An Oxford Anthology*, ed. Roger Lonsdale. *TLS* (10–16 Nov. 1989), 1228.

DOODY, MARGARET ANNE. 'Tit for Tat', rev. of *Eighteenth-Century Women Poets: An Oxford Anthology*, ed. Roger Lonsdale. *London Review of Books* (21 Dec. 1989), 4.

GREER, GERMAINE. 'No Laments for Dead Birds', rev. of *Eighteenth-Century Women Poets: An Oxford Anthology*, ed. Roger Lonsdale. *Daily Telegraph* (21 Oct. 1989), Weekend sect., p. XIII.

JUMP, HARRIET DEVINE. '107 Grandmothers', rev. of *Eighteenth-Century Women Poets: An Oxford Anthology*, ed. Roger Lonsdale. *Oxford Magazine*, no. 55 (Hilary Term 1990), 15.

MUNNS, JESSICA. Rev. of *The Prostituted Muse: Images of Women and Women Dramatists 1642–1737*, by Jacqueline Pearson. *Restoration and 18th Century Theatre Research*, ser. 2/4 (1989), 64.

PORTER, PETER. 'Disturbing the Augustan Peace', rev. of *The New Oxford Book of Eighteenth-Century Verse*, ed. Roger Lonsdale. *TLS* (22 Feb. 1985), 187–8.

PRITCHARD, R. E. 'A Lettered Bride', rev. of *Eighteenth-Century Women Poets: An Oxford Anthology*, ed. Roger Lonsdale. *PN Review*, 16/4 (1990), 60–1.

ROGERS, PAT. 'Puellilia', rev. of *Mothers of the Novel: One Hundred Good Women Writers Before Jane Austen*, by Dale Spender. *London Review of Books* (7 Aug. 1986), 11.

RUTHERFORD, MALCOLM. 'Light on Female Bards', rev. of *Eighteenth-Century Women Poets: An Oxford Anthology*, ed. Roger Lonsdale. *Financial Times* (16 Dec. 1989), Weekend sect., p. x.

THOMPSON, E. P. 'Happy Families', rev. of *The Family, Sex and Marriage in England 1500–1800*, by Lawrence Stone. *New Society* (8 Sept. 1977), 499.

TOMALIN, CLAIRE. 'A Buried Treasury of Wicked Wits', rev. of *Eighteenth-Century Women Poets: An Oxford Anthology*, ed. Roger Lonsdale. *The Independent* (7 Oct. 1989), 34.

WILLIAMSON, KARINA. Rev. of *Eighteenth-Century Women Poets: An Oxford Anthology*, ed. Roger Lonsdale. *Essays in Criticism* (forthcoming).

Radio Broadcast

BBC Radio 3. 'Critics' Forum', transcript of discussion of *Eighteenth-Century Women Poets: An Oxford Anthology*, ed. Roger Lonsdale (7 Oct. 1989).

Books, Articles, and Theses

ABRAMS, M. H. *The Mirror and the Lamp: Romantic Theory and the Critical Tradition.* Oxford: Oxford University Press, 1953.

ADBURGHAM, ALISON. *Women in Print: Writing Women and Women's Magazines from the Restoration to the Accession of Victoria.* London: George Allen & Unwin, 1972.

ADDISON, JOSEPH. *Cato: A Tragedy.* London, 1713.

AKENSIDE, MARK. *The Pleasures of the Imagination.* London, 1744.

ALLISON, K. J., BERESFORD, M. W., and HURST, J. G. *The Deserted Villages of Northamptonshire.* Department of English Local History Occasional Papers, no. 18. Leicester: Leicester University Press, 1966.

ARIÈS, PHILIPPE. *The Hour of Our Death*, trans. Helen Weaver. London: Allen Lane, 1981.

ASHRAF, PHYLLIS MARY. *Introduction to Working Class Literature in Great Britain.* 2 vols. Berlin: Ministerium für Volksbildung, Hauptabteilung Lehrbildung, 1978-9.

ASSHETON, WILLIAM. *A Method of Devotion for Sick and Dying Persons.* London, 1706.

ASTELL, MARY. *A Serious Proposal to the Ladies.* London, 1694-7.

—— *Some Reflections Upon Marriage.* London, 1700; 2nd edn., 1703.

AUBIN, ROBERT ARNOLD. *Topographical Poetry in XVIII-Century England.* The Modern Language Association of America Revolving Fund Series, 6. New York: Modern Language Association, 1936; New York: Kraus Reprint Corporation, 1966.

AUERBACH, NINA. *Communities of Women: An Idea in Fiction.* Cambridge, Mass. and London: Harvard University Press, 1978.

BACKSCHEIDER, PAULA R. *Daniel Defoe: His Life.* Baltimore and London: The Johns Hopkins University Press, 1989.

BAKER, ANNE ELIZABETH. *Glossary of Northamptonshire Words and Phrases.* 2 vols. London, 1854.

BAKER, DAVID ERSKINE. *Biographia Dramatica: Or, A Companion to the Playhouse*, rev. Isaac Reed and Stephen Jones. 3 vols. London, 1764; rev. edn., 1812.

BAKER, GEORGE. *The History and Antiquities of the County of Northampton.* 2 vols. London, 1822-41.

BAMFORD, FRANCIS, ed. *Dear Miss Heber: An Eighteenth Century Correspondence*, pref. Georgia Sitwell, introd. Sacheverell Sitwell. London: Constable, 1936.

BANCKS, JOHN. *The Weaver's Miscellany: Or, Poems on Several Subjects.* London, 1730.

BARBAULD, ANNA LAETITIA, ed. *The Correspondence of Samuel Richardson.* 6 vols. London, 1804.

Bibliography

BARRELL, JOHN. *The Dark Side of the Landscape: The Rural Poor in English Painting 1730–1840.* Cambridge: Cambridge University Press, 1980.

—— *English Literature in History 1730–80: An Equal, Wide Survey.* London: Hutchinson, 1983.

—— *The Idea of Landscape and the Sense of Place 1730–1840: An Approach to the Poetry of John Clare.* Cambridge: Cambridge University Press, 1972.

BARROW, ISAAC. *Of Contentment, Patience and Resignation to the Will of God.* London, 1685.

BATE, WALTER JACKSON. *The Burden of the Past and the English Poet.* London: Chatto & Windus, 1971.

BEATY, NANCY LEE. *The Craft of Dying: A Study in the Literary Tradition of the Ars Moriendi in England.* Yale Studies in English, 175. New Haven, Conn., and London: Yale University Press, 1970.

BENTLEY, ELIZABETH. *Genuine Poetical Compositions on Various Subjects.* Norwich, 1791.

BERGER, JOHN. 'Past Seen from a Possible Future', in Nikos Stangos (ed.), *Selected Essays and Articles: The Look of Things*, 211–21. Harmondsworth: Penguin, 1972.

BLACKWELL, THOMAS. *An Enquiry into the Life and Writings of Homer.* London, 1735.

BLAND, WILFRED. 'Susanna Highmore's Literary Reputation', *Proceedings of the American Philosophical Society*, 122 (1978), 377–84.

BLENCOWE, MRS, ed. *The Casket: A Miscellany.* London, 1829.

BLOOMFIELD, ROBERT. *Collected Poems (1800–1822)*, ed. Jonathan N. Lawson. 5 vols. in one. Gainesville, Fla.: Scholars Facsimiles, 1971.

BLUNDEN, EDMUND. 'A Northamptonshire Poetess: Glimpses of an Eighteenth-Century Prodigy', *Journal of the Northamptonshire Natural History Society*, 28 (1936), 59–74. Reprint with manuscript revisions in the Bodleian Library, 2795 e. 274.

—— and MELLOR, BERNARD. *Wayside Poems of the Early Eighteenth Century.* Hong Kong: Hong Kong University Press, 1964.

BOND, DONALD F., ed. *The Tatler.* 3 vols. Oxford: Clarendon Press, 1987.

BONNELL, THOMAS F. 'Bookselling and Canon-Making: The Trade Rivalry over The English Poets, 1776–1783', in *Studies in Eighteenth-Century Culture*, 19, Proceedings of The American Society for Eighteenth-Century Studies (East Lansing, Mich.: Colleagues Press, 1989), 53–69.

BOSWELL, JAMES. *Boswell's Life of Johnson*, ed. G. B. Hill, rev. L. F. Powell. 6 vols. Oxford: Clarendon Press, 1934–50.

BOURNE, HENRY. *Antiquitates Vulgares: Or, The Antiquities of the Common People.* Newcastle, 1725.

BOWLES, CAROLINE. 'The Birth-Day, A Poem', *Blackwood's Edinburgh Magazine*, 41 (Dec. 1836–June 1837), 404–28.

BOWLES, THOMAS. *A Compendious and Rational Institution of the Latin Tongue*. Oxford, 1740. Rev. edn., *Aristarchus: Or, A Compendious and Rational Institution of the Latin Tongue*. London, 1748.

—— *Grammaticæ Latin Syntaxis Commentariis Illustrata: Or, the Fundamental Rules of the Latin Grammar Made Plain and Easy*. Northampton, 1738.

—— *A Sermon on the Gradual Advances, and Distinct Periods of Divine Revelation*. Northampton, 1738.

BOWLES, WILLIAM LISLE. *Scenes and Shadows of Days Departed*. London, 1835.

BRAGG, MARION K. *The Formal Eclogue in Eighteenth-Century England*. University of Maine Studies, ser. 2/6. Orono, Me.: The University Press, 1926.

BREVAL, JOHN. *The Art of Dress*. London, 1717.

BRIDGES, JOHN. *The History and Antiquities of Northamptonshire*, ed. Peter Whalley. 2 vols. Oxford, 1791.

BROWNE, ALICE. *The Eighteenth Century Feminist Mind*. Brighton: Harvester, 1987.

BROWNE, ISAAC HAWKINS. *De Animi Immortalitate*. London, 1754.

—— *The Immortality of the Soul*, trans. Richard Grey. London, 1754.

BROWNELL, MORRIS. 'Poetical Villas: English Verse Satire of the Country House, 1700–1750', in J.D. Browning (ed.), *Satire in the 18th Century*, 9–51. Publications of the McMaster University Association for 18th Century Studies, 10. New York and London: Garland Publishing, 1983.

BRYANT, JOHN FREDERICK. *Verses*. London, 1787.

BURKE, PETER. *Popular Culture in Early Modern Europe*. London: Temple Smith, 1978.

BUTLER, MARILYN. *Literature as a Heritage: Or, Reading Other Ways*. Inaugural Lecture delivered 10 Nov. 1987. Cambridge: Cambridge University Press, 1988.

BUTLER, SAMUEL. *Hudibras*, ed. John Wilders. Oxford: Clarendon Press, 1967.

C., R. *The Triumphant Weaver: Or, The Art of Weaving Discussed and Handled*. London, 1682.

CAESAR, JULIUS. *Julius Caesar's Commentaries*, trans. Martin Bladen. London, 1705.

CARTER, JEFFERSON MATTHEW. 'The Unlettered Muse: The Uneducated Poets and the Concept of Natural Genius in Eighteenth-Century England', Ph.D. thesis, University of Arizona, 1972.

CASTLE, TERRY. *Masquerade and Civilization: The Carnivalesque in*

Eighteenth-Century English Culture and Fiction. Stanford, Calif.: Stanford University Press, 1986.

CHALKER, JOHN. *The English Georgic: A Study in the Development of a Form.* London: Routledge & Kegan Paul, 1969.

CHILDS, FENELA ANN. 'Prescriptions for Manners in English Courtesy Literature, 1690–1760, and their Social Implications', D.Phil. thesis, Oxford University, 1984.

CLARE, JOHN. *The Prose of John Clare*, eds. J. W. Tibble and Anne Tibble. London: Routledge & Kegan Paul, 1951.

CLARKE, JOHN. *The Book of Brackley: The First Thousand Years.* Buckingham: Barracuda Books, 1987.

—— *Yesterday's Brackley—The Last 300 Years.* Buckingham: Barracuda Books, 1990.

COLE, JOHN. *Memoirs of Mrs. Chapone.* London, 1839.

—— *Popular Biography of Northamptonshire.* London, 1839.

COLEY, W. B. 'Notes toward a "Class Theory" of Augustan Literature: The Example of Fielding', in Frank Brady, John Palmer, and Martin Price. (ed.), *Literary Theory and Structure: Essays in Honor of William K. Wimsatt*, 313–50. New Haven, Conn., and London: Yale University Press, 1973.

COLLIER, MARY. *The Woman's Labour: An Epistle to Mr Stephen Duck.* London, 1739.

COLLINS, J. CHURTON, ed. *A Treasury of Minor British Poetry.* London and New York, 1896.

COLMAN, GEORGE, and THORNTON, BONNELL, ed. *Poems by Eminent Ladies.* London, 1755. Rev. edn., *Poems by the Most Eminent Ladies of Great Britain and Ireland.* London, c.1775.

COOPER, NICHOLAS. *Aynho: A Northamptonshire Village.* Banbury Historical Society, 20. Banbury: Leopard's Head Press and Banbury Historical Society, 1984.

COWPER, WILLIAM. *The Letters and Prose Writings of William Cowper*, ed. James King and Charles Ryskamp, 5 vols. (Oxford: Oxford University Press, 1979–86).

CRABBE, GEORGE. *The Complete Poetical Works*, gen. ed. Norma Dalrymple Champneys; ed. Norma Dalrymple Champneys and Arthur Pollard. 3 vols. Oxford: Clarendon Press, 1988.

CREECH, THOMAS. *The Idylliums of Theocritus.* Oxford, 1684.

DAVIES, KATHLEEN M. 'The Sacred Condition of Equality: How Original were Puritan Doctrines of Marriage?', *Social History*, no. 5 (May 1977), 563–80.

DAVIS, ROSE MARY. *Stephen Duck, The Thresher-Poet.* University of Maine Studies, ser. 2/8. Orono, Me.: The University Press, 1926.

DEFOE, DANIEL. *A Brief State of the Question, Between the Printed and*

Painted Callicoes and the Woollen and Silk Manufacture. London, 1719.

—— *Roxana*, ed. Jane Jack. London, New York, and Toronto: Oxford University Press, 1964; paperback edn., 1981.

DELL, HENRY, ed. *A Select Collection of the Psalms of David.* London, 1756.

Dictionary of National Biography. 22 vols. London, 1885–1901.

DIXON, SARAH. *Poems on Several Occasions.* Canterbury, 1740.

DODSLEY, ROBERT. *Servitude: A Poem*, introd. and postscript Daniel Defoe. London, 1729.

DOODY, MARGARET ANNE. *The Daring Muse: Augustan Poetry Reconsidered.* Cambridge: Cambridge University Press, 1985.

—— 'Swift among the Women', *Yearbook of English Studies*, 18 (1988), 68–92.

DRELINCOURT, CHARLES. *The Christian's Defence Against the Fears of Death*, trans. M. D'Assigny. London, 1675.

DUBOIS, DOROTHEA. *Poems on Several Occasions.* Dublin, 1764.

DUBROW, HEATHER. 'The Country-House Poem: A Study in Generic Development', *Genre*, 12 (1979), 153–79.

DUCK, STEPHEN. *Poems on Several Occasions.* London, 1736.

—— and COLLIER, MARY. *The Thresher's Labour (1736) and The Woman's Labour (1739).* Augustan Reprint Society Publication 230, ed. Moira Ferguson. Los Angeles: William Andrews Clark Memorial Library, 1985.

DUFF, WILLIAM. *An Essay on Original Genius.* London, 1767.

DUNCOMBE, JOHN. *The Feminiad.* London, 1754. Facsimile, Augustan Reprint Society Publication 207, ed. Jocelyn Harris. Los Angeles: William Andrews Clark Memorial Library, 1981.

DYCE, ALEXANDER, ed. *Specimens of British Poetesses.* London, 1825.

EAGLETON, TERRY. *The Function of Criticism: From* The Spectator *to Post-Structuralism.* London: Verso Editions and NLB, 1984.

EAVES, T. C. DUNCAN, and KIMPEL, BEN D. *Samuel Richardson: A Biography.* Oxford: Clarendon Press, 1971.

EGERTON, SARAH FYGE. *The Female Advocate.* London, 1686.

—— *Poems on Several Occasions.* London, 1703.

EHRENPREIS, IRVIN. 'Letters of Advice to Young Spinsters', in Irvin Ehrenpreis and Robert Halsband, *The Lady of Letters in the Eighteenth Century: Papers Read at a Clark Library Seminar, January 18, 1969*, 1–27. Los Angeles: William Andrews Clark Memorial Library, 1969.

—— 'Poverty and Poetry: Representations of the Poor in Augustan Literature', in *Studies in Eighteenth-Century Culture*, 1. Proceedings of the American Society for Eighteenth Century Studies, 3–35. Cleveland and London: The Press of Case Western Reserve University, 1971.

ELAND, GEORGE. 'Molly Leapor—Poetess', *Northampton County Magazine*, 5 (1932), 116–19.
——, ed. *Purefoy Letters 1735–1753*. 2 vols. London: Sidgwick & Jackson, 1931.
ELIAS, A. C. 'A Manuscript Book of Constantia Grierson's', *Swift Studies*, 2 (1987), 33–56.
ELTON, OLIVER. *A Survey of English Literature 1730–1780*. 2 vols. London: Edward Arnold, 1928.
ERDMAN, DAVID. 'Editor's Epigraph', *Bulletin of the New York Public Library*, 77 (1974), 289.
ERSKINE-HILL, HOWARD. *The Social Milieu of Alexander Pope: Lives, Example and the Poetic Response*. New Haven, Conn., and London: Yale University Press, 1975.
FABRICANT, CAROLE. 'The Aesthetics and Politics of Landscape in the Eighteenth Century', in Ralph Cohen (ed.), *Studies in Eighteenth-Century British Art and Aesthetics*, 49–81. Berkeley, Los Angeles, and London: University of California Press, 1985.
—— 'Binding and Dressing Nature's Loose Tresses: The Ideology of Augustan Landscape Design', in *Studies in Eighteenth-Century Culture*, 8. Proceedings of the American Society for Eighteenth Century Studies, 109–35. Madison and London: The University of Wisconsin Press, 1979.
—— *Swift's Landscape*. Baltimore and London: The Johns Hopkins University Press, 1982.
FADERMAN, LILLIAN. *Surpassing the Love of Men: Romantic Friendship and Love Between Women from the Renaissance to the Present*. New York: William Morrow and Company, 1981.
FAIRCHILD, HOXIE NEALE. *Religious Trends in English Poetry*. 6 vols. New York: Columbia University Press, 1939–68. Vol. ii: *1740–1780: Religious Sentimentalism in the Age of Johnson*, 1942.
FALCONER, WILLIAM. *The Shipwreck*. London, 1762.
FARMER, RICHARD. *An Essay on the Learning of Shakespeare*. Cambridge, 1767.
FEINGOLD, RICHARD. *Nature and Society: Later Eighteenth Century Uses of the Pastoral and Georgic*. Hassocks: The Harvester Press, 1978.
FERGUSON, MOIRA. 'Resistance and Power in the Life and Writing of Ann Yearsley', *The Eighteenth Century: Theory and Interpretation*, 27 (1986), 247–68.
FIGES, EVA. *Sex and Subterfuge: Women Novelists to 1850*. London and Basingstoke: Macmillan, 1982.
FINCH, ANNE. *The Poems of Anne Countess of Winchilsea*, ed. Myra Reynolds. Chicago: University of Chicago Press, 1903.
FORRESTER, ERIC G. *A History of Magdalen College School, Brackley,*

Northamptonshire, 1548–1949. Buckingham: E. N. Hillier and Sons, 1950.

Foss, Michael. *The Age of Patronage: The Arts in Society 1660–1750*. London: Hamish Hamilton, 1971.

Foster, J. *Alumni Oxonienses 1715–1886*. 4 vols. Oxford, 1888.

Fowler, Alastair. 'Country House Poems: The Politics of a Genre', *The Seventeenth Century*, 1 (1986), 1–14.

Foxon, D. F. *English Verse 1701–1750*. 2 vols. Cambridge: Cambridge University Press, 1975.

Fraser, Antonia. *The Weaker Vessel: Woman's Lot in Seventeenth-Century England*. London: Weidenfeld & Nicolson, 1984.

Frye, Northrop. 'Towards Defining an Age of Sensibility', *ELH* 23 (1956), 144–52.

Gay, John. *Dramatic Works*, ed. John Fuller. 2 vols. Oxford: Clarendon Press, 1983.

—— *John Gay: Poetry and Prose*, ed. Vinton A. Dearing, asst. ed. Charles E. Beckwith. 2 vols. Oxford: Clarendon Press, 1974.

The Gentleman's Magazine, 1731–

Gillis, John R. 'Married but not Churched: Plebeian Sexual Relations and Marital Nonconformity in Eighteenth-Century Britain', in Robert P. MacCubbin (ed.), *'Tis Nature's Fault: Unauthorized Sexuality during the Enlightenment*, 31–42. Cambridge and New York: Cambridge University Press, 1987.

Gittings, Clare. *Death, Burial and the Individual in Early Modern England*. London and Sydney: Croom Helm, 1984.

Goldsmith, Oliver. *The Collected Works of Oliver Goldsmith*, ed. Arthur Friedman. 5 vols. Oxford: Clarendon Press, 1966.

Göller, Karl Heinz. 'The Emancipation of Women in Eighteenth-Century English Literature', *Anglia*, 101 (1983), 78–98.

Gray, Thomas. *The Complete Poems of Thomas Gray, English, Latin and Greek*, ed. H. W. Starr and J. R. Hendrickson. Oxford: Clarendon Press, 1966.

Greenberg, Janelle. 'The Legal Status of the English Woman in Early Eighteenth-Century Common Law and Equity', in *Studies in Eighteenth-Century Culture*, 4. Proceedings of the American Society for Eighteenth Century Studies, 171–81. Madison and London: University of Wisconsin Press, 1975.

Greer, Germaine, Hastings, Susan, Medoff, Jeslyn, and Sansone, Melinda, ed. *Kissing the Rod: An Anthology of Seventeenth-Century Women's Verse*. London: Virago, 1988.

Grey, Richard. *An Answer To Mr. Warburton's Remarks on Several Occasions*. London, 1744.

Grigson, Geoffrey, ed. *Before the Romantics: An Anthology of the Enlightenment*. London: George Routledge & Sons, 1946.

GROSVENOR, BENJAMIN. *Observations on Sudden Death*. London, 1720.
GRUNDY, ISOBEL. 'Samuel Johnson: A Writer of Lives Looks at Death', *Modern Language Review*, 79 (1984), 257-65.
GUBAR, SUSAN. 'The Female Monster in Augustan Satire', *Signs*, 3 (1977), 380-94.
HALSBAND, ROBERT. 'Ladies of Letters in the Eighteenth Century', in Irvin Ehrenpreis and Robert Halsband, *The Lady of Letters in the Eighteenth Century: Papers Read at a Clark Library Seminar, January 18, 1969*, 29-55. Los Angeles: William Andrews Clark Memorial Library, 1969.
—— 'Woman and Literature in 18th Century England', in Paul Fritz and Richard Morton (ed.), *Woman in the 18th Century and Other Essays*, 55-71. Publications of the McMaster University Association for 18th Century Studies, 4. Toronto and Sarasota, Fla.: Samuel Stevens Hakkert, 1976.
HANDS, ELIZABETH. *The Death of Amnon*. Coventry, 1789.
HARDING, DIANA. 'Education in Northants in the 18th Century', Ph.D. thesis, University of Newcastle upon Tyne, 1969.
HARRIS, JOCELYN. *Jane Austen's Art of Memory*. Cambridge: Cambridge University Press, 1989.
—— *Samuel Richardson*. Cambridge: Cambridge University Press, 1987.
—— 'Sappho, Souls, and the Salic Law of Wit', in Alan C. Kors and Paul J. Korshin (ed.), *Anticipations of the Enlightenment in England, France, and Germany*, 232-58. Philadelphia: University of Pennsylvania Press, 1987.
HECHT, J. JEAN. *The Domestic Servant Class in Eighteenth-Century England*. London: Routledge & Kegan Paul, 1956.
HIBBARD, G. R. 'The Country House Poem of the Seventeenth Century', *Journal of the Warburg and Courtauld Institutes*, 19 (1956), 159-74.
HILL, BRIDGET. 'A Refuge from Men: The Idea of a Protestant Nunnery', *Past & Present*, no. 117 (Nov. 1987), 107-30.
—— *Women, Work and Sexual Politics in Eighteenth-Century England*. Oxford: Basil Blackwell, 1989.
HOBSBAWM, E. J., and SCOTT, JOAN WALLACH. 'Political Shoemakers', *Past & Present*, no. 89 (Nov. 1980), 86-114.
HOLD, TREVOR, ed. *A Northamptonshire Garland: An Anthology of Northamptonshire Poets with Biographical Notes*. Northampton: Northamptonshire Libraries, 1989.
HOLT (née WISEMAN), JANE. *Antiochus the Great: Or, The Fatal Relapse*. London, 1702.
—— *A Fairy Tale*. London, 1717.
HOULBROOKE, RALPH, ed. *Death, Ritual and Bereavement*. London and New York: Routledge in association with The Social History Society of the United Kingdom, 1989.

HUFTON, OLWEN. 'Women without Men: Widows and Spinsters in Britain and France in the Eighteenth-Century', *Journal of Family History*, 9 (1984), 355-76.
HUNT, JOHN DIXON. *The Figure in the Landscape: Poetry, Painting, and Gardening during the Eighteenth-Century*. Baltimore and London: The Johns Hopkins University Press, 1976.
ISER, WOLFGANG. *The Implied Reader: Patterns of Communication in Prose Fiction from Bunyan to Beckett*. Baltimore and London: The Johns Hopkins University Press, 1974.
JANSSEN, ANKE. 'Frühe Lyrikerinnen des 18. Jahrhunderts in ihrem Verhältnis zur Poetik und zur *Poetic Diction*', *Anglia*, 99 (1981), 111-33.
JEMMAT, CATHERINE. *Miscellanies, in Prose and Verse*. London, 1766.
JOHNSON, SAMUEL. *The Yale Edition of the Works of Samuel Johnson*. 15 vols. to date. New Haven, Conn.: Yale University Press, 1958.
—— *The Letters of Samuel Johnson with Mrs Thrale's Genuine Letters to Him*, ed. R. W. Chapman. 3 vols. Oxford: Clarendon Press, 1952.
—— *Lives of the English Poets*, ed. George Birkbeck Hill. 3 vols. Oxford: Clarendon Press, 1905.
JONES, HENRY. *Poems on Several Occasions*. London, 1749.
JONES, M. G. *The Charity School Movement: A Study of Eighteenth Century Puritanism in Action*. Cambridge: Cambridge University Press, 1938.
JONES, MARY. *Miscellanies in Prose and Verse*. Oxford, 1750.
KAMES, HENRY HOME, Lord. *Elements of Criticism*. 2 vols. 9th edn. Edinburgh, 1817.
KEN, THOMAS. *The Works of Thomas Ken*. 4 vols. London, 1721.
KENNY, VIRGINIA C. *The Country-House Ethos in English Literature 1688-1750: Themes of Personal Retreat and National Expansion*. Brighton: Harvester, 1984.
KETTLEWELL, JOHN. *Death Made Comfortable: Or The Way to Dye Well*. London, 1695.
KLAUS, H. GUSTAV. *The Literature of Labour: Two Hundred Years of Working-Class Writing*. Brighton: Harvester, 1985.
—— 'Stephen Duck und Mary Collier. Plebejische Kontro-Verse über Frauenarbeit vor 250 Jahren', *Gulliver*, 10 (1981), 115-23.
KORSHIN, PAUL J. 'Types of Eighteenth-Century Literary Patronage', *Eighteenth Century Studies*, 7 (Summer 1974), 453-73.
KOWALESKI-WALLACE, BETH. 'Milton's Daughters: The Education of Eighteenth-Century Women Writers', *Feminist Studies*, 12 (1986), 275-93.
KUIST, JAMES M. *The Nichols File of The Gentleman's Magazine*. Madison and London: University of Wisconsin Press, 1982.

KUSSMAUL, ANN. *Servants in Husbandry in Early Modern England.* Cambridge: Cambridge University Press, 1981.

The Lady's Poetical Magazine: Or, Beauties of British Poetry. 4 vols. London, 1781-2.

LANDRY, DONNA. *The Muses of Resistance: Laboring-Class Women's Poetry in Britain, 1739-1796.* Cambridge Studies in Eighteenth-Century Literature and Thought. Cambridge: Cambridge University Press, 1990.

—— 'The Resignation of Mary Collier: Some Problems in Feminist Literary History', in Felicity Nussbaum and Laura Brown (ed.), *The New Eighteenth Century: Theory, Politics, English Literature*, 99-120. New York and London: Methuen, 1987.

LEAPOR, MARY. *Poems Upon Several Occasions.* 2 vols. London, 1748-51.

—— 'The Rural Maid's Reflexions', *London Magazine*, 16 (1747), 45.

LENNOX, CHARLOTTE. *The Female Quixote*, ed. Margaret Dalziel. London, New York, and Toronto: Oxford University Press, 1970.

LEWIS, ESTHER. *Poems Moral and Entertaining.* Bath, 1789.

LEWIS, JOSEPH [LANCELOT POVERTY-STRUCK]. *The Miscellaneous and Whimsical Lucubrations of Lancelot Poverty-struck.* London, 1758.

LOCKE, JOHN. *Two Treatises of Government*, ed. Peter Laslett. Cambridge: Cambridge University Press, 1960; 2nd edn., 1967.

LONSDALE, ROGER, ed. *Eighteenth-Century Women Poets: An Oxford Anthology.* Oxford and New York: Oxford University Press, 1989.

—— ed. *The New Oxford Book of Eighteenth-Century Verse.* Oxford and New York: Oxford University Press, 1984.

LOVEJOY, A. O. 'Monboddo and Rousseau', in *Essays in the History of Ideas*, 38-61. Baltimore: The Johns Hopkins Press, 1948.

—— CHINARD, GILBERT, BOAS, GEORGE, and CRANE, RONALD S., gen. ed. *A Documentary History of Primitivism and Related Ideas.* 1 vol. only: A. O. Lovejoy and George Boas, *Primitivism and Related Ideas in Antiquity.* Baltimore: The Johns Hopkins Press, 1935.

LOWERSON, JOHN R. 'Enclosure and Farm Holdings in Brackley, 1829-51', *Northamptonshire Past and Present*, 6 (1978), 33-48.

MCCLUNG, WILLIAM A. *The Country House in English Renaissance Poetry.* Berkeley, Los Angeles, and London: University of California Press, 1977.

MCGONIGLE, PETER J. 'Stephen Duck and the Text of *The Thresher's Labour,*' *The Library*, ser. 6/4 (1982), 288-96.

MACK, MAYNARD. *Alexander Pope: A Life.* New Haven, Conn., and London: Yale University Press in association with W. W. Norton & Company, 1985.

MCMANNERS, JOHN. *Death and the Enlightenment: Changing Attitudes to*

Death among Christians and Unbelievers in Eighteenth-Century France. Oxford: Oxford University Press, 1981.

MAHL, MARY R., and KOON, HELENE, ed. *The Female Spectator: English Women Writers Before 1800.* Bloomington, Ind. and London: The Feminist Press, 1977.

MALCOLMSON, ROBERT W. *Life and Labour in England 1700–1780.* Hutchison Social History of England. London: Hutchison, 1981.

—— *Popular Recreations in English Society 1700–1850.* Cambridge: Cambridge University Press, 1973.

MALINS, EDWARD. *English Landscaping and Literature 1660–1840.* London: Oxford University Press, 1966.

Man Superior to Woman. London, 1739.

MARSHALL, DOROTHY. *The English Domestic Servant in History.* Historical Association Publications, gen. ser. 13. London: George Philip & Son, 1949.

MASTERS, MARY. *Poems on Several Occasions.* London, 1733.

MAYO, RICHARD. *A Present For Servants From their Ministers, Masters, Or Other Friends, Especially in Country Parishes.* London, 1693.

MENDELSON, SARA HELLER. '"The Weightiest Business: Marriage in an Upper-Gentry Family in Seventeenth-Century England', *Past & Present*, no. 85 (Nov. 1979), 126–35.

MESSENGER, ANN. ' "Daughter of Shenstone"? Being a Brief Life of Mary Whateley Darwall', *Bulletin of Research in the Humanities*, 87 (1986–7), 462–81.

—— *His and Hers: Essays in Restoration and Eighteenth-Century Literature.* Lexington, Ky.: The University of Kentucky Press, 1986.

—— 'Women Poets and the Pastoral Trap: The Case of Mary Whateley', in Frederick M. Keener and Susan E. Lorsch (ed.), *Eighteenth Century Women and the Arts*, 93–105. Westport, Conn.: Greenwood Press, 1988.

MITCHELL, L. G., ed. *The Purefoy Letters 1735–53.* London: Sidgwick and Jackson, 1973.

MONK, SAMUEL H. *The Sublime: A Study of Critical Theories in XVIII-Century England.* New York: Modern Language Association of America, 1935.

MONTAGU, ELIZABETH. *An Essay on the Writings and Genius of Shakespeare.* London, 1769.

MONTAGU, MARY WORTLEY. *The Complete Letters of Lady Mary Wortley Montagu*, ed. Robert Halsband. 3 vols. Oxford: Oxford University Press, 1965–7.

—— *Essays and Poems and Simplicity, A Comedy*, ed. Robert Halsband and Isobel Grundy. Oxford: Clarendon Press, 1977.

The Monthly Review, 1749–1845.

MOORE, PAUL HENRY. 'Death in the Eighteenth-Century Novel 1740–1800', D.Phil. thesis, Oxford University, 1986.
NAMIER, LEWIS, and BROOKE, JOHN. *The House of Commons 1754–1790*. 2 vols. London: HM Stationery Office, 1964.
NEESON, J. M. 'Common Right and Enclosure in Eighteenth Century Northamptonshire', Ph.D. thesis, University of Warwick, 1978.
—— 'The Opponents of Enclosure in Eighteenth-Century Northamptonshire', *Past & Present*, no. 105 (Nov. 1984), 114–39.
NELSON, HENRY. *A New Poem on the Ancient and Loyal Society of Journey-Men Taylors*. Dublin, 1725.
NEUBURG, VICTOR E. *Popular Education in Eighteenth Century England*. London: Woburn Press, 1971.
—— *Popular Literature: A History and Guide from the Beginning of Printing to the Year 1897*. Harmondsworth: Penguin, 1977.
Northamptonshire Poll Books from 1702–1831. Northampton, 1832.
NOVAK, MAXIMILIAN, ed. *English Literature in the Age of Disguise*. Berkeley and London: University of California Press, 1977.
NUSSBAUM, FELICITY. *The Brink of All We Hate: English Satires on Women 1660–1750*. Lexington, Ky.: University of Kentucky Press, 1984.
O'CONNOR, MARY CATHERINE. *The Art of Dying: The Development of the Ars Moriendi*. Columbia University Studies in English and Comparative Literature, 156. New York: Columbia University Press, 1942.
ONG, WALTER J. 'The Writer's Audience is Always a Fiction', in *Interfaces of the Word: Studies in the Evolution of Consciousness and Culture*, 53–81. Ithaca, NY and London: Cornell University Press, 1977.
OSBORN, JAMES M. 'Spence, Natural Genius and Pope', *Philological Quarterly*, 45 (1966), 123–44.
PATTON, JULIA. *The English Village: A Literary Study 1750–1850*. New York: Macmillan, 1919.
PAULSON, RONALD. *Popular and Polite Art in the Age of Hogarth and Fielding*. University of Notre Dame Ward-Phillips Lectures in English Language and Literature, 10. Notre Dame, Ind. and London: University of Notre Dame Press, 1979.
PEARSON, JACQUELINE. *The Prostituted Muse: Images of Women and Women Dramatists 1642–1737*. Hemel Hempstead: Harvester-Wheatsheaf, 1988.
PEDERSON, SUSAN. 'Hannah More Meets Simple Simon: Tracts, Chapbooks, and Popular Culture in Late Eighteenth-Century England', *Journal of British Studies*, 25 (1986), 84–113.
PERRY, RUTH. *The Celebrated Mary Astell: An Early English Feminist*. Chicago and London: University of Chicago Press, 1986.

PEVSNER, NIKOLAUS. *Northamptonshire*, rev. Bridget Cherry. *The Buildings of England*, ed. Nikolaus Pevsner and Judy Nairn. Harmondsworth: Penguin, 1961; rev. edn., 1973.

PHILIPS, AMBROSE. *The Poems of Ambrose Philips*, ed. M. R. Segar. The Percy Reprints, 14. Oxford: Basil Blackwell, 1937.

PHILLIPS, PATRICIA. *The Adventurous Muse: Theories of Originality in English Poetics 1650–1760*. Studia Anglistica Upsaliensia, 53. Uppsala: Uppsala University, 1984.

PHILLIPS, THOMAS. 'Pedigree of Blencowe of Marston St. Lawrence, Co. Northamptonshire', *Genealogia: A Collection of Pedigrees of Families*, n.p., c.1871.

POLLAK, ELLEN. *The Poetics of Sexual Myth: Gender and Ideology in the Verse of Swift and Pope*. Chicago and London: University of Chicago Press, 1985.

POPE, ALEXANDER. *The Twickenham Edition of the Works of Alexander Pope*, gen. ed. John Butt. 11 vols. London: Methuen, 1939–68.

PORTER, ROY. *Disease, Medicine and Society in England 1550–1860*. London: Macmillan, 1987.

—— 'Making Faces: Physiognomy and Fashion in Eighteenth-Century England', *Études Anglaises: Grande Bretagne, États-Unis*, 38 (1985), 383–96.

—— and PORTER, DOROTHY. *In Sickness and in Health: The British Experience 1650–1850*. London: Fourth Estate, 1988.

POWELL, DAVID. 'Five Best Poets of Northamptonshire', *Northamptonshire and Bedfordshire Life*, 2 (Apr.–May 1972), 22–4.

Proposals for Printing by Subscription The Poetical Works, Serious and Humorous, Of Mrs. Leapor, lately Deceased. London, 1747. Damaged copy at Bodleian Library, Ballard MS 42, fo. 24b.

REY, CLAUDIUS. *A Further Examination of the Weavers Pretences*. London, 1719.

—— *Observations on Mr. Asgill's Brief Answer To A Brief State of the Question Between the Printed and Painted Callicoes*. London, 1719.

—— *The Weavers True Case*. London, 1719; 2nd edn., 1719.

REYNOLDS, MYRA. *The Learned Lady in England 1650–1760*. Boston, Mass. and New York: Houghton Mifflin, 1920.

RICHARDSON, RUTH. *Death, Dissection and the Destitute*. London and New York: Routledge & Kegan Paul, 1987.

RICHARDSON, SAMUEL. *Pamela: Or, Virtue Rewarded*, ed. Peter Sabor, introd. Margaret Anne Doody. Harmondsworth: Penguin, 1980.

RILEY, JAMES C. *Sickness, Recovery and Death: A History and Forecast of Ill Health*. London: Macmillan, 1989.

RIVERS, ISABEL. *The Poetry of Conservatism 1600–1745: A Study of Poets and Public Affairs from Jonson to Pope*. Cambridge: Rivers Press, 1973.

Rizzo, Betty. 'Christopher Smart, The "C.S." Poems, and Molly Leapor's Epitaph', *The Library*, ser. 6/5 (1983), 21–31.

—— 'Found: Joseph Lewis, Elusive Author of *Mother Midnight's Comical Pocket-Book*', *Bulletin of the New York Public Library*, 77 (1974), 281–7.

—— 'Joseph Lewis in REAL CALAMITY', *Bulletin of Research in the Humanities*, 81 (Spring 1978), 84–9.

—— 'Molly Leapor: An Anxiety for Influence', *The Age of Johnson*, 4 (forthcoming).

—— 'The Patron as Poet Maker: The Politics of Benefaction', in *Studies in Eighteenth-Century Culture*, 20, Proceedings of the American Society for Eighteenth-Century Studies (East Lansing, Mich.: Colleagues Press, 1990), 241–66.

Rogers, Katherine Lyle M. *Feminism in Eighteenth-Century England*. Brighton: Harvester, 1982.

—— *The Troublesome Helpmate: A History of Misogyny in Literature*. Seattle and London: University of Washington Press, 1966.

Rogers, Pat. *Literature and Popular Culture in Eighteenth Century England*. Brighton: Harvester, 1985.

Rowe, Nicholas. *The Dramatick Works of Nicholas Rowe, Esq.* 2 vols. London, 1720.

Rowton, Frederick, ed. *The Female Poets of Great Britain*. London, 1848.

Rumbold, Valerie. *Women's Place in Pope's World*. Cambridge Studies in Eighteenth-Century English Literature and Thought, 2. Cambridge: Cambridge University Press, 1989.

Saintsbury, George, ed. *The Receipt Book of Mrs. Ann Blencowe, A.D. 1694*. London: The Adelphi, Guy Chapman, 1925.

Sale, William M., Jr. *Samuel Richardson: Master Printer*. Cornell Studies in English, 37. Ithaca, NY: Cornell University Press, 1950.

Sales, Roger. 'The Literature of Labour and "The Condition of England Question"', Ph.D. thesis, Cambridge University, 1975.

—— 'The Politics of Pastoral', in Kathleen Parkinson and Martin Priestman (ed.), *Peasants and Countrymen in Literature*, 91–104. Roehampton: The English Department of the Roehampton Institute of Higher Education, 1982.

Sambrook, A. J. 'The English Lord and the Happy Husbandman', *Studies on Voltaire and the Eighteenth Century*, 57 (1967), 1357–75.

—— 'An Essay on Eighteenth-Century Pastoral, Pope to Wordsworth (I)', *Trivium*, 5 (1970), 21–35.

—— 'An Essay on Eighteenth-Century Pastoral, Pope to Wordsworth (II)', *Trivium*, 6 (1971), 103–15.

Serjeantson, R. M., and Atkins, W. Ryland D., ed. *The Victoria History of the County of Northampton*. 4 vols. to date. London, 1902– .

SHARPE, J. A. 'Plebeian Marriage in Stuart England: Some Evidence from Popular Literature', *Transactions of the Royal Historical Society*, ser. 5/36 (1986), 69-90.
SHERBO, ARTHUR. 'Another Reply, This Time to Betty Rizzo', *Bulletin of the New York Public Library*, 77 (1974), 288.
—— 'The Case for Internal Evidence (I): Can *Mother Midnight's Comical Pocket-Book* be Attributed to Christopher Smart?', *Bulletin of the New York Public Library*, 61 (1957), 373-82.
SHERLOCK, WILLIAM. *A Practical Discourse Concerning Death.* London, 1689.
—— *A Practical Discourse Concerning a Future Judgement.* London, 1692.
SITTER, JOHN. *Literary Loneliness in Mid-Eighteenth Century England.* Ithaca, NY and London: Cornell University Press, 1982.
SITWELL, GEORGE. *A Brief History of Weston Hall, Northamptonshire, and of the Families that Possessed it.* London: p.p., 1927.
SITWELL, OSBERT. *Left Hand, Right Hand!* 5 vols. London: Macmillan, 1945-50.
SITWELL, SACHEVERELL. *For Want of the Golden City.* London: Thames and Hudson, 1973.
SLATER, MIRIAM. 'A Rejoinder', *Past & Present*, no. 85 (Nov. 1979), 136-40.
—— 'The Weightiest Business: Marriage in an Upper-Gentry Family in Seventeenth-Century England', *Past & Present*, no. 72 (Aug. 1976), 25-54.
SMART, CHRISTOPHER. *The Midwife*, i (1750).
—— *The Poetical Works of Christopher Smart*, ed. Karina Williamson and Marcus Walsh, 5 vols. (Oxford: Oxford University Press, 1980-).
SNELL, K. D. M. *Annals of the Labouring Poor: Social Change and Agrarian England, 1660-1900.* Cambridge: Cambridge University Press, 1985.
'SOPHIA'. *Woman Not Inferior to Man.* London, 1739.
—— *Woman's Superior Excellence over Man.* London, 1740.
SOUTHEY, ROBERT. 'An Introductory Essay on the Lives and Works of Our Uneducated Poets', in John Jones, *Attempts in Verse*, 1-168. London, 1831.
—— ed. *Specimens of the Later English Poets.* 3 vols. London, 1807.
SPACKS, PATRICIA MEYER. '"Always at Variance": Politics of Eighteenth-Century Adolescence', in Patricia Meyer Spacks and W. B. Carnochan, *A Distant Prospect: Eighteenth-Century Views of Childhood*, 3-22. Los Angeles: William Andrews Clark Memorial Library, 1982.

Bibliography 231

—— *The Female Imagination: A Literary and Psychological Investigation of Women's Writing*. London: George Allen & Unwin, 1976.
—— *Gossip*. New York: Alfred P. Knopf, 1985.
SPECK, W. A. 'Brackley: A Study in the Growth of Oligarchy', *Midland History*, 3 (1975–6), 30–41.
SPENCE, JOSEPH. *A Full and Authentic Account of Stephen Duck, The Wiltshire Poet*. London, 1731.
SPENCER, JANE. *The Rise of the Woman Novelist from Aphra Behn to Jane Austen*. Oxford: Basil Blackwell, 1986.
SPUFFORD, MARGARET. *Small Books and Pleasant Histories: Popular Fiction and its Readership in Seventeenth-Century England*. London: Methuen, 1981.
SQUIRE, JOHN, ed. *A Book of Women's Verse*. Oxford: Clarendon Press, 1921.
STANHOPE, PHILIP DORMER. *The Letters of the Earl of Chesterfield to his Son*, ed. Charles Strachey. London, 1901.
STANTON, JUDITH PHILLIPS. 'Statistical Profile of Women Writing in English from 1660 to 1800', in Frederick M. Keener and Susan E. Lorsch (ed.), *Eighteenth-Century Women and the Arts*, 247–54. Westport, Conn.: Greenwood Press, 1988.
STEPHENS, JOHN CALHOUN, ed. *The Guardian*. Lexington: The University Press of Kentucky, 1982.
STONE, LAWRENCE. *The Family, Sex and Marriage in England 1500–1800*. London: Weidenfeld & Nicolson, 1977.
SUTHERLAND, JAMES. *A Preface to Eighteenth-Century Poetry*. Oxford: Clarendon Press, 1948.
SWIFT, JONATHAN. *The Correspondence of Jonathan Swift*, ed. Harold Williams. 5 vols. Oxford: Oxford University Press, 1963–5.
—— *Directions to Servants and Miscellaneous Pieces 1733–1742*, ed. Herbert Davis. Oxford: Basil Blackwell, 1964.
—— *The Poems of Jonathan Swift*, ed. Harold Williams. 3 vols. Oxford: Oxford University Press, 1958.
SYMONDS, EMILY MORSE [GEORGE PASTON]. *Mrs. Delany (Mary Granville): A Memoir*. London: Grant Richards, 1900.
TATERSAL, ROBERT. *The Bricklayer's Miscellany: Or, Poems on Several Subjects*. 2nd edn. London, 1734.
TAYLOR, JEREMY. *The Rule and Exercises of Holy Dying*. London, 1651.
—— *The Rule and Exercises of Holy Living*. London, 1650.
The Taylors answer to Vulcan's Speech. Dublin, 1725.
TEFT, ELIZABETH. *Orinthia's Miscellanies*. London, 1747.
THICKNESSE, PHILIP. *Memoirs and Anecdotes*. Dublin, 1790.
THOMAS, KEITH. 'Age and Authority in Early Modern England', *Proceedings of the British Academy*, 62 (1976), 205–48.

—— 'The Meaning of Literacy in Early Modern England', in Gerd Baumann (ed.), *The Written Word: Literacy in Transition* 96–131. The Wolfson College Lectures, 1985. Oxford: Clarendon Press, 1986.

—— 'The Place of Laughter in Tudor and Stuart England', *Times Literary Supplement* (21 Jan. 1977), 77–81.

THOMPSON, E. P. 'Eighteenth-Century English Society: Class Struggle Without Class?', *Social History*, 3 (1978), 133–65.

TILLOTSON, JOHN. *The Works of the Most Reverend Dr. John Tillotson.* 2 vols. London, 1712.

TINKER, CHAUNCEY BREWSTER. *Nature's Simple Plan: A Phase of Radical Thought in the Mid-Eighteenth Century.* Princeton, NJ: Princeton University Press, 1922; London: Humphrey Milford, Oxford University Press, 1922.

TODD, JANET. *Feminist Literary History: A Defence.* Cambridge: Polity Press, 1988.

—— *Sensibility: An Introduction.* London and New York: Methuen, 1986.

—— *The Sign of Angellica: Women, Writing and Fiction 1660–1800.* London: Virago, 1989.

—— *Women's Friendship in Literature.* New York: Columbia University Press, 1980.

——, ed. *A Dictionary of British and American Women Writers 1660–1800.* London: Methuen, 1984.

TRUMBACH, RANDOLPH. *The Rise of the Egalitarian Family: Aristocratic Kinship and Domestic Relations in Eighteenth-Century England.* New York, San Francisco, and London: Academic Press, 1978.

TURNER, JAMES G. *The Politics of Landscape: Rural Scenery and Society in English Poetry 1630–1660.* Oxford: Basil Blackwell, 1979.

—— 'The Sexual Politics of Landscape: Images of Venus in Eighteenth-Century English Poetry and Landscape Gardening', in *Studies in Eighteenth-Century Culture*, 11, Proceedings of the American Society for Eighteenth Century Studies, 343–66. Madison: University of Wisconsin Press, 1982.

TUVESON, ERNEST LEE. *The Imagination as a Means of Grace: Locke and the Aesthetics of Romanticism.* Berkeley and Los Angeles: University of California Press, 1960.

UNWIN, RAYNER. *The Rural Muse: Studies in the Peasant Poetry of England.* London: George Allen & Unwin, 1954.

UVEDALE, THOMAS. *The Death-Bed Display'd.* London, 1727.

VAISEY, DAVID, ed. *The Diary of Thomas Turner 1754–1765.* Oxford: Oxford University Press, 1984.

VINER, JACOB. 'Satire and Economics in the Augustan Age of Satire', in Henry Knight Miller, Eric Rothstein, and G. S. Rousseau (ed.), *The*

Augustan Milieu: Essays Presented to Louis A. Landa, 77–101. Oxford: Clarendon Press, 1970.

Vulcan's Speech. Dublin(?), 1725.

WALLAS, ADA. *Before the Bluestockings*. London: George Allen & Unwin, 1929.

WALLIS, JOHN. 'An Extract of a Letter', *Philosophical Transactions*, 14 (20 Dec. 1684), 800–1.

WARBURTON, WILLIAM. *Remarks on Several Occasional Reflections*. London, 1744.

WARD, A. W., and WALLER, A. R., ed. *The Cambridge History of English Literature*. 15 vols. Cambridge: Cambridge University Press, 1907–27. Vol. xi, 1914.

WARD, EDWARD. *Works*. 4 vols. London, 1703–9.

WATTS, ISAAC. *Hymns and Spiritual Songs 1707–1748*, ed. Selma L. Bishop. London: The Faith Press, 1962.

WELLEK, RENÉ. *A History of Modern Criticism 1750–1950*. 6 vols. London: Jonathan Cape, 1955–86. Vol. i: *The Later Eighteenth Century*, 1955.

WHATELEY, MARY. *Original Poems on Several Occasions*. London, 1764.

WHISTON, JOHN. *Directions for a Proper Choice of Authors to Form a Library*. London, 1766.

WHITING, C. E. *Nathaniel Lord Crewe Bishop of Durham (1674–1721) and his Diocese*. London: SPCK, 1940.

WHITNEY, LOIS. *Primitivism and the Idea of Progress in English Popular Literature of the Eighteenth Century*. Baltimore: The Johns Hopkins Press, 1934.

WILLEY, BASIL. *The Eighteenth Century Background: Studies on the Idea of Nature in the Thought of the Period*. London: Chatto & Windus, 1940.

WILLIAMS, CAROLYN. 'The Changing Face of Change: Fe/male In/constancy', *British Journal for Eighteenth-Century Studies*, 12 (1989), 13–28.

WILLIAMS, IOLO, ed. *The Shorter Poems of the Eighteenth Century*. London: William Heinemann, 1923.

WILLIAMS, RAYMOND. *The Country and the City*. London: Chatto & Windus, 1973.

WILLIAMSON, KARINA. 'Joseph Lewis, "our Doggrel Author"', *Bulletin of Research in the Humanities*, 81 (Spring 1978), 74–83.

WOODHOUSE, JAMES. *The Life and Poetical Works of James Woodhouse (1735–1820)*, ed. R. I. Woodhouse. 2 vols. London, 1896.

WRIGHTSON, KEITH. *English Society 1580–1680*. London: Hutchinson, 1980.

YEARSLEY, ANN. *Poems, on Several Occasions*. Prefatory letter, Hannah More. London, 1785.

—— *Poems, on Various Subjects*. London, 1787.
YOUNG, EDWARD. *Night Thoughts*, ed. Stephen Cornford. Cambridge: Cambridge University Press, 1989.
The Young Gentleman and Lady Instructed. 2 vols. London, 1747.
Z., A. 'Leapor's Unhappy Father', *Notes and Queries*, ser. 1/7 (1853), 382–3.
—— 'Tragedy by Mary Leapor', *Notes and Queries*, ser. 1/9 (1854), 104.

Index

Abrams, M. H. 157 n., 158 n.
Addison, Joseph 170, 174, 179–80
'Advice to Myrtillo' 151
'Advice to Sophronia' 15, 90, 153
aequa mens 79
agriculture 8, 59, 105–7, 123–45
   see also labouring poets, pastoral
Akenside, Mark 35, 160
Allison, K. J. 16 n.
Amis, Kingsley 35–6
Anglesey, Earl of 68–9
anthologies 31–7, 47–50, 205
Apocrypha 168
Ariès, Phillippe 186 n.
Aristotle 74
ars moriendi 198
'Artemisia', *see* Freemantle, Bridget
Ashraf, Phyllis Mary 99, 101
Assheton William 198 n.
Astell, Mary 45, 53, 178
Atkins, W. Ryland D. 2 n.
Aubin, Robert Arnold 137
Auerbach, Nina 86
'August 1746' 21
Aynho 7, 17, 24

Backscheider, Laura 109 n.
Bailey, Bruce 15 n.
Baillie, Joanna 49, 207
Baker, David Erskine 21 n.
Baker, George 1, 2, 4, 5, 11, 15, 19, 20, 28–9, 34–5
Ballard, George 10 n., 48
Bamford, Francis 12 n.
Bancks, John 101, 104–5
Barbauld, Anna Laetitia Aikin 26 n., 48
Barber, Mary 26, 31, 54, 207
Barnardiston, Arthur 11, 12
Barnardiston, Mary 11, 12, 13
Barnardiston family 24
Barrell, John 126
Barron, Janet 36 n.
Barrow, Isaac 197, 199
Bate, Walter Jackson 157 n.
Baumann, Gerd 166 n.
BBC 36 n.
Beaty, Nancy Lee 198 n.

beauty, standards of 86–96
   see also body, cultural attitudes
'The Beauties of the Spring' 32
Beckwith, Charles E. 106 n.
Behn, Aphra 31, 39, 43, 62
Bennett, John 105
Berger, John 125–6
Bishop, Selma L. 202 n.
Blackwell, Thomas 158–9
Blackwood's Edinburgh Magazine 32
Bladen, Martin 170
Blair, Robert 172, 188
Blamire, Susanna 49, 207
Bland, Wilfred 26 n.
Blencowe, Anne 5, 12, 13
Blencowe, Betty 12
Blencowe, John 4, 6
Blencowe, Sir John 5, 6, 10–11
Blencowe, Mrs 25
Blencowe, Jr, R. W. 25
Blencowe family 6, 10, 11, 16, 24–5, 172
Bloomfield, Robert 105, 136
Blunden, Edmund 28 n., 31 n., 33–4, 128, 167, 169
Boas, George 157 n.
body, cultural attitudes 54–5, 74, 86–97, 187, 196
   see also death; hygiene; physiognomy; sickness
Bond, Donald F. 180 n.
Bonnell, Thomas 205 n.
Boswell, James 93 n., 111 n., 198 n.
Bourne, Henry 194
Bowles, Elizabeth Lisle 13, 166–7
Bowles, Thomas 2–3, 166–8
Bowles, Thomas, jr 3
Bowles, William Lisle 3, 35
Brackley:
   social and historical background 1–4, 6, 8, 9, 135, 192
   parish register 4, 5, 8, 22, 192
Brady, Frank 150 n.
Bragg, Marion K. 92 n.
Breval, John 94
Bridges, John 16 n.
Bridgewater, Dukes of 1–2
Brooke, John 2 n.

Index

Brown, Laura 120 n.
Browne, Alice 53 n., 62 n.
Browne, Isaac Hawkins 3, 19, 23, 27, 28
Bryant, John Frederick 101, 105
Burke, Peter 104
Burney, Fanny 39, 49
Butler, Marilyn 206–7
Butler, Samuel 174–6

C., R. 104 n.
Caesar, Julius 168, 170
Cambridge University 46
Candler, Ann 110
canon, literary 34, 37, 38, 84 n., 106, 205–6
  see also anthologies
Carnochan, W. B. 188 n.
Carter, Elizabeth 26, 28, 39, 43, 46, 48
Cartwright family 17, 24
  see also Aynho
cast clothes 117
Castle, Terry 36 n., 88, 95
Cato the Censor 168, 170
Cato of Utica 168, 170
'Celadon to Mira' 182, 195–6, 201
celibacy 60, 63–4, 76
  see also spinsters
Centlivre, Susanna 26, 46
Chapman, R. W. 149 n.
Chapone, Hester Mulso 35, 48
'The Charms of Anthony' 131–2
Chaucer, Geoffrey 171
Chauncy, Elizabeth 15
Chauncy, Richard 15–16
Chauncy, Toby 15–16
Chauncy, William Henry 16, 117–18
Chauncy family 15–16, 17, 91–2, 153
cheese-cakes 15
Cherry, Bridget 16 n.
Chesterfield, Earl of, see Stanhope, Philip Dormer, Earl of Chesterfield
Childs, Fenela Ann 89 n., 93 n., 94 n.
Chinard, Gilbert 157 n.
Chudleigh, Lady Mary 48
Churchill, Charles 208
Cibber, Colley 21, 177–8
'Cicely, Joan, and Deborah' 21
Cicero 168, 170
Clare, John 33–4, 35, 59
Clarke, John 1, 9, 20, 29 n., 166, 184, 204

Cleves, Anne of 16
Cohen, Ralph 132 n.
Coke, Sir Edward 184
Cole, John 35
Coley, W. B. 150
'Colinetta' 25, 144–5, 178
Collier, Mary 101, 110, 119–21
Collins, J. Churton 32
Colman, George 31, 32, 48
'Complaining Daphne' 59–60
Congreve, William 173
'The Consolation' 77, 153, 193, 202
constancy 74–81
contagion 187
  see also sickness; small-pox
contentment 196–8
cookbook 11–12
  see also Weston Hall
Cooper, Nicholas 7 n., 17 n.
Cooper, Richard 9, 166, 183–4
Cornford, Stephen 188 n.
cosmetics 88–9
  see also body, cultural attitudes
costume 88–9, 91
  see also body, cultural attitudes
'Corydon. Phillario. or, Mira's Picture' 81, 92–6, 174
counter-pastoral 95, 105, 106
  see also pastoral, agriculture
country house poems 137–42
court of piepowder 1
Cow Close 6
Cowley, Hannah 49
Cowper, William 31–2
Crabbe, George 100, 105, 208
craft poetry 104–5
Crane, Ronald S. 157 n.
Creech, Thomas 169
Crewe, Nathaniel 2, 3, 20
'Crito', see Duncombe, John
Cromwell, Thomas 16
'The Crucifixion and Resurrection' 32
'The Cruel Parent' 67–9
'Crumble Hall' 15–16, 115, 137–44, 153, 181
Cumberland, Duke of 21
customs, see popular culture

Dalrymple-Champneys, Norma 105 n.
D'Assigny, M. 198 n.
Davies, Kathleen M. 40 n.
Davis, Herbert 113 n.
Davis, Rose Mary 107 n.

Index

Dearing, Vinton A. 106 n.
death, cultural attitudes 186–204
  see also body, cultural attitudes
dedications 151
  see also patronage
Defoe, Daniel 45, 109, 112, 119 n., 183
Dell, Henry 31
Dictionary of National Biography 5, 33, 73
dirt 55, 93–7
'The Disappointment' 15, 77, 91, 117, 152
dissenters 2
division of labour 118–19, 123
Dixon, Sarah 74–5
Doddridge, Phillip 2
Dodsley, Robert 104, 112, 119
domestic service 10–17, 43, 44, 113–23, 125, 188
  see also kitchen maid; labouring poets
Doody, Margaret Anne 36, 47, 55, 58, 95, 96–7, 114 n., 177, 178
'Dorinda at her Glass' 89–90, 181
dowries 44–5, 64, 76
Drelincourt, Charles 198 n.
Dryden, John 10, 85, 170, 171, 172–3
Dubois, Lady Dorothea 68–9
Dubrow, Heather 138 n.
Duck, Stephen 35, 100–12, 119–21, 135–6, 177–8
Duff, William 158
Duncombe, John 4, 23–4, 30–1, 47, 48, 162–3
D'Urfey, Thomas 176
Dyce, Alexander 32

Eagleton, Terry 109
economics and literary criticism 102–13
  see also agriculture; domestic service; labouring poets; landscape; patronage
Edgcote House 15–17, 91, 153
Edgeworth, Maria 39
education:
  labourers 100, 124, 166
  primitivism 157–65
  universities 45–6, 99
  women 45–6, 49, 75
  see also Leapor, Mary, education
Edwards, Thomas 26, 29, 153
Edwy (Eadwig) 73–4

Egerton, Sarah Fyge 48, 69
Ehrenpreis, Irvin 102, 143
Eland, George 6, 7, 8 n., 24, 29 n., 35, 166, 191–2
elections 2, 24
Elton, Oliver 33
enclosure 135–6, 142–5
'An Enquiry' 179–80
'An Epistle to Artemisia. On Fame' 15, 17, 91, 118–21, 153, 163, 174, 181, 190
'The Epistle of Deborah Dough' 81, 115–16, 175–6
'An Epistle to a Lady' 35, 79, 183, 184–5, 189, 200–4
epitaphs 19, 27–8
Erdman, David 149 n.
Erskine-Hill, Howard 138
'An Essay on Friendship' 33, 76–80
'An Essay on Happiness' 197–8
'An Essay on Hope' 33, 129
'An Essay on Woman' 35, 64–7, 153
executions 21

Fabricant, Carole 126 n., 132, 138 n.
Faderman, Lillian 84
Fairchild, Hoxie Neale 34, 200
Falconer, William 99
Farewell, George 207
Farmer, Richard 159
fathers, representation of 52–3, 67–70
Feingold, Richard 145 n.
femme sole 44
'Fidelia' 81
Fielding, Henry 114, 183
Fielding, Sarah 26
'The Fields of Melancholy and Chearfulness' 172
Figes, Eva 41
'Florimelia, the First Pastoral' 127
Forrester, Eric G. 2 n.
Forster, Margaret 36 n.
Foss, Michael 150 n.
Foster, J. 16 n.
Fowler, Alastair 137
'The Fox and the Hen' 171
Foxon, David 104, 109 n.
Freemantle, Bridget:
  biography 19–21
  dedications 151
  friendship with ML 17–22, 79, 84, 86, 168

Freemantle, Bridget (*cont.*):
  letter 4, 8–10, 18–20, 26–8, 30, 52, 92, 145, 151, 162–3, 164, 193
  ML's education 8–10, 162–3
  ML's epitaph 27–8
  ML's implied reader 77, 125
  ML's manuscripts 26–7, 153
  ML's originality 164–5
  ML's social criticism 154
  styled 'Artemisia' 19
Freemantle, Mary 19, 20, 189
Freemantle, Thomas 19, 20
Friedman, Oliver 143 n.
'The Friend in Disgrace' 147–8
friendship, female 50, 74–85, 90, 96–7, 201
  see also lesbianism
Frizzle, Henry 101
Frye, Northrop 40

Garrick, David 23, 27
Gay, John 106, 131, 178–9
Gentleman's Magazine 14, 15, 16, 23, 25, 27, 30, 31, 48, 75, 142, 163
georgics 106
Gillis, John R. 42
Gittings, Clare 186 n.
Goldsmith, Oliver 143–4
Göller, Karl Heinz 47 n.
Goose Green 6
gossip 80–4, 96
graveyard poetry 188, 193
Gray, Thomas 49, 124, 188, 201, 209
Green, George Smith 102
Greenberg, Janelle 42
Greer, Germaine 36 n., 39 n.
Grey, Bridget 3
Grey, Richard 3, 20
Grierson, Constantia 46, 110, 112
Griffith, Ralph 25
  see also *Monthly Review*
Grigson, Geoffrey 34
Grosvenor, Benjamin 187
Grundy, Isobel 55 n., 198 n.

Halsband, Robert 55 n., 87 n., 110
Hands, Elizabeth 98, 110
Hanover, House of 20
Harris, Jocelyn 47, 53, 87
Harrison, Susannah 110
harvest feasts 134–6
Haywood, Eliza 26
'The Head-Ach' 96

Heber, Mary 12
Hecht, J. J. 114, 117, 122–3
Hendrickson, J. R. 124 n.
Henry V 16
heterosexuality 50–1, 60, 85–6
Hibbard, G. R. 137
Highmore, Susanna 23, 26, 28
Hill, Bridget 17, 42–3, 44, 45 n., 114 n.
Hill, George Birkbeck 93 n., 201
Hinton, Northamptonshire 1, 3, 4, 5, 19, 20
Hobsbawm, E. J. 104 n.
Holbech family 24
Hold, Trevor 15, 35
Home, Henry, Lord Kames 161
Homer 168–9
Horace 170
Houlbrooke, Ralph 186 n.
Hudibrastics 175
Huften, Olwen 44, 64
hygiene 93
  see also body, cultural attitudes
'An Hymn to the Morning' 32, 34, 85–6

improvement 126, 132–45
  see also landscape
incarnation 96–7, 130
'The Inspired Quill' 180, 184
Irwin, Anne, Viscountess 75
Iser, Wolfgang 77 n.

J—, Mrs, *see* Susanna Jennens
Jacobitism 20–1
Janssen, Anke 47 n.
Jemmat, Catherine 43
Jennens, Richard 11
Jennens, Richard, jr 11
Jennens, Susanna 10–14, 16, 24, 27, 77, 151, 153
Jennens family 12, 13, 24
Johnson, John 31
Johnson, Samuel:
  attitudes towards death 187, 198
  attitudes towards marriage 42
  'Betty Broom' 119
  Gray's 'Elegy' 201
  literary circle 48
  patronage 148–9, 151
  primitivism 161
  scriblerian tradition 208
  Smart's hygiene 93
  Woodhouse's poetry 111

Index

jointures 44
Jones, Henry 23, 101, 105, 112
Jones, John 100
Jones, Mary 48, 54, 60, 207
Jones, M. G. 166
Josephus 171
Jump, Harriet Devine 36 n.

Kames, Henry Home, Lord 161
Ken, Thomas 198 n.
Kenny, Virginia C. 138 n.
Kettlewell, John 198 n.
Killigrew, Anne 85
King, James 32 n.
King, William 177
kitchen maid (job description) 17, 114–15
Klaus, H. Gustav 101–2
Kors, Alan C. 47 n.
Korshin, Paul 150
Kowaleski-Wallace, Beth 39
Kuist, James M. 14 n., 23 n.
Kussmaul, Ann 119

labouring poets:
 conflict with employers 119–21
 environment 130
 historical and literary background 98–113
 pastoral 126–7
 primitivism 107, 158, 160–1
 women 46, 110
 see also agriculture; canon, literary; domestic service; education; natural genius; patronage
Lancashire canals 1
land, common 134, 142, 145
 see also agriculture
Landry, Donna 31 n., 32 n., 36, 50–2, 60, 68, 70, 85–6, 120 n., 139–40, 142, 185
landscape 123–45
 see also agriculture; counter-pastoral; labouring poets; pastoral
landscape painting 126
Laslett, Peter, 53 n.
Latin 9, 45, 167–8, 184
Law, William 2
Lawson, Jonathan N. 136 n.
Leapor, Alice 5
Leapor, Anne 4, 8–9, 52, 188–92, 203
 see also Sharman family
Leapor, Elizabeth 4–5, 6

Leapor, Mary:
 birth 4
 cooking 115–16, 177
 death 22, 52, 193
 death, expectation of 79, 97, 172, 186–204
 dedications 151
 dismissal 15, 17, 68, 91–2, 117–21
 domestic service 10–14, 16–17, 113–23
 early writing 8–9, 14, 27
 education 8–10, 12, 31–2, 65, 158–85
 epitaph and gravestone 27–8
 freehold 24
 health 21–2
 housework 18, 97
 Latin, knowledge of 167–8, 184
 law, knowledge of 183–4, 193–5
 literary fashions 48, 208–9
 manuscripts 13, 26–7
 marriage, views of 50–67, 70–4
 plagiarism (alleged) 164–5
 Pope, attitude towards, 76–81, 180–2
 prosody 33, 34, 167–8
 publication 21–9
 reading 10, 11, 13, 93–4, 162–85
 religious opinions 2–3, 78–80, 90, 97, 181, 189, 195–204
 reputation, literary 18, 25–6, 29–37, 98, 207
 subscription 3, 19, 21–5, 52, 145, 147, 150–6
 subscription proposals 10, 20, 23, 162
 women's friendship, views of 74–86
 women writers, knowledge of 178
 works, *see* titles
Leapor, Philip 4–10, 22, 24, 27–9, 52, 192–3
Leapor, Philip (ML's grandfather) 4
Leapor family 5–6, 10
Lennox, Charlotte 26, 46, 48
lesbianism 51, 60, 82, 84–6
L'Estrange, Roger 170
Lewis, Esther 96–7, 207
Lewis, Joseph 102, 149
'The Libyan Hunter' 182
Lincoln College, Oxford 19–20
Locke, John 53
London Magazine 22
Lonsdale, Roger 84 n.
 ECV 35–6, 205, 206

Lonsdale, Roger (*cont.*)
  ECWP 36, 47–50, 55, 103 n., 169, 181, 206 n.
Lovejoy, A. O. 157 n.
Lowerson, John R. 2 n., 135
Lucian 176
Lucretius 171

McClung, William A. 138 n.
McGonigle, Peter J.
Mack, Maynard 106
McManners, John 186 n.
Magdalen College, Oxford 2, 9, 166, 204
Malcolmson, Robert W. 114, 134
Mallet, David 173–4
Manley, Delarivière 43
'Man the Monarch' 52–4, 153
marriage, companionate 40–3, 44, 51
Marshall, Dorothy 122
Marshall, Jeremy 139 n.
Marston St Lawrence, Northamptonshire 1, 4–5
Masters, Mary 110, 164–5
may-fly, image of 78
Mayo, Richard 118
measles 22
Mellor, Bernard 34
Mendelson, Sara Heller 41 n.
Messenger, Ann 39
Mill, John Stuart 83
Miller, Henry Knight 102 n.
Milton, John 172
'Mira to Octavia' 61–4, 153
'Mira's Will' 24, 35, 183, 193–5
mirrors 88–90
'The Mistaken Lover' 55–8, 91–2, 170
Mitchell, L. G. 8, 17 n.
Modern Language Association (MLA) 39
Mollington, Oxfordshire 11
Monk, Samuel H. 157 n.
Montagu, Elizabeth 46, 49, 159–60
Montagu, Lady Mary Wortley 45, 47, 55, 87, 178
'The Month of August' 32, 33, 51, 132–6, 153, 169
Monthly Review 25, 29–30, 111–12
Moore, Paul Henry 186 n.
'Mopsus' 19, 145–7, 163, 171, 175
'The Moral Vision' 196
Munns, Jessica 40
'The Muses Embassy 14, 177

Nairn, Judy 16 n.
Namier, Lewis 2 n.
natural genius 9, 10, 31–2, 107, 158–65
  see also education; labouring poets
Neeson, J. M. 135 n.
Nelson, Henry 104
Neo-Classicism 208
Neuberg, Victor 166
'A New Ballad' 34
Newton, John 20, 127
Nonsense Club 32
Northamptonshire 2, 34–5, 59, 135
Novak, Maximilian 95
Nussbaum, Felicity 120 n.

O'Connor, Sister Mary Catherine 198 n.
'An Ode on Mercy' 23, 27
Ong, Walter J. 77 n.
'On Mr Pope's Universal Prayer' 181
'On Patience. To Stella' 196–7
'On the Death of a justly admir'd Author' 182
'On Sickness' 200
'On Winter' 127–9
'Ophelia' 142
Osborn, James M. 157 n.
Otway, Thomas 173, 190
Ouse 6
Ovid 169–70, 170
Oxford English Dictionary 139

Paine, James 4
Paine, Thomas 4
Palmer, John 150 n.
Parkhurst, L. 8 n.
'Parthenissa', *see* Jennens, Susanna
'Parthenissa's Answer' 13
pastiche of ML 30
pastorals 20, 25, 126, 131, 135–6, 143–5, 146
  see also agriculture; counter-pastoral; labouring poets
patronage 107–9, 145–56, 161
  see also economics and literary criticism; labouring poets; subscription publishing
Patton, Julia 142 n.
Pearson, Jacqueline 40
peasant poetry 99
'The Penitent' 24, 151
Perry, Ruth 84–5
Pevsner, Nikolaus 16 n.

pewter 17, 116
Philips, Ambrose 106, 127–8, 169, 178
Philips, John 106
Phillips, Katherine 43
Phillips, Patricia 157 n.
Phillips, Thomas 25 n.
'Phoebus to Artemisia' 20
physiognomy 88, 91–2, 196
  see also body, cultural attitudes
physiology 74
  see also, body, cultural attitudes
Pilkington, Laetitia 43
Piozzi, Hester Thrale 49
Pitt, William 29
Plato 170
Plutarch 171
Pollard, Arthur 105 n.
poor, deserving 102, 152
Pope, Alexander:
  education 10
  'Epistle to Burlington' 137–8, 142
  'Epistle to a Lady' 74–6, 78–81
  female desire 44
  iambics 34
  influence on ML 34, 81, 180–2
  labouring poets 111–12
  pastorals 106
  scriblerian tradition 207–8
  translation of Sappho 169
  see also Amis, Kingsley; 'Celadon to Mira'
popular culture 104–5, 134–6, 175–6, 194
Porter, Dorothy 186 n., 196
Porter, Peter 35
Porter, Roy 88, 94, 186 n., 187, 196
Poverty-struck, Lancelot, see Lewis, Joseph
Powell, David 35 n.
Powell, L. F. 93 n.
'A Prayer for the Year, 1745' 192
Price, Martin 150 n.
primitivism 107, 157–65
  see also education; labouring poets; natural genius
Prior, Matthew 177
Pritchard, R. E. 36 n.
Probyn, Lady 12
'The Proclamation of Apollo' 169–70
'Proper ingredients for the Head of a Beau' 58
'The Proposal' 13, 83, 176
'Proserpine's Ragout' 34, 176

prospect poems 126
Purefoy, Elizabeth 6
Purefoy, Henry 6, 7–8, 8, 183
Purefoy Letters, see Eland, George; Mitchell, L. G.
puritans 2
Pythagoras 180

'The Question' 81

rationalism 53
'A Request to the Divine Being' 31, 200
Rey, Claudius 109
Reynolds, Myra 33, 38 n., 46, 86
Richardson, Ruth 186 n., 187
Richardson, Samuel:
  education 45
  publisher 19, 23, 25–7, 112 153
  literary circle 32, 48
  ML's reading 183
  Pamela 114, 116
Riley, James C. 186 n., 192 n.
'The Rival Brothers' 31
Rivers, Isabel 139 n.
Rizzo, Betty 4, 6, 13, 19, 24, 25 n., 27, 28, 35, 69, 71, 78, 149 n., 155 n., 159 n., 163, 165–6, 173, 178
Roberts, James 25
Rogers, Katherine 41, 43, 53 n.
Rogers, Pat 47, 108
romantic love 54–64, 84–6
  see also celibacy; lesbianism; marriage, companionate; seduction
Romanticism 49, 83, 101, 186, 208
Rothstein, Eric 102 n.
Rousseau, G. S. 102 n.
Rowe, Elizabeth 43, 48, 188
Rowe, Nicholas 69–72, 173, 178
Rowton, Frederick 32
'The Rural Maid's Reflexions', see 'To Lucinda'
Rutherford, Malcolm 36
Ryskamp, Charles 32 n.

Sabor, Peter 114 n.
'The Sacrifice' 123
Saintsbury, George 12, 33
Sale, William 26
Sambrook, A. J. 100, 107 n., 108, 142 n., 143–4
Sapphic textuality, *see* lesbianism

242 Index

Sappho 85–6, 169
scriblerian tradition 207–9
seduction 43–4, 59, 134
Segar, M. R. 128 n.
Seneca 170
sensibility 48, 85–6, 208
Serjeantson, R. M.
Seward, Anna 48
Shakespeare, William 46, 127, 159–60, 171–2
Shalstone, Buckinghamshire 6
Sharman family 4, 9
Sharpe, J. A. 41 n.
Shenstone, William 112, 155
Sherbo, Arthur 149 n.
Sherlock, William 198 n., 199
Sherman, Margaret 4, 9
shoemakers 104–5
sickness 21–2, 187–204
  see also body, cultural attitudes
'Silvia and the Bee' 32, 34, 81–2
Sitter, John 83–4
Sitwell, Edith 11
Sitwell, George 11, 12, 13, 116
Sitwell, Georgia 12
Sitwell, Osbert 11
Sitwell, Sacheverell 10, 11, 186
Slater, Miriam 41 n.
small-pox 17, 83, 192
Smart, Christopher 25, 28, 32, 59 n., 93, 205, 209
Smith, Charlotte 48
Smith, David Nichol 33
'Song to Cloe, playing on her Spinnet' 81–2
'Sophia' 53–4, 178
'Sophronia' 15, 77, 91, 115–19, 125, 192
Southey, Robert 32, 100
'The Sow and the Peacock' 58, 170
Spacks, Patricia Meyer 83, 188
Speck, W. A. 2 n.
The Spectator 169
Spence, Joseph 107
Spender, Dale 47 n.
spinsters 44, 64
  see also celibacy
spouting-clubs 111
Spufford, Margaret 41 n.
Squire, John 33
Stangos, Nikos 126 n.
Stanhope, Philip Dormer, Earl of Chesterfield 24, 94, 112, 148, 167

Stanton, Judith Phillips 41 n.
Starr, H. W. 124 n.
Steane, Northamptonshire 1
Steele, Richard 179–80
Stephens, John Calhoun 131 n.
Stone, Lawrence 40–1
Strachey, Charles 167 n.
'Strephon to Celia: A modern Love Letter' 58
Stuart, House of 3, 21
subscription publishing 19, 21–5, 48, 145–56
Sulgrave, Northamptonshire 4
'A Summer's Wish'
Sutherland, James 38, 64
Swift, Jonathan:
  Directions to Servants 113–14
  female body, representation of 54–8, 89–90
  influence on ML 55–8, 178, 193–5
  influence on women writers 43, 96
  labouring poets, attitude towards 110–12
Symonds, Emily Morse 28 n.

Tatersal, Robert 101, 108, 130
Taylor, Jeremy 197, 198 n., 203–4
teeth 94
Teft, Elizabeth 87–8
'The Temple of Love'
Theocritus 169
Thicknesse, Philip 3 n.
'The Third Chapter of the Wisdom of Solomon' 199–200
Thomas, Keith 88, 166, 167 n., 192
Thompson, E. P. 41 n.
Thomson, James 173–4, 183
Thornton, Bonnell 31–2, 48
Thorp Mandeville 11
Tibble, Anne 59 n.
Tibble, J. W. 59 n.
Tickell, Thomas 106, 131
Tillemans, Peter 15
Tillotson, John 202
Tinker, Chauncey Brewster 157 n.
'To Artemisia' 82–3, 123, 177
'To Lucinda' 22, 27, 124–5, 163, 184
Todd, Janet 45 n., 46–7, 69, 85, 103 n., 164
Tollet, Elizabeth 31, 48
Tomalin, Claire 47
Tories 2, 20
Trumbach, Randolph 40 n.

Index

Turner, James G. 132 n., 138 n.
Turner, Thomas 189
Tuveson, Ernest Lee 157 n.
The Unhappy Father 21, 30, 69–73, 121–2, 170, 172, 173, 190–1

unfinished play (Edwy) 73–4, 77, 173–4
Unwin, Rayner 99 n., 100–1, 110, 111 n., 154
'Upon her Play being returned to her' 21, 33
Uvedale, Thomas 198 n., 199

Vaisey, David 189 n.
Viner, Jacob 102
Virgil 167, 169–70
'The Visit' 80–1, 90–1, 153

W. 14, 16
  see also Chauncy, William Henry
W—, Miss 55
Wallach, Joan 104 n.
Waller, A. R. 33 n.
Wallis, John 5, 16
Walsh, Marcus 59 n.
Walsh, Octavia 48
Warburton, William 3
Ward, A. W. 33 n.
Ward, Edward 103, 176–7
Watts, Isaac 202
'The Way of the World' 148, 173
Weaver, Helen 186 n.
weavers 104–5
Weeks, James Eyre 101, 105
Welch, Mrs 12
Welchman, John, junior 177, 204
Welchman, John, senior 2, 177, 183–4, 204
Wellek, René 157 n., 159, 161 n.
Wesley, Samuel 45
Weston, Northamptonshire 4, 11
Weston Hall:
  history 10–13
  library 10, 170–83
  ML's employment 10–14
  manuscript poems 12–13, 77, 164, 178
  pewter 116
  see also Jennens, Susanna
Whalley, Peter 16 n.
Whateley, Mary 75–6, 207
Whiston, John 37

White, Thomas Holt 14, 23
Whitney, Lois 157 n.
widows 12, 44
Wilders, John 175 n.
Willey, Basil 157 n.
Williams, Anna 48
Williams, Carolyn 74
Williams, Harold 110 n.
Williams, Helen Maria 48
Williams, Iolo 33
Williams, Raymond 101, 107, 125, 137
Williamson, Karina 36 n., 59 n., 149 n., 205, 206
Winchilsea, Anne Finch, Countess of 31, 36, 38, 47, 48, 87
Wiseman, Jane Holt 103, 110
women:
  constancy 74–81
  friendship 74–85
  education 45–6
  legal status 42, 44
  marriage and family 40–3, 44, 50–74
  moral standards 43–4
  obedience 42–3, 52–4
  occupations 43–4
  see also body, cultural attitudes; celibacy; lesbianism; seduction
women poets:
  book trade 41
  historical and literary background 38–50
  eighteenth century studies 37, 38–40, 46–50, 205–9
  labouring class 38, 42, 46, 84, 110
  see also anthologies; canon, literary; women
woodcuts 29
Woodhouse, James:
  canon, literary 207
  labouring poet 100, 101, 105, 111, 112
  patronage 155
  primitivism 161
Woodhouse, R. I. 155 n.
Wordsworth, William 25, 49, 102, 113
working-class literature 98–9
  see also labouring poets
Worsley coal mines 1
Wright, Mehetabel 45, 48
Wrightson, Keith 41 n.

Yearsley, Ann 100, 101, 110, 112, 152, 160–1
Young, Edward 172, 188